2004

MEXICAN HIGHLAND CULTURES

MEXICAN HIGHLAND CULTURES

ARCHAEOLOGICAL RESEARCHES AT TEOTIHUACAN, CALPULALPAN, AND CHALCHICOMULA IN 1934–35

Sigvald Linné

Foreword by Staffan Brunius
Introduction by George L. Cowgill

THE UNIVERSITY OF ALABAMA PRESS
Tuscaloosa and London

Originally published in 1942 by The Ethnographical Museum of Sweden

Typeface is AGaramond

∞
The paper on which this book is printed meets the minimum requirements of American National Standard for Information Science–Permanence of Paper for Printed Library Materials, ANSI Z39.48–1984.

Library of Congress Cataloging-in-Publication Data

Linné, Sigvald, 1899–
Mexican highland cultures : archaeological researches at Teotihuacan, Calpulalpan, and Chalchicomula in 1934–35 / Sigvald Linné ; foreword by Staffan Brunius ; introduction by George L. Cowgill.
p. cm.
Originally published: Stockholm : Ethnographical Museum of Sweden, 1942.
Includes bibliographical references and index.
ISBN 0-8173-1295-1 (cloth : alk. paper) — ISBN 0-8173-5006-3 (paper : alk. paper)
1. Teotihuacán Site (San Juan Teotihuacán, Mexico) 2. Ciudad Serdán
(Mexico)—Antiquities. 3. Calpulalpan (Tlaxcala, Mexico)—Antiquities. 4. Excavations
(Archaeology)—Mexico. 5. Mexico—Antiquities. I. Title.

F1219.1.T27L56 2003
972'.401—dc21

2002041618

British Library Cataloguing-in-Publication Data available

CONTENTS

FOREWORD
The Early Swedish Americanist Tradition and the Contributions of Sigvald Linné (1899–1986)
Staffan Brunius

In the 1920s the university and the ethnographical museum of Gothenburg (Göteborg), the busy seaport city, were the institutions to attend for an academically competent and internationally well respected Swedish education in American Indian cultures. This high quality ethnographical-anthropological training was the result of one man's extraordinary achievements—those of baron Erland Nordenskiöld (1877–1932), the prominent Swedish americanist. Since the end of the 1890s Erland Nordenskiöld had devoted his life to South America, first as a zoologist but soon turning to ethnography, archaeology, and (ethno-)history. His extensive fieldwork, his productive authorship, his devotion to students, and his professional museum experience made him a respected and beloved teacher and supervisor.

Many of Erland Nordenskiöld's students would, indeed, over time make acclaimed americanist contributions of their own. These students included Sven Lovén (1875–1948), Karl Gustav Izikowitz (1903–1984), Gösta Montell (1899–1975), Gustaf Bolinder (1888–1957), Alfred Metraux (1902–1963), Stig Rydén (1908–1965), Henry S. Wassén (1908–1996), and Sigvald Linné.

Through their teacher they would not only receive theoretical and, in most cases, fieldwork training, they would also be familiar with archival research and museum work. Following the example of Erland Nordenskiöld, most of these students would as americanists concentrate almost exclusively on South America, except for Sigvald Linné who primarily, but certainly not exclusively, focused his research work on Lower Central America and Mesoamerica.

Erland Nordenskiöld's importance to the high standing of Swedish americanist research during the first half of the 1900s can not be underestimated. However, it must be emphasized that Nordenskiöld was not the first Swede to study the American Indian.

If we expand the meaning of the "americanist" concept, we find that such interest in Sweden traces its roots to the New Sweden colony (1638–1655) that covered approximately the present state of Delaware. From the colony derive documents with ethnographical

This foreword is reprinted in the companion volume by Sigvald Linné, *Archaeological Researches at Teotihuacan, Mexico*.

information, (ethno-)historical sources that have proved to be important for the study of the Lenape (Delaware) Indians. In Sweden this early interest was, not surprisingly, mostly limited to the absolute upper echelon of the Swedish society and often manifested in the time typical of *Kunst und Wunderkammer* (Art and miracle chambers) established in the castles and mansions of the royalty and aristocracy. The very earliest American Indian collections in Sweden were, indeed, "curiosities" from this very period—a fact that would catch the attention of the broadly oriented Sigvald Linné later in his career (see, for example, his articles *Drei alte Waffen aus Nordamerika im Staatlichen Ethnographischen Museum in Stockholm* [1955] and *Three North American Indian Weapons in the Ethnographical Museum of Sweden* [1958]).

From the 1700s and onward, ethnographical and Precolumbian collections from the Americas were increasingly gathered and systematically organized at universities and various cabinets of naturalia, such as at the Royal Swedish Academy of Sciences founded in 1739.

In the 1800s Swedish travelers visited the New World in greater numbers and sometimes described in accounts their meetings with Indians. One of those travelers was Fredrika Bremer (1801–1865) in the early 1850s. Then in the latter part of the 1800s true americanist efforts with published results were made by Swedish natural scientists, early archaeologists, and ethnographers, including such people as Carl Bovallius (1849–1907), working primarily in Costa Rica and Nicaragua in the 1880s and later in northern South America; Eric Boman (1867–1925), working in Argentina and adjacent areas; Gustaf Nordenskiöld (1868–1895), the elder brother of Erland Nordenskiöld, working in the early 1890s in Mesa Verde in the southwestern United States; Axel Klinckowström (1867–1933), working in the early 1890s in northeastern South America; and Carl V. Hartman, working in the 1890s in northern Mexico, Costa Rica, and El Salvador. Instrumental for Carl V. Hartman's pioneering archaeological work in Costa Rica was Hjalmar Stolpe (1841–1905). Stolpe was himself a natural scientist, archaeologist, and an americanist, and he had researched American Indian ornamental art as well as the archaeology of Peru during the Swedish Vanadis-expedition that circumnavigated the world from 1883 to 1885.

Erland Nordenskiöld had an important influence on Linné, but Hjalmar Stolpe's influence can not be underestimated either. Influenced by currents abroad, Hjalmar Stolpe in the early 1870s helped promote the founding of a Swedish anthropological society, later The Swedish Society for Anthropology and Geography. Its prestigious journal *Ymer* became attractive for the early americanists in Sweden. Furthermore, impressed by what he had seen in Copenhagen, Hjalmar Stolpe was instrumental in the founding of an ethnographical museum in Stockholm, which traces its roots via the Museum of Natural History to the previously mentioned cabinet of naturalia of The Royal Academy of Sciences. Hjalmar Stolpe became the first director of this ethnographical museum in 1900, which today is The National Museum of Ethnography (Etnografiska Museet). It was at this very museum that Linné began his work in 1929 and for which he was the director from 1954 to 1966.

Through the museum, he would publish his major works, and many of his shorter articles appeared in its journal *Ethnos,* first published in 1936.

Linné recognized the importance of history—the history of learning, the history of ethnography-anthropology, and particularly the history of americanist research, especially as it had developed in Sweden. He had detailed knowledge about the *Kunst und Wunderkammer* and cabinet of naturalia periods, about his americanist predecessors, about Hjalmar Stolpe's ambitious ethnographical exhibition venture in Stockholm from 1878 to 1879, about the contents of the Swedish contributions to and the network of contacts that developed at the American-Historical Exhibition in Madrid 1892, and about the organization of and contributions at the International Congress of Americanists held in Stockholm in 1894 and in Gothenburg (together with Haag) in 1924.

This historical knowledge was probably an expression of a sincere intellectual curiosity; however, the academic training under Erland Nordenskiöld also emphasized the importance of using (ethno-)historical sources in archaeological and ethnographical research. One of Linné's major publications, *El Valle y La Ciudad de Mexico en 1550* (1948), which discussed the oldest preserved map of Mexico City kept at Uppsala University library, certainly reflects his interest in history. Already in 1939 Linné had presented his initial research about the contents and the background of the map at International Congress of Americanists held in Mexico City, one of the many international congresses and conferences in which he participated.

When Linné approached Erland Nordenskiöld in Gothenburg in the mid-1920s he had already left behind studies in the natural sciences (chemistry). Obviously Nordenskiöld made a deep impression, because from then on Linné changed his focus of study to archaeology and ethnography of the Americas. Nevertheless, he always recognized the importance of the natural sciences, and his first major graduate work, *The Technique of South American Ceramics* (1925), included microscopic analysis. It received fine reviews from Alfred Kroeber in *American Anthropologist,* and much later, in 1965, it was praised as a "major pioneer work" in a volume from the "Ceramics and Man" symposium held in 1961 at Burg Wartenstein.

The following major work as a student for Erland Nordenskiöld was his dissertation, *Darien in the Past: The Archaeology of Eastern Panama and Northwestern Colombia* (1929), based on fieldwork during Erland Nordenskiöld's last expedition in 1927 to Colombia and Panama. Again reviews in *American Anthropologist* praised the work: Alfred Kroeber wrote that "the Göteborg technique and standard of scholarship are thoroughly upheld." Interestingly enough, the great authority Doris Stone maintained as late as 1984 that Linné's work from 1929 was still the best for that particular area.

In 1929 Linné moved from the west coast of Sweden back to his native Stockholm, having received a position at the ethnographical museum. The previous director of the museum, Costa Rica expert Carl V. Hartman, had retired, and the africanist Gerhard Lindblom was the recently appointed new director. Much work was needed to organize the museum after the move from central Stockholm to a new location at an adjacent recreational area. But Linné also worked with Precolumbian/archaeological collections from Lower Central America purchased earlier by Carl V. Hartman. Besides studying the rich collections at the museum, he would throughout the years study Precolumbian collections in Europe during his vacations. Over time his knowledge about Precolumbian art and the acquisitions contexts of such collections grew to become, simply expressed, immense.

One reason why Linné began to look toward Mesoamerica was that the museum had fine Precolumbian collections, specifically, the Edvin Paulson collection, from this culture area. No Swede had previously done serious field archaeology in Mesoamerica. The fact that Sweden had excellent diplomatic relations with Mexico and that Swedish business interests were well established in Mexico had significant implications for Linné's archaeological research at Teotihuacan in 1932. He received support from Swedish diplomats and from such firms as The Mexican Match Company and the L. M. Ericsson Telephone Company as well as from the Royal Swedish Academy of Sciences and the J. A. Wahlberg Foundation/The Swedish Society for Anthropology and Geography. Several important professional colleagues also gave him advice and assistance, including Manuel Gamio, Ignacio Marquina, Eduardo Noguera, Sylvanus Morley, Gustav Stromsvik, Frans Blom, and George C. Vaillant, who Linné especially held in high esteem. This support was important, particularly during his travels to numerous sites outside the Valley of Mexico, such as to the Yucatán Peninsula. Considering that his actual excavations of the large Xolalpan public structure at Teotihuacan lasted only about four months, the results were impressive. Two years later, in 1934, Linné's report, *Archaeological Researches at Teotihuacan, Mexico,* was published through the museum with funding from the Humanistic Foundation in Stockholm and from the previously mentioned Swedish-American businessman Edvin Paulson. In 1935 George C. Vaillant in *American Anthropologist* praised Linné for "the presentation of a technical field excavation in such terms that anyone can follow his text and see the relationship between details of position of specimens and the larger problems of history and anthropology."

The expedition of 1932 proved so successful and promising that a new Teotihuacan venture was soon under way. The following individuals and groups were again instrumental for the realization of Linné's new project: the Swedish diplomatic representation in Mexico under C. G. G. Anderberg; the courtesy of Mexican authorities; the business firms Compañía Mexicana de Cerillos y Fósforos, South America; and Empresa de Teléfonos Ericsson, South America. Important support also came from The Vega Foundation/The Swedish Society for Anthropology and Geography and the Swedish-Mexican Society in Stockholm as well as from private persons such as the previously mentioned A. E. Paulson. Again, the intention was to excavate at Teotihuacan but also at other places in and around the Valley of Mexico. Furthermore, the project included ethnographical explorations that were the particular concern of Gösta Montell, a fellow student under Erland Nordenskiöld in Gothenburg and later a colleague at the museum in Stockholm.

The excavations primarily involved the large Tlamimilolpan public structure, similar in type to the Xolalpan house ruin, which further indicated the former true urban character of that huge archaeological site from mainly the Classic period. In 1942 the museum published Linné's report *Mexican Highland Cultures. Archaeological Researches at Teotihuacan, Calpulalpan and Chalchicomula in 1934/35.* In 1950 Richard Woodbury concluded in *American Antiquity* that "this report is a 'must' for all who are interested in Americas high cultures." Gösta Montell also published the results—a book about Mexico and its native peoples and cultures, written for the Swedish general public.

The Mexican authorities permitted Linné to bring the vast majority of the archaeological finds from both expeditions to Sweden, where they were carefully cataloged. (These finds also characterize the ethnographical collections.) His Teotihuacan finds have been represented in various exhibitions, including the important "Teotihuacan: City of the Gods" exhibition in 1993 in San Francisco. The detailed reports and the correctly cataloged collections still provide a rich data base for new research and interpretations, like the recently published work from 2001 on the Teotihuacan figurines by Sue Scott.

Linné's *Zapotecan Antiquities and the Paulson Collection in the Ethnographical Museum of Sweden* (1938) published by the museum is another major work that again demonstrates his interest in Precolumbian art. This research on identifying the iconography of Zapotecan funerary urns seems not as well known as his Teotihuacan reports. It nevertheless received fine comments by the acclaimed archaeologists Alfonso Caso and Ignacio Bernal in their important work *Urnas de Oaxaca* (1952).

The Teotihuacan excavations in the 1930s was the last of Linné's big fieldwork projects; however, Linné made some later field visits in 1947–48 to Guerrero, which at that time was little known archaeologically. Interestingly enough, as mentioned in his article *Archaeological Problems in Guerrero,* published in the museum journal *Ethnos* (1952), he saw a connection with the Olmec culture, which was increasingly beginning to be archaeologically identified.

Over the years Linné published numerous scientific and popular articles but also books for the general public, particularly those about the Precolumbian cultures of Mesoamerica. He gave, of course, public lectures at the museum. As associate professor and later professor of general and comparative ethnography, a position that went with the museum directorship, he had many students; however, only a few would pursue his Mesoamericanist interest, such as Anna-Britta Hellbom, the former curator of the Americas at the ethnographical museum in Stockholm. Linné made formal complaints about the impossible workload that included administration, teaching, and supervising students, in addition to being the museum director. After his final retirement in 1969 the museum directorship was indeed officially separated from university positions.

The contributions of Linné resulted not only in fine reviews but also in various marks of distinction, including the Anders Retzius medal in 1937 in Sweden, the Loubat prize in 1943, and the Sparrman medal in 1972. In 1951 he was awarded an honorary doctorate in Mexico, and in 1957 he received The Huxley Memorial Medal in England.

In 1994 the 48th International Congress of Americanists was held in Stockholm and

Uppsala. During a session about Swedish americanists, arranged by The Swedish Americanist Society and led by Åke Hultkrantz who is a famous expert on North American Indian religions and shamanism, the contributions of Linné were of course emphasized. Sigvald Linné had the academic integrity and good judgement not to generalize far from the basic findings, even when it was from archaeology, ethnography, or (ethno-)history. Linné is foremost remembered as an archaeologist, but he also mastered the broad cultural background for his conclusions, whether the data came from excavations, ethnography, archives, or the libraries. For us of a younger generation who had the great privilege to meet Linné as retired, living in Helsingborg in the very southern part of Sweden, he was a living encyclopedia with a great sense of humor and generosity. It is no wonder that he had been popular among his crew members from the contemporary local population during the Teotihuacan excavations, and his contributions to this day are remembered and valued.

For a Sigvald Linné bibliography, please see Staffan Brunius, Not Only From Darien to Teotihuacan—the Americanist Contributions of Sigvald Linné, *Acta Americana [Journal of the Swedish Americanist Society]* 1, no. 1 (1993).

INTRODUCTION TO THE
2003 EDITION

George L. Cowgill

In 1934 and 1935 Swedish anthropologist/archaeologist Sigvald Linné, aided by his wife and Gösta Montell, carried out archaeological surveys and excavations in the vicinities of Chalchicomula (Ciudad Serdán) in east-central Puebla, Calpulalpan in the state of Tlaxcala, and the site of Tlamimilolpa in Teotihuacan. This was the second of his two archaeological expeditions to this region. As in his previous work at Teotihuacan in 1932 (Linné 1934), he was greatly aided by the advice of George C. Vaillant of the American Museum of Natural History, as well as by eminent Mexican archaeologists, including Alfonso Caso, Manuel Gamio, Ignacio Marquina, and Eduardo Noguera.

Both Kent Flannery and René Millon have observed, verbally if not in print, that our ideas have finite lifetimes, but good data are good forever. Even if there is no such thing as "pure" data free of any interpretive presuppositions, this insight is basically true. The present volume and Linné's earlier report on his 1932 work at Xolalpan (site 2:N4E2 of the Teotihuacan map [Millon et al. 1973]) and Las Palmas (14:N3E2) are cases in point. Linné made excellent use of the literature available to him, and most of his ideas were well-reasoned and often quite astute, given the knowledge and intellectual climate of the time. But he emphasized that the archaeology of Mesoamerica was barely beginning and that it was to be expected that there would be vast changes in our understandings of the pre-Conquest past. He would surely have been very disappointed if many of his ideas and interpretations had not been superseded. This has indeed been the case. Today they have an honorable place in the history of archaeological thought, but on their account alone, there would be little reason for republication of his reports, long out of print. His data are another story. To be sure, there is no evidence that he ever used screens, and he paid little attention to potsherds or other artifacts that were not part of grave offerings or of exceptional interest as individual objects. His field methods fell considerably short of today's standards, but they compare favorably with other field practices of the time and, for that matter, those of many more recent projects. He published plans of the excavated part of Tlamimilolpa (Plate 1 and p. 111) and what he called "somewhat schematized" (p. 108) cross-sections of a portion of the ruin centered around Room 1 (pp. 110–111), and some plans and sections of details (p. 119). He published a cross-section of Cache 1 (p. 121), but no drawings of any of the thirteen graves he encountered. Photos of excavated rooms and other architecture are on pp. 97, 101, 103, and 117. He identified three construction stages. It is interesting to compare his stratigraphic information with the profiles of a number of deep but areally limited test excavations published by Millon (1992). Linné published almost no physical anthropological data. Contextual data on finds not associated with graves are often rather vague. I suspect that an attempt to construct a Harris diagram for Tlamimilolpa would confront one with a number of irresolvable ambiguities, but the effort would be instructive.

We need not belabor the quantities and kinds of data that Linné did not report. The fact is that what he *did* report is of exceptional and lasting importance. His discussions of the things that interested him are keenly observed, well illustrated, and highly informative. After an extensive review of data on Teotihuacan grave lots, Sempowski (1994:27) says Linné's "reports on and illustrations of the artifactual offerings associated with particular burials are unparalleled in their systematic presentation." Even today, with all the advances since the 1930s, very few Teotihuacan apartment compounds have been excavated as extensively as Tlamimilolpa and also had the results published as fully as Linné did. Manzanilla (1993) is a major exception, although full reports of some other meticulous excavations of relatively large parts of compounds are in various stages of preparation. Thus, a great deal of the information in this book is of permanent interest, especially for Teotihuacan specialists, but also for all other Mesoamericanists and for scholars interested in comparative studies of early complex societies.

In November 1934 through January 1935 Linné carried out surface reconnaissance in the vicinity of Chalchicomula (now Ciudad Serdán) in eastern Puebla, roughly 170 km from Teotihuacan and not far from the border of the state of Veracruz, and trenched a mound in this district near Aljojuca. A major finding was that Teotihuacan-related materials were nearly absent. He considered, correctly, that most of the materials were related to what Vaillant called the "Cuicuilco-Ticomán" culture, although he delicately suggested that Vaillant's estimate of a date ca. A.D. 400–700 might be too recent. Today we would date them to the Late Preclassic, in the last few centuries B.C. Linné correctly related some polychrome sherds to Postclassic Cholula, but saw almost nothing he considered Aztec. He saw, probably correctly, some connections with Gulf Lowlands ceramics. Although he found some Thin Orange Ware (his "yellowish-red" ware) he no longer thought it had been made in this region (as he had in 1934). For good reason, in the light of his data, he doubted whether there had been a Teotihuacan outpost in this region. In passing, he mentioned Cantona—a site of considerable recent interest—as among sites that "may be described as cities" (p. 49).

Given that Thin Orange, which we now know was made in southern Puebla (Rattray 1990a) began to be imported to Teotihuacan at least as early as the first century A.D., it does not seem that Linné found very much in the Ciudad Serdán region that could be attributed to the long interval between the Late Preclassic and the Late Postclassic. I do not know whether this hiatus has been borne out by later research. However, Linné considered the region environmentally marginal (although it was far from uninhabited in the 1930s) and this may explain the apparent paucity of Classic to Early Postclassic occupation.

The situation was far different in western Tlaxcala state, where Linné surveyed and made limited excavations at three sites 2.5 to 15 km east of Calpulalpan in March 1935 while Montell was supervising work at Tlamimilolpa. The three sites were Las Colinas (where Linné worked most intensively), and near San José Zoquiapan and San Nicolás el Grande. Probably his most notable find was an elaborately decorated mold-impressed bowl in Grave II at Las Colinas, the celebrated "Calpulalpan vessel" that continues to be the subject of much iconographic analysis and speculation. Linné recognized that both the architecture and nearly all the ceramics he found at these sites were virtually identical to that of Teotihuacan itself. Today it would be interesting to do compositional analyses of the ceramics to determine what proportion of the ceramics was locally made and whether some are imports from the Teotihuacan Valley. Calpulalpan is only about 40 km from Teotihuacan and can be reached without traversing any difficult terrain. It was very clearly within the Teotihuacan cultural sphere, and there is little doubt that it was within the Teotihuacan regional state. It is about 70 km from Cholula, whose political relationship to Teotihuacan remains enigmatic.

Excavations at Tlamimilolpa began on 11 February 1935, with a crew that before long totaled "21 men and an errand boy" (p. 92), and concluded on 22 April. Linné's report, published in 1942, makes use of a good deal of literature published after 1935, showing that he was keeping well informed about developments in Mesoamerica. However, it is useful to set his work at Tlamimilolpa in the context of research since 1942. This is not the place for a general review of current knowledge about Teotihuacan. For that, see Cowgill (2000), Millon (1992), and the numerous publications cited therein. Here, I summarize information gathered since 1942 that pertains specifically to the site of Tlamimilolpa.

During the initial stage of the Teotihuacan Mapping Project (Millon 1973; Millon et al. 1973), in the course of discovering the outer limits of the urban zone, Tlamimilolpa was revisited on 6 and 7 September 1962, by a team consisting of James Bennyhoff, Joseph Marino, Charles Fletcher, and Pedro Baños. Notes and a small surface collection were made. It was visited again between June and August 1966, by a team composed of René Millon, Warren Barbour, and Arnulfo de Lucio, when further notes and larger collections were made. In 1983 Evelyn Rattray carried out further excavations at the site. Rattray (1989) includes a preliminary report on these excavations.

Linné was emphatic in saying that in the limited time available, he had been unable to reach any of the outer edges of the Tlamimilolpa ruins. Unlike the Xolalpan ruin, he found the plan of Tlamimilolpa puzzling, and later students have continued to be puzzled. Linné frequently refers to the long and narrow access-ways, which make a number of right-angle turns, as "alleys," and it seems clear that he tended to think of the site as a crowded urban neighborhood. Millon (1976) interprets it as a single large apartment compound, with outer walls only four to eight meters beyond the limits of Linné's plan on the north, west, and south, and 16 m beyond on the east. This makes it overall about 95 m east-west by ca. 62 m north-south, for a total area of about 5,890 m². Linné believed that Tlamimilolpa's plan changed considerably over time and that it grew by accretion. Nevertheless, he laments that he did not have time to explore earlier construction stages very much. Millon (1976:218–220, 224) acknowledges fragmentary evidence for accommodating increased size in domestic groups by subdividing existing apartments or single rooms, and he recognizes that Linné's plan could be interpreted as representing growth by accretion rather than from a preconceived plan; however, he finds this unlikely and thinks it was at least partly the result of a preconceived plan. Probably only additional excavations carried to subsoil over large areas (perhaps still possible) could resolve this issue.

Angulo (1987) argues plausibly but not conclusively for changes in the layout of the Tetitla apartment compound (1:N2W2). At Tlajinga 33 (33:S3W1), Widmer (1987) shows clear evidence for major changes over time in its layout. Tlajinga 33 may be an atypical case, but at present the degree to which most Teotihuacan apartment compounds approximated their present layouts from the beginning remains an open question. We are still very short of excavations of Teotihuacan apartment compounds in which large areas are excavated down to subsoil with rigorous attention to discerning the entire construction sequence.

An important Mapping Project finding was the proportions of sherds and other artifacts of various types and periods found on the surface of Tlamimilolpa, as determined by the ca. 750 rim and feature sherds from the 1962 and 1966 surface collections, phased by approximately the criteria of Rattray (2001). This information goes some way toward making up for the absence of this kind of data from the stratigraphically distinct layers excavated by Linné—the more so since the extensive recycling of earlier material in later building fill at Teotihuacan means that sherds from the earliest occupations in the vicinity are well-represented in surface collections. In round numbers, the percentages of the 607 phased sherds are as follows:

pre-Patlachique	none
Patlachique (ca. 110–111 b.c.)	none
Tzacualli (ca. a.d. 1–125)	2%
Miccaotli (ca. a.d. 125–200)	5%
Tlamimilolpa* (ca. a.d. 200–350)	12%
Xolalpan (ca. a.d. 350–550)	20%
Metepec (ca. a.d. 550–650)	7%
Coyotlatelco (ca. a.d. 650–850)	12%

* For better or worse, both the Tlamimilolpa and Xolalpan apartment compounds have been used as names of phases in the Teotihuacan ceramic sequence. In this introduction I use the terms in both senses. I believe the context always makes it clear which sense I mean.

| Mazapan (ca. A.D. 850–1050) | 3% |
| Aztec (ca. A.D. 1050–1600) | 40% |

To judge from the above figures and those from collections from other sites in the area, the site of Tlamimilolpa was a good kilometer beyond the eastern margin of Patlachique phase occupation. There was probably a sparse occupation somewhere in the vicinity, if not exactly at this site, in the Tzacualli phase, although Tlamimilolpa was at the eastern margin of occupation during this and all succeeding Teotihuacan Period phases. Miccaotli phase occupation was also probably only moderate in the vicinity, but ceramics of the Tlamimilolpa and Xolalpan phases are more abundant, and the decrease in the Metepec phase does not seem drastic (if ceramics of this phase have been identified correctly, and bearing in mind that this phase may have lasted only about half as long as each of the two preceding phases). Linné noted that Mazapan phase ceramics were far less abundant than at Xolalpan or Las Palmas, while there was a far greater quantity of Aztec at Tlamimilolpa. Both of these observations are borne out by the TMP surface collections, although Aztec ceramics occur in such enormous quantities in some other parts of the TMP survey area (Garraty 2000) that the Tlamimilolpa concentration does not stand out by comparison. Linné (this volume, p. 178) recognized that Coyotlatelco phase ceramics were present, some almost identical to examples shown by Tozzer (1921), whereas others differ. Nevertheless, for reasons unclear to me, he considered Coyotlatelco foreign to Teotihuacan. Subsequent research, including neutron activation analyses (Crider 2002) shows conclusively that it was produced locally.

Linné recognized that two vessels purchased locally and alleged to have been found in a field in San Martín de las Pirámides (just north of San Francisco Mazapan) were in fact foreign (this volume, p. 178 and figs. 318–319, p. 175). He thought they might have come from Cholula. However, one of them clearly comes from northwestern Mexico or the southwestern United States and is possibly Ramos Polychrome (Randall McGuire, personal communication, 1980). It is interesting to speculate about how such a vessel found its way to Teotihuacan. The other vessel is of a type unfamiliar to me but certainly is not in any local style.

One of the most valuable aspects of Linné's volumes is their relatively full discussions of grave lots and high-quality illustrations of many of the finds. Phases assigned to the 13 Tlamimilolpa burials in recent publications on Teotihuacan grave lots (Rattray 1992; Sempowski 1994) are best summarized by the following table:

Burial	Sempowski	Rattray
1	Late Tlamimilolpa	Late Tlamimilolpa
2	Late Xolalpan	Metepec
3	Xolalpan	unphased

4	Late Xolalpan	Late Xolalpan
5	Xolalpan-Metepec	Late Tlamimilolpa
6	Xolalpan-Metepec	not included
7	unphased	Late Tlamimilolpa
8	unphased	not included
9	unphased	Early Xolalpan
10	unphased	Early Xolalpan
11	unphased	Early Xolalpan
12	unphased	not included
13	Xolalpan	Late Xolalpan

Several of the burials in Tlamimilolpa were of infants and had few offerings, and Sempowski and Rattray tend to treat them as unphased or omit them altogether. The only pronounced discrepancy in their phasings is for Burial 5. Linné (this volume, pp. 135–136) illustrates some of the obsidian but none of the four ceramic vessels (other than miniatures) from this burial, and I cannot resolve this discrepancy, although his discussion of the context suggests that it may pertain to construction Stage III.

By far the largest and most significant of these grave lots is the one from Burial 1. In terms of sheer quantity of objects, this is probably still the richest documented Teotihuacan burial outside of sacrificial burials at the Feathered Serpent Pyramid (Temple of Quetzalcoatl) (Cabrera et al. 1991) and the Moon Pyramid (Cabrera and Sugiyama 1999). However, as Millon (1976:219–220) notes, it is "impressive more for the quantity than the quality of its offerings." It includes a curious mixture of ceramics most typical of the Early Tlamimilolpa phase or earlier, with others typical of the Late Tlamimilolpa phase. It includes a number of direct-rim cylinder tripods, a form absent among the tens of thousands of sherds from the fill and offerings of the Feathered Serpent Pyramid (except for a few possible examples among foreign sherds of probable Gulf origins), which is Early Tlamimilolpa. Burial 1 also includes a *copa,* a small spouted pitcher on a pedestal base (fig. 211, p. 128). No evidence of *copas* (or the "Copa Ware" from which *copas* and some direct-rim cylinder vases were made, probably locally) was found in the Feathered Serpent Pyramid materials, and the form is not thought to be earlier than Late Tlamimilolpa. Of two *candeleros* Linné illustrates (p. 129), one is single chambered and the other is an early version of a two-chambered *candelero* that is still visibly the result of joining two single-chambered *candeleros,* rather than fusing them into a single body, as is typical of Xolalpan and Metepec phase *candeleros.* No traces of any *candeleros* of any kind were found in the Feathered Serpent Pyramid fill. *Candeleros* are most typical of the Xolalpan and Metepec phases but are thought to have begun to be made in small quantities in Late Tlamimilolpa times. The composite censer found in fragments in Burial 1 (figure 315, p. 171—see Berrin and Pasztory [1993:44, 219] for a far more informative illustration) has some early features, including hand-modeling rather than molding of many of the ornaments, and an early-looking "Tlaloc" type nose-pendant. At the same time, there are numerous cylinder vases with outflaring rims, nubbin supports, and sides that are either vertical or narrow slightly toward the top. This vase form is quite common in the Miccaotli and Early Tlamimilolpa phases but is thought to have virtually disappeared thereafter, being replaced by direct-rim cylinder vases with relatively large circular or rectangular supports. It is unexpected to see so many of the two vase forms in association. All in all, it seems likely that Burial 1 dates to a very early subphase of Late Tlamimilolpa. However, the Teotihuacan ceramic chronology is still subject to refinement. Neither Sempowski nor Rattray have made the bases for their chronological assignments of Tlamimilolpa graves entirely explicit. It is desirable to do a systematic and intensive seriation analysis of the several hundred Teotihuacan grave lots now available for study. In any such analysis, the contents of Tlamimilolpa Burial 1 will play a large role.

By 1942 Linné knew of the results from Jorge Acosta's first season at Tula, where ceramics similar to those identified as Mazapan at Teotihuacan were reported. This enabled Linné to clearly identify Teotihuacan with the earlier of the "Toltecs" described in sixteenth-century chronicles; earlier than the "Toltecs" associated with Tula and with central Mexican elements in Lowland Maya sites such as Chichén Itzá.

Linné continued to be interested in Mesoamerican archaeology long after 1942, and he published one of the first radiocarbon dates for Teotihuacan (Linné 1956), an (uncalibrated) date of A.D. 235 plus/minus 65 years for Burial 1. Calibration would make this date a little later, well within the current estimate of ca. A.D. 200–350 in calendar years for the Tlamimilolpa phase, and quite consistent with an early Late Tlamimilolpa date. This article is also significant because in 1942 Linné, who by then could use the five-stage sequence for Teotihuacan proposed by Vaillant (unavailable in 1934), suggested that the Tlamimilolpa ruin was probably somewhat later than that at Xolalpan (this volume, p. 186). However, by 1956, based on the tripod vessels in Burial 1, Linné argued for the reverse sequence. Of course, both sites were probably occupied continuously from at least Late Tlamimilolpa through the Metepec phases, but Linné certainly had it right in 1956 as regards the sequence of ceramic phases named after these sites by Pedro Armillas.

Linné illustrates a number of imported sherds from the Lowland Maya and Gulf Lowlands, including some fine examples of Early Classic polychrome basal flange bowls (p. 179). Subsequent reconnaissance and excavations at Tlamimilolpa (Rattray 1989) have recovered a good many more sherds from both regions. Tlamimilolpa is only a short distance north of the "Merchants'" enclave, where even higher proportions of foreign ceramics (up to 3 percent Maya and 6 percent Gulf) have been found in excavations (Rattray 1990b).

As in his earlier report on Xolalpan, Linné was struck by the apparent scarcity of utilitarian ceramics and other evidence of food preparation at Tlamimilolpa (p. 169). This is probably one of the reasons why so many scholars could think of Teotihuacan as an "empty" ceremonial city with little permanent population, even through the 1950s. Nevertheless, the Mapping Project surface collection found that about 20 percent of the Teotihuacan

Period sherds from Tlamimilolpa were from burnished ollas and another 14 percent from utilitarian San Martín Orange Ware, mostly craters (a much higher proportion of San Martín Orange than at Xolalpan). It is somewhat hard to understand why there is such a large discrepancy in these findings. The best explanation I can think of is that Linné's workmen were under the impression that plain unslipped sherds were of no interest, and Linné failed to note in the field that they were not being collected. More recent excavations in Teotihuacan apartment compounds have found ample evidence of domestic activities. Taken together with the Mapping Project surface collections, there is no reasonable doubt that Tlamimilolpa had a sizable number of residents who carried out a full range of domestic activities there.

The socioeconomic status of the occupants of Tlamimilolpa was perhaps relatively low, although it may have varied somewhat over time and among different apartments within the excavated area. Millon (1976:219–220) notes that it has "a crowded, cramped appearance when compared with other compounds." He suggests that, like site B in the La Ventilla district, it "may have been occupied by people of relatively low status who lived in crowded tenement-like quarters." He suggests (Millon 1976:227) that at least six status levels can tentatively be identified at Teotihuacan, and he would place the occupants of Tlamimilolpa and La Ventilla B in the lowest of these. However, I note that Linné (pp. 115–116) found traces of mural paintings in seven rooms and one patio at Tlamimilolpa, and this might suggest a higher status for at least some occupants. Incidentally, although Linné offers no interpretation of the one mural fragment in good enough condition to be illustrated (figure 190, p. 116), it looks like the feet and lower legs of a frontal human figure wearing tufted sandals.

A great deal more could be done with Linné's collections from Tlamimilolpa. Most of the material is at the National Museum of Ethnography, in Stockholm, while some of the finer pieces are in Mexico, at the Museo Nacional de Antropología or the Teotihuacan site museum. Scott's (1993, 2001) studies of figurines are impressive examples of what can be done with these materials.

There are also recent publications that show some of Linné's finds in greater detail or in different aspects. A notable example is the catalog of the 1993 show at the DeYoung Museum in San Francisco (Berrin and Pasztory 1993). Objects from Tlamimilolpa include the important composite censer from Burial 1 on pp. 44 and 219 (pp. 171 and 173, this volume), two *floreros* from Burial 1 on p. 238 (p. 128, this volume), one of the vases with outflaring lip and nubbin supports from Burial 1 on p. 249 (127, this volume), two of the painted clay masks found under floor 3 of Room 1 on pp. 219 and 220 (plates 3 and 4, this volume), a half-conical figurine from Burial 2 on p. 230 (p. 133, this volume), a "puppet" figurine from Burial 13 on pp. 232–233 (p. 140, this volume), a direct-rim cylinder vase from Cache 1 on p. 249 (p. 142, this volume), an unusual two-chambered *candelero* in the shape of a fish from Room 38 on p. 267 (p. 122, this volume), and a direct-rim cylinder vase purchased by Linné that he considered possibly from the Tuxtlas region of southern

Veracruz on p. 257 (p. 94, this volume). On pp. 234 and 235 are three clay stamps collected by Linné. A so-called "plastersmoother"* is shown on p. 123 and is attributed ambiguously to the Stockholm museum but is in all probability from one of Linné's excavations.

ACKNOWLEDGMENTS

The University of Alabama Press is to be congratulated on making Linné's valuable books widely available again.

LITERATURE CITED

Angulo V., Jorge
  1987   Nuevas consideraciones sobre los llamados conjuntos departamentales, especialmente Tetitla. In *Teotihuacan: Nuevos Datos, Nuevas Síntesis, Nuevos Problemas,* edited by E. McClung de Tapia and E. C. Rattray, pp. 275–315. Instituto de Investigaciones Antropológicas, Universidad Nacional Autónoma de México, Mexico City.
Berrin, Kathleen, and Esther Pasztory (editors)
  1993   *Teotihuacan: Art from the City of the Gods.* Thames and Hudson, New York.
Cabrera Castro, Rubén, Saburo Sugiyama, and George L. Cowgill
  1991   The Templo de Quetzalcoatl Project at Teotihuacan: A Preliminary Report. *Ancient Mesoamerica* 2(1):77–92.
Cabrera Castro, Rubén, and Saburo Sugiyama
  1999   El Proyecto Arqueológico de la Pirámide de la Luna. *Arqueología* 21:19–33.
Cowgill, George L.
  2000   The Central Mexican Highlands from the Rise of Teotihuacan to the Decline of Tula. In *The Cambridge History of the Native Peoples of the Americas, Volume II: Mesoamerica, Part 1,* edited by R. E. Adams and M. J. MacLeod, pp. 250–317. Cambridge University Press, Cambridge.
Crider, Destiny
  2002   *Coyotlatelco Phase Community Structure at Teotihuacan.* Manuscript on file, Department of Anthropology, Arizona State University, Tempe, Arizona.
Garraty, Christopher
  2000   Ceramic Indices of Aztec Eliteness. *Ancient Mesoamerica* 11(2):323–340.

* These stone objects doubtless played some role in fashioning the plastered surfaces of walls and floors, but their vesicular texture makes them ill-suited for finishing and polishing and better suited to some abrading operation. Just how they were used remains a puzzle.

Linné, Sigvald

  1934   *Archaeological Researches at Teotihuacan, México.* The Ethnographical Museum of Sweden, Stockholm.

  1956   Radiocarbon dates in Teotihuacan. *Ethnos* 21(3–4):180–193.

Manzanilla, Linda (editor)

  1993   *Anatomía de un Conjunto Residencial Teotihuacano en Oztoyahualco.* Instituto de Investigaciones Antropológicas, Universidad Nacional Autónoma de México, Mexico City.

Millon, René

  1973   *The Teotihuacan Map. Part One: Text.* University of Texas Press, Austin.

  1976   Social Relations in Ancient Teotihuacan. In *The Valley of Mexico: Studies in Pre-Hispanic Ecology and Society,* edited by Eric R. Wolf, pp. 205–248. University of New Mexico Press, Albuquerque.

  1992   Teotihuacan Studies: From 1950 to 1990 and Beyond. In *Art, Ideology, and the City of Teotihuacan,* edited by J. C. Berlo, pp. 339–429. Dumbarton Oaks, Washington, D.C.

Millon, René, R. Bruce Drewitt, and George L. Cowgill

  1973   *The Teotihuacan Map. Part Two: Maps.* University of Texas Press, Austin.

Rattray, Evelyn C.

  1989   El barrio de los comerciantes y el conjunto Tlamimilolpa: Un estudio comparativo. *Arqueología* 5:105–129.

  1990a New Findings on the Origins of Thin Orange Ceramics. *Ancient Mesoamerica* 1(2):181–195.

  1990b The Identification of Ethnic Affiliation at the Merchants' Barrio, Teotihuacan. In *Etnoarqueología: Primer Coloquio Bosch-Gimpera,* edited by Y. Sugiura and M.-C. Serra, pp. 113–138. Instituto de Investigaciones Antropológicas, Universidad Nacional Autónoma de México, Mexico City.

  1992   *The Teotihuacan Burials and Offerings: A Commentary and Inventory.* Vanderbilt University Publications in Anthropology, No. 42, Nashville, Tennessee.

  2001   *Teotihuacan: Ceramics, Chronology, and Cultural Trends.* Instituto Nacional de Antropología e Historia and University of Pittsburgh, Mexico City and Pittsburgh.

Scott, Sue

  1993   *Teotihuacan Mazapan Figurines and the Xipe Totec Statue: A Link Between the Basin of Mexico and the Valley of Oaxaca.* Vanderbilt University Publications in Anthropology, No. 44, Nashville, Tennessee.

  2001   *The Corpus of Terracotta Figurines from Sigvald Linné's Excavations at Teotihuacan, Mexico (1932 & 1934–35) and Comparative Material.* The National Museum of Ethnography, Monograph Series 18, Stockholm.

Sempowski, Martha L.

  1994   Mortuary Practices at Teotihuacan. In *Mortuary Practices and Skeletal Remains at*

Teotihuacan, by Martha L. Sempowski, Michael W. Spence, and Rebecca Storey, pp. 1–314. University of Utah Press, Salt Lake City.

Tozzer, Alfred M.
  1921   *Excavation of a Site at Santiago Ahuitzotla, D. F., Mexico.* Smithsonian Institution, Washington, D.C.

Widmer, Randolph J.
  1987   The Evolution of Form and Function in a Teotihuacan Apartment Compound: The Case of Tlajinga 33. In *Teotihuacan: Nuevos Datos, Nuevas Síntesis, Nuevos Problemas,* edited by E. McClung de Tapia and E. C. Rattray, pp. 317–368. Instituto de Investigaciones Antropológicas, Universidad Nacional Autónoma de México, Mexico City.

MEXICAN HIGHLAND CULTURES

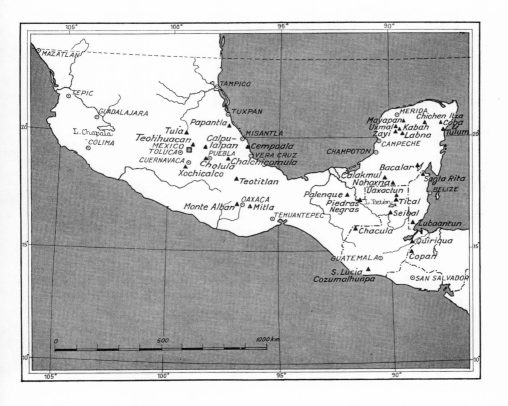

Fig. 1. Important archaeological sites in central and southern Mexico and in northern Central America. The sites are marked with triangles.

TO THE MEMORY

OF

ERLAND NORDENSKIÖLD

P R E F A C E

Erland Nordenskiöld, to whose memory this work is dedicated, was a singularly inspiring teacher, an ingenious researcher, the re-creator of a museum, and a brilliant field-worker. To him, the author owes a heavy debt of gratitude as a pupil, as a member of his sixth and last South-American expedition, and as a fellow-worker at the ethnographical section of the Gothenburg Museum, which under Nordenskiöld's direction attained world-renown. What I learnt from him I have to the best of my ability endeavoured to put into practice, and to whatever humble extent I may have succeeded, to him falls the greater part of the credit.

To Nordenskiöld, field-work did not mean random reconnoiterings, with accident and luck as their principal assets. It was always clear to him that theoretical studies alone put into the explorer's hand the divining-rod telling him what to look for, and where. The acquisition of collections for his museum was his delight and passion, and in working them up he was constantly finding new problems which he attacked with a combination of the critical attitude of a man of science and the imagination of an artist. Problems acted on him as a perpetual spur, and no sooner had he solved one than he propounded new ones for himself and for future investigators.

When a museum sends out an archaeological expedition to foreign lands, not only scientific results are expected but also collections capable of illustrating the ancient cultures concerned. I think the latter task was accomplished as far as was possible, and in this result we are also indebted to the Mexican authorities who with much sympathetic understanding allowed the collections to be taken out of the country. As regards the scientific results, this book is intended to illustrate to what extent exploration of the cultures of ancient Mexico has been advanced through our expedition.

7

C O N T E N T S

INTRODUCTION

In 1932 the Ethnographical Museum of Sweden sent an archaeological expedition to Mexico at the suggestion of the then Swedish envoy to Mexico, Mr. C. G. G. Anderberg. Through a series of fortunate circumstances, not least thanks to the exceeding courtesy of the Mexican authorities and the interested, diligent and conscientious work rendered by our Indian helpers, we — my wife and I — succeeded in attaining valuable results. This encouraged Mr. Anderberg and the director of the Museum, Professor Gerhard Lindblom, to try and bring about a continuation of the enterprise.

As members of this second expedition to Mexico were selected the author and Dr. Gösta Montell. This time too, financial backing was forthcoming from Compañía Mexicana de Cerillos y Fósforos, S. A., and from Empresa de Teléfonos Ericsson, S. A. Several members of the staff of the latter company, particularly Mr. Anders Lilliehöök and Mr. Torsten Tranberg, most kindly furthered our work in many ways. The expedition also received support from the Swedish Society for Anthropology and Geography (the Vega Foundation), the Lars Hierta Memorial Foundation, and the Swedish-Mexican Society at Stockholm. Generous contributions were also received from the then Director-in-Chief of the SKF Ball-Bearing Co., now Swedish Minister to the United Kingdom, Mr. Björn Prytz, and Mr. A. E. Paulson, of New York and Puebla, long-standing patron of the Museum. The latter gentleman also assisted us in various ways in Mexico, besides enriching the expedition's collections with valuable ethnographical and archaeological gifts. The Swedish America-Mexico Line granted a heavy reduction of fares to and from Mexico as well as free home transport of our collections.

To all those who rendered the expedition possible and facilitated its work: to Swedish and Mexican authorities and institutions, Swedish industrial concerns, private persons in Sweden and fellow-countrymen in Mexico, I wish to express my sincere thanks for all the courtesy, kindness and hospitality shown.

According to the plan drawn up in advance, the main objective of the expedition was to proceed with the exploration of the Teotihuacan culture and its area of distribution. Our working programme also included comparative studies at the principal ruined sites in and about the Valley of Mexico. Towards meeting our

Museum's requirements in the way of exhibitable material, we were also to acquire archaeological type collections illustrative of the culture during different epochs of the antiquity of the Valley, from the Early Cultures (Archaic) to the period of the Aztec domination. An especially valuable addition to our Museum's collections we were, thanks to Minister Anderberg's generosity, fortunate enough to obtain through the intermediation of the Mexican National Museum. The owner of a very large collection of beautiful, well preserved and interesting clay vessels, figurines, etc., from Chupícuaro in the State of Guanajuato wished to dispose of it by sale, and this was permitted after the National Museum had selected out certain objects that were considered unique. By this arrangement both institutions were enriched with material that otherwise, by way of curio-venders, certainly would have been broken up and scattered among tourists, thereby becoming lost to scientific study.

The ethnographical exploration of Mexico has been deplorably neglected, which is only natural seeing that that remaining part of the original Indian culture which was not swept away by the storms of the Conquest, has largely survived intact into our times. Modern means of communication, above all the bus traffic, no doubt have a far more levelling effect than the Government's progressive policy for the raising of the Indian population's standard of living. Even if ethnographers cannot be said to be about at the eleventh hour, their work is nevertheless highly important. Many archaeological elements can only be ethnographically explained and thereby given a certain measure of life. To ethnographical studies and collecting work, a comparatively large space had accordingly been allotted in our programme. This department was the principal concern of Dr. Gösta Montell who has already published minor sections of the extensive material, and when his time allows, intends to carry his studies further.

On the journeys that we devoted to ethnographical research and collecting, and on archaeological excursions, mainly in the Valley of Mexico, as well as in the reconnoitring venture at Calpulalpan and vicinity, we received most valuable assistance from Mrs. Helga Larsen, Miss Bodil Christensen and Mr. Ola Apenes, all of them residents of Mexico City. It was only their intimate knowledge of the country and the natives that enabled us to acquire extensive and scientifically important material as well as archaeological collections, valuable for comparative studies, from already known working sites. In the passing away, on May 11th, 1938, of Mrs. Larsen science suffered a great loss, for few scientists in Mexico possess her qualifications for field work among the Indians, whose full confidence she always commanded, and fewer still are those who are her equals in fervent enthusiasm for their work.

We also owe a great debt of gratitude to Dr. and Mrs. George Vaillant, of the National Museum of Natural History. In word and deed they ever smoothed the path for us. And it was from them that, among other things, we received the impulse for the exploration of the Calpulalpan region, a work for which we unfortunately could spare only a restricted time. As on my previous expedition, also now Dr. Alfonso Caso, Dr. Manuel Gamio, Sr. Ignacio Marquina and Sr. Eduardo Noguera were most kind and gave much valuable advice and information.

Dr. Montell and I left Stockholm on September 20th, 1934, and returned on June 15th of the following year. While waiting for the issue of our excavating license we made a series of journeys to places of archaeological and ethnographical interest in and about the Valley of Mexico and to the Chalchicomula district, in the extreme southeast of the State of Puebla. The latter journey I made in the company of Mr. Evert Paulson, then technical director of the L. M. Ericsson telephone station at Puebla, and thanks to the interest he took, and his knowledge of local conditions, valuable acquaintances were made and agreements entered upon as regards excavations.

By the kind courtesy of Sr. José Reygadas Vértiz, director of Departamento de Monumentos, Secretaría de Educación Pública (Ministry of Public Education of the Mexican Government), we first obtained permission to excavate on land belonging to Hacienda de Jalapaxco and neighbouring tracts in the Chalchicomula district. These excavations were carried out during December 1934 and January of the year following. While working here we were the guests of the hacienda owner, Sr. Antonio Trespalacios, who showed us most generous hospitality and afforded us all possible assistance.

Having completed our work at Chalchicomula, we applied for and obtained further permits to excavate. In the beginning of February we located our operations to Teotihuacan. As in 1932, even this time Departamento de Monumentos placed rooms at our disposal in its administration building and provided space for our collections in the store-room of the Teotihuacan Museum. Our friends since our first expedition, the local superintendent Sr. José Pérez and his wife, rendered us many valuable services during our stay at this place, and the pleasant hours we spent in their delightful home are among the brightest memories of our journey. At Teotihuacan work was pursued uninterruptedly and with a large working staff until the end of April, when, for lack of time and funds, we were obliged to return to Sweden.

While Dr. Montell directed the work at Teotihuacan, I — accompanied by Mrs. Larsen and Miss Christensen — occupied myself with archaeological reconnaissances in the neighbourhood of Calpulalpan. With that town for our base, we carried out a series of investigations as well as a trial excavation productive of valuable results, and also certain researches that practically only amounted to taking test samples.

The publication of the present work has exclusively been rendered possible by a grant from the Humanistic Foundation (Humanistiska Fonden). The working up of the material has been delayed for several reasons, the principal one being my having — before I was able to give my full attention to it — to compile a monograph on Zapotecan antiquities (No. 4 of this series) and to write an explanatory text, etc., to the earliest map of the Valley of Mexico, in the possession of the library of the Uppsala University. Circumstances owing to the political situation have prevented the publication of the work.[1]

Even in the present instance Dr. Nils Odhner of the National Museum of Natural History, Stockholm, has zoologically determined the mollusk material brought together in the course of the excavations. The recovered whale bone was also identified by him. Dr. Nils Zenzén of the same institution has determined stone objects from a mineralogical point of view and also carried out petrographic examination of pottery fragments. Miss Elisabeth Strömberg of the Nordical Museum has technically examined textiles of the archaeological material.

Drawings and water colours of objects have with usual minute exactness been executed by the artist, Mr. Axel Hjelm, and maps and plans by Miss Anna-Lisa Dahlén, both of Gothenburg. The fair-copying of the plan, sections and building details of the ruin at Tlamimilolpa, San Juan Teotihuacan, from drawings made from measurements on the spot, is the work of Miss Dahlén in close collaboration with the author.

To my fellow-worker at the office, Miss Ingeborg Törnblom, I am greatly indebted not only for the typing of manuscripts, etc., but also for undertaking that dreariest part of the work in the production of a book, the proof-reading.

The translation into English of the Swedish manuscript has, as in the case of the works referred to above, been carried out by Mr. Magnus Leijer, of Gothenburg.

[1] During the time that has passed since the conclusion of the expedition in 1935, certain of the results thereby attained have been published. Wholly or partly founded on the material gained through the expedition, the following publications have so far appeared:

S. Linné. The expedition to Mexico sent out in 1934—35 by the Ethnographical Museum of Sweden. 1. The archaeological investigations (Ethnos, vol. 1, pp. 39—48, Stockholm 1936).

G. Montell. The expedition to Mexico sent out in 1934—35 by the Ethnographical Museum of Sweden. 2. The ethnographical investigations (Ethnos, vol. 1, pp. 60—66, Stockholm 1936).

G. Montell. Mexikanskt indianliv i forntid och nutid. 220 pp., 48 pls., Stockholm 1936.

S. Linné. Hunting and fishing in the Valley of Mexico in the middle of the 16th century (Ethnos, vol. 2, pp. 56—64, Stockholm 1937).

S. Linné. Statens etnografiska museums expedition till Mexico 1934—35. De arkeologiska undersökningarna (Ethnos, vol. 2, pp. 267—300, 3 pls., Stockholm 1937).

G. Montell. Statens etnografiska museums expedition till Mexico 1934—35. De etnografiska undersökningarna (Ethnos, vol. 2, pp. 301—318, Stockholm 1937).

S. Linné. American roof-apex caps of clay (Ethnos, vol. 3, pp. 18—32, Stockholm 1938).

G. Montell. Yaqui dances (Ethnos, vol. 3, pp. 145—166, Stockholm 1938).

S. Linné. A Mazapan grave at Teotihuacan, Mexico (Ethnos, vol. 3, pp. 167—178, Stockholm 1938).

S. Linné. Blow-guns in ancient Mexico (Ethnos, vol. 4, pp. 56—61, Stockholm 1939).

S. Linné. Fornamerikansk konst och kultur (Ymer, vol. 59, pp. 1—28, Stockholm 1939).

S. Linné. Dental decoration in aboriginal America (Ethnos, vol. 5, pp. 2—28, 1 pl., Stockholm 1940).

S. Linné. Teotihuacan symbols (Ethnos, vol. 6, pp. 174—186, Stockholm 1941).

PART I

ARCHAEOLOGICAL RESEARCHES AND EXCAVATIONS IN THE DISTRICT OF CHALCHICOMULA, STATE OF PUEBLA

When, in the middle of August 1519, Hernando Cortés with his small army of bold adventurers set out from Villa Rica de la Vera Cruz to march, via Tlaxcala, upon Tenochtitlán-Mexico, he laid his route first by way of Jalapa and then through a mountain pass south of Cofre de Perote. According to Krickeberg, from Ixhuacán they could not take the direct route via Quimixtlán and Jalapaxco, as this was held by Aztec forces, and therefore struck through the trackless wilderness west of Cofre de Perote.[1] That any suitable road existed by way of Jalapaxco does not appear very probable, although there might have been one just west of this, via the present-day localities of Aljojuca or El Seco. (The new-built motor road Puebla—Jalapa—Vera Cruz runs through the latter of the above mentioned places.) These regions were late in coming under Aztec dominion, probably not until the reign of Ahuitzotl, 1486—1502.[2] This may perhaps explain why — with one or two exceptions which, however, are by no means absolutely certain — we did not find any traces of Aztec pottery. I have not, however, been able to unearth any detailed record of the Chalchicomula district, either from the time immediately preceding, or following upon, the conquest. Nor is there much of interest to be gathered from the scanty data we have of the colonial era.

[1] Krickeberg 1918—22: 10.

[2] It is, however, remarkable that the place-names with exception for occasional Spanish ones — and meaningless renamings of a very late date — are Mexican. Peñafiel (1897, vol. 2: 91, 19, 147, 30, 262) gives the translation of the place-names referred to in the following:

Chalchicomula. Chalchi-comul-la, síncopa de la palabra mexicana Chalchi-tlacomula, barranca de chalchihuites ó piedras verdes; radicales: *chalchihuitl* y *tlacomulli* ó *tlacomolli*, barranca. According to "Guía ilustrada de México a Veracruz" (7a. edición, 1931 p. 53), in pre-Spanish times this place was known as Xachiculco, which in Mexican means "Rincón informe de arena", though other interpretations have also been advanced (Palacios 1917: 297). In most recent times the place — for reasons not readily understood — has been again renamed, now Ciudad Serdán, after a revolutionary, whose memory was thought worthy of being in this way saved from oblivion.

Aljojuca. A-xoxuh-can, Atla-xoxouh-can, en mexicano; lugar de agua verde; radicales: *atl*, agua; *xoxouhqui* ó *xuxuhqui*, verde; *can*, final de lugar.

Jalapasco. Xal-apaz-co, de origen mexicano; Apazco del arenal; componentes: *xalli*, arena, *apaztli*, lebrillo de barro, y *co*, final de lugar.

Atenco. Atempa ó Atempan, del idioma mexicano, sinónimo de Atenco; en la ribera; compuesto de *atl*, agua, y *tem-pa*, orilla.

Tepetitlan. Tepe-titlan, de lengua mexicana; lugar situado entre los cerros.

15

The first to pursue archaeological research in these parts was Dupaix. He depicts a pyramid,[3] fig. 2, and writes as follows: "I, William Dupaix, late an officer in the Mexican dragoons, left this capital (México) on the fifth of January 1805, having been commanded by His Majesty to proceed to the investigation of whatever monuments of antiquity might be still in existence in this kingdom, of a date anterior to that of the conquest" ... He is on his way from Cordova, back to Mexico City, his route from the former place being, however, unknown. From "the country-house called San Antonio" he passed through San Andrés Chalchicomula via Acatzingo to Cholula.

"At the country-house called San Antonio, formerly San Andrés Chachicomula, I saw an ancient edifice; and two miles further to the north of the country-house an oratory four stories high, in a pyramidal form, resting upon an oblong base. The highest story, which I conjecture was a small covered oratory, is now destroyed. Twelve years ago when I visited this spot it was in existence. The stairs, which were facing the west, are also demolished, as well as the other sides, which corresponded to the cardinal points. The basement story was coated with volcanic stones regularly squared, and the upper stories were plastered and bright. The exact dimensions of these ancient edifices cannot always be ascertained, some local circumstances occasionally rendering the operation impracticable; but every care has been taken in giving the admeasurements in such cases with the nearest possible approximation to accuracy. The human form lives its appointed time and disappears for ever, leaving behind it its likeness: but the monuments of Mexican grandeur sink into decay without the chance of restoration or reproduction, and the time is fast approaching when their entire destruction will be effected."[4]

On his expedition to Mexico 1902—1903, Eduard Seler paid a short visit to the Hacienda de Jalapaxco, in the district of Chalchicomula. The object of this visit was to study an archaeological collection which had been brought together by the manager of the hacienda, Sr. Honorato J. Carrasco.[5] It appears that this gentleman, on his own stating, had opened a large number of grave-mounds in the neighbourhood. To those activities of his, Seler refers in terms that are, perhaps, rather too complaisant: "eine Sammlung ... durch Ausgrabungen zusammengebracht hatte, die er seit dem Jahre 1895 in systematischer Weise ... vorgenommen hatte".[6] This large collection, for the housing of which parts of the hacienda buildings had been adapted as a museum, was purchased by Seler, on his 1910—1911 expedition, for Museum für Völkerkunde, Berlin. Much of the material contained in this collection has been published by Seler in his monograph on Teotihuacan[7] as it includes, among other things a multitude of extremely interesting objects of purely Teotihuacan type. In the report on my excavations at Teotihuacan in 1932, I had frequent occasions to refer to this Jalapaxco material

[3] Kingsborough 1831, vol. 4: part 1, pl. 7. Later he depicts with minor modifications the same pyramid in "Antiquités Mexicaines". Also reproduced in an edition of Prescott (1937: fig. 107, p. 895).
[4] Kingsborough 1831, vol. 6: 421, 426—427; Spanish version, vol. 5: 217.
[5] Seler 1904: 265.
[6] Seler 1915: 443.
[7] Seler 1915: 405—585.

Fig. 2. Temple-pyramid. Chalchicomula district. According to Dupaix.

in connection with the comparative studies. As, however, the collection in question also includes material belonging to an earlier archaeological level as well as such as indicates connection with the peoples that lived on the Atlantic coast, I was inclined to suppose that excavations at this place might yield links between the Teotihuacan culture and those earlier ones. Our working programme was accordingly made to include researches at, and around, Jalapaxco.

RECONNAISSANCES IN THE CHALCHICOMULA DISTRICT

In November 1934 I made a short reconnoitring tour of the Chalchicomula district for the purpose of ascertaining the existence of any important ancient monuments. It then appeared that the most likely area was situated between hacienda San Diego Jalapaxco and the village of San Jerónimo Aljojuca.[1] What information we obtained from Sr. Carrasco, whom we succeeded in locating, was in part incorrect and in part impossible of verification owing to the prevailing

[1] Seler gives the name of the place as San Rodrigo Aljojuca. The local tutelary saint is, and always was, San Jerónimo. It is by this name the village is referred to in Alonso Ponce's travelling account of 1584 (Ponce 1873, vol. 2: 503).

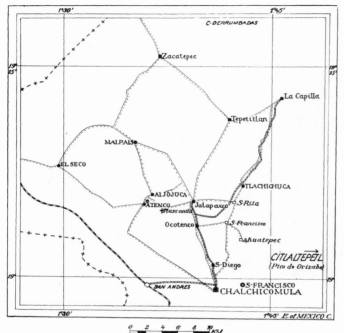

Fig. 3. The district of Chalchicomula, eastern section of the State of Puebla.

political situation. Sr. Carrasco had become well advanced in years, and had lived at the capital for the last decades, and did not take much interest in Jalapaxco. Provided with the requisite excavating license, Dr. Montell and I in December left together for Jalapaxco, where we enjoyed the most generous hospitality of its owner, Sr. Antonio Trespalacios. Besides continuing our reconnoitring in various parts of the Chalchicomula district, we concentrated on examinations of mounds, or, as they are here called, teteles,[2] round about Aljojuca. The turn of the year we spent in and around Mexico City, but January saw us back again at Jalapaxco. Here we excavated a tetele near the village of Aljojuca, and super- ficially studied an area of apparently untouched teteles at hacienda Santa Cecilia Tepetitlán. While walking over the ground, we studied and collected vast numbers of surface finds of pottery fragments. Some 10,000 of these thereby passed through our hands, subsequently proving to be of great value in our attempts at drawing conclusions as to the early culture of this region.

[2] Corruption of Mexican, *tlaltelli*. Lehmann (1922: 286) translates the word *tlatilli*: "Steinhügel". The name for mounds containing graves, or have been foundations of temples or other buildings, and at all events in the latter case are ruins of structures of pyramidal character, varies; *mogotes* in Oaxaca, *cu*, *cues* or *cuecillos* among the Maya Indians and their linguistic kinsmen, *teteles* in the central highlands. Cu, cues, sometimes has been supposed an Arawak loan-word from Haiti or Cuba (Friederici 1926: 35).

18

Fig. 4. "Crater-lake", so-called jalapaxco. Near San Jerónimo Aljojuca.

The Chalchicomula district is situated in the eastern part of the State of Puebla, and borders on the State of Vera Cruz, see sketch map, fig. 3. This border is partly a geographical one: the volcano of Citlaltépetl (Pico de Orizaba), the highest mountain of Mexico, which attains nearly 5,700 m, Sierra Negra, south of it, and the mountains north of Citlaltépetl, which in Cofre de Perote, 4,085 m, reach their highest altitude. This region thus borders on the slope towards the lowland of the Atlantic coast. The northern and central portions of the area are largely composed of plains with an approximate level of 2,500 m above the sea. Here and there high mountains rather abruptly overtop the flat country. As, however, they are strangely enough not shown on the Mexican Ordnance Survey map, which is the basis of the sketch map here reproduced, they have had to be omitted.

Everywhere earlier traces of volcanic activity can be observed, and particularly in the neighbourhood of Cofre de Perote immense lava beds are found. Typical of the region are higher or lower conical mountains which once were volcanoes (Citlaltépetl showed signs of activity even as late as the 19th century). Characteristic, too, are "jalapaxcos" (or xalapascos), mostly circular, crater-like hollows, often found on the plains themselves; reminiscences of the turbulent past of these volcanic regions. They attain considerable dimensions, even up to 1,800 m in

19

diameter, some of them partly filled with water.[3] Hacienda de Jalapaxco stands on the edge of a waterless crater of this kind, and 2 km east of this place is one still larger. The name of the hacienda is an apposite one, "jalapaxco" meaning, as already mentioned, "by (the edge of) the sand-bowl". Between the villages of Aljojuca and Atenco there is a water-bearing jalapaxco, fig. 4, measuring well over 500 m in diameter and 190 m in depth, $^1/_3$ of which is filled with water. Further north some more of the same type are found. This is mentioned as early as by Antonio de Herrera, who in 1596 was appointed Historiador de Indias.[4]

In modern times Chalchicomula has become an important agricultural centre, whose great haciendas above all produce large quantities of maize and wheat. In latter years, the compulsory partitioning of haciendas into small holdings has, at any rate for the present, paralysed production. Its population is given as ca. 70,000.

No artifacts were found by us on the plains, and our questioning among the local natives regarding the existence of finds yielded unanimously negative answers. The haciendas, like the town of Chalchicomula and its surrounding residential area, are supplied with water from the melted snows of Citlaltépetl by means of extensive aqueducts. The region around Aljojuca obtains its water from the water-bearing jalapaxco, but is otherwise devoid of any natural water supply. If natural conditions, rainfall etc., have not changed in post-Columbian times and the centuries next preceding the conquest, it is difficult to understand how human beings could have lived in these tracts during the dry season, except at Aljojuca and other jalapaxcos that are now dry. Naturally, here as in the Valley of Mexico, disafforestation must have caused deterioration of climate. Possibly even the pre-Spanish population knew how to turn to account the water from the melting snows of the eternal snow region of the volcano.

It may not, however, be altogether improbable that the population made periodical migrations to regions that were water-bearing in the dry season, as, inter alia, is the case in north-western Mexico. Thus the Pápago, adapting themselves to climatic conditions, go in for a sort of seasonal nomadism. In the dry season

[3] Ordóñez 1905.

[4] Herrera (dec. II, lib. X, cap. XXII) accounts for them in detail. It is worthy of note that even in our days the idea prevails that the level of the water is regulated by a subterranean river. Herrera writes: "EN Los terminos de Tecamachalco, y Cachulac, junto a vna aldea dicha Aljoxucan, en lo alto de vn zerro, ay vna laguna que desde lo alto hasta baxar al agua, ay mas de ciento y cinquenta estados, y por vn lado por vna veredilla, baxan los naturales a coger agua, y los ganados a abreuar. No se cria pescado en ella, ni otra fauandija: no crece con las aguas del inuierno, ni mengua con la seca del verano. No se le ha hallado fondo, y presumen que le passa por de baxo vn rio, que va a responder diez leguas, en tierra mas baxa, que llaman Aolizapàn. El agua es muy fria, y de color azul, y porque la del rio es de la misma manera, se tiene esta presunciõ por cosa cierta. Esta en los mismos terminos otra laguna, a tres leguas de la sobredicha, en tierra rasa, y la llaman de Tlachac, y se puede andar a la redonda, y llegar los cauallos a beuer en ella. Tiene vna legua de box, y es tan hondable, que no se le halla suelo: cria ciertos pescadillos blancos, tan grandes como el dedo de la mano, muy sabrosos. Y vna legua esta otra laguna que llaman de Alchichicàn, que quiere dezir, agua amarga: esta en llano, boxa dos leguas: los ganados la beuen, y los engorda: no la hallan suelo, y el agua es muy clara, y no cria pescado, ni otra cosa: con el viento leuanta grandes olas, y haze resaca como la mar, ni tampoco crece ni mengua, como la primera: y ay en su comarca llanos de mas de doze leguas, con grãdes montes, y pastos para ganados ouejunos."

20

Fig. 5. Tetele, at Barrio San Francisco; sacked by treasure hunters.

they live in villages with a sufficient water supply. When the rainy season sets in, they move to villages on the open plains, where they have their cultivations and where they remain till harvest-time, and subsequently repair to places where the water supply will not fail them during the rainless months.[5]

The portion of the Chalchicomula visited by us is roughly bordered by a line running through El Seco—Zacatepec—Tepetitlán—Chalchicomula—El Seco. Our actual studies encompassed a considerably more restricted area, and only the region between Jalapaxco and Aljojuca formed the subject of our special researches. As our researches were principally of a reconnoitring character, the list given in the following of ancient monuments does by no means claim to be complete. These monuments were throughout of a similar kind, namely teteles, earth mounds that had probably served as foundations for dwellings or temples. Their size varies from 2 to 10 m in height, and from 10 to 50 m in width. Their measurements can only be given very approximatively, as all of them are in a more or less demolished state. They are mainly earth-built and throughout appear — unless of circular base — to have been cased with stone, which as a rule was unworked. It is not impossible that the stone may have been dressed, in parts, but carried away and used for building purposes in modern times, as is usual in Mexico. The earth contains artifacts, chiefly potsherds, which were found in it prior to its being used for building material. Thin, horizontal layers of lime, generally met with in the upper parts of the structure and with interspaces of a few decimeters, may be supposed to have served a constructive purpose, viz. that of binding the rather loose earth together. In addition, the mounds contain graves. The shape of the base varies, but is as a rule circular or square.

[5] Hoover 1935: 259.

The teteles have for the most part been stripped of their stone casing, and subsequently planted with maguey. In many cases they have even been ploughed over and planted with maize. In consequence, they have not only been broken up so as to make it impossible to ascertain either their original shape or dimensions, but are even at times difficult to distinguish from natural hillocks. In some cases they have been almost entirely obliterated. In the teteles, the soil is better than that of the fields that have been cultivated for centuries but never manured, which contributes to their continued obliteration. Further effective destruction has been wrought them through the systematic grave-rifling practised in latter days. In this, the teteles were cut through with wide trenches, with the earth thrown up on either side, and this has inspired the local inhabitants to complete the devastation by spreading the soil over the fields. The excavation enterprise carried out by Sr. Carrasco, already referred to, can only be described as archaeological waste-thrift. Before his time, the ravaging appears to have been mainly superficial, although even Dupaix, as we know, complained of rapid devastation as early as the opening years of the 19th century. With the exception of teteles at Tepetitlán, there now remain only some very few of those we have seen that have escaped final obliteration through these quasi-archaeological researches. Treasure hunts carried out by the natives will probably have worked less damage, as they have generally been concerned with teteles that were already trenched.

At the present time there seem to be about 55 more or less obliterated teteles in existence, and at the following places: Barrio San Francisco (east of the town of Chalchicomula), 10; between San Diego and Ahuatepec, 4; San Francisco, 1(?); Santa Rita, 2; Aljojuca, 23; Tepetitlán, 15. "Atlas arqueológico de la República Mexicana" includes a number of localities in the Chalchicomula district, which we did not visit.[6] Atzitzintla, some 15 km south-east of San Andrés Chalchicomula, is said to have 9 teteles; Paso Nacional, about 16 km east of Tepetitlán, contains teteles in numbers not stated, and the same applies to Tepeticpac in the northeastern corner of the district. Other localities given in the above publication are no doubt included in our list, although under different names. Between Atenco and El Seco there are at least 6 teteles, but lack of time prevented their inspection. From the above it will therefore be seen that the total number of so far known teteles in the entire district amounts to at least 75, but the actual figure may well be supposed to lie considerably higher.

Owing to local conditions — or rather malconditions — resulting from the cutting up of the landed estates, we found that only at Aljojuca and Tepetitlán would it be possible, without the military escort offered by the Governor of the State, to carry out excavations. Strangely enough, even as early a writer as Dupaix refers to certain difficulties attached to working in these parts. Unfortunately we did not learn of the existence of the ancient remains at Tepetitlán until our

[6] Marquina 1939: 185 seq.

Fig. 6. Stone ring, from a ball court. Barrio San Francisco.

preparations for excavating at Aljojuca had been completed. Lest the comprehensive programme already drawn up for our expedition be thrown into confusion, we were compelled to restrict ourselves to the latter excavation. As is practically always the case with archaeological work in Mexico, no problems are definitely solved by an excavation: on the contrary, paths previously unknown are apt to open out. In the end it became clear that not until one or more of the teteles at Tepetitlán had been thoroughly examined, would it be possible to bring into full light the pre-Spanish culture and history of these regions, that is to say, as far as archaeology is able to dispel the gloom that is overspreading epochs before the coming of the white man.

Teteles at Barrio San Francisco, many of which were of considerable size, appeared to have been pillaged pretty severely, fig. 5. Strangely enough, in the courtyard of a house by the side of a tetele was found a stone ring, which in all probability was originally used at a ball court, fig. 6. This is all the more remarkable, seeing that the pottery studied by us, though admittedly only consisting of rather plain surface finds, was of the same kind as that of the Aljojuca region. No trace of either Aztec, Cholula or Teotihuacan ceramics was found. Our visit was, however, far too hurried to allow of any pretense at solving the pottery problem. Unfortunately we could get no information as to how or where the stone ring had been recovered. Ball games, with special courts and rings serving for "goals", were of fairly common occurrence from the Maya in the south to the Tarascans in the north.[7] They still survive, although in a modified form, even farther north, as among the Tarahumare. To what particular culture this stone ring should be referred, would seem impossible to determine, but as the game is of great antiquity and ball courts occurred among Zapotecs and Huaxtecs, it does by no means of necessity indicate Aztec influence.

[7] Cf. Blom 1932: 485—530.

23

North of Barrio San Francisco, as far as and including Santa Rita, the teteles were of minor interest. Some were found out on the plains, others, like those of San Francisco, on the slopes of the foothills of Citlaltépetl. On the road from Chalchicomula to Tlachichuca, roughly abreast of Ahuatepec, there is a very large tetele, without doubt the largest in the district. Immediately adjoining it, however, there stands a newly built village, inhabited by so-called Agraristas. The inimical disposition of those gentry barred any detailed study of the remains in question. Further on, account will be given of the ancient remains at hacienda Tepetitlán.

The village of Aljojuca is situated on the north-western side of a mountain-range, with a S.W.—N.E. orientation. Rising from the south-western part of it are some conical mountain peaks, by the side of which lies Tlaxcantla, formerly a convent of exquisite beauty, now in ruins. The range slopes north-eastward and almost imperceptibly merges into the all but level plain extending between Jala-paxco and Tepetitlán. Close by Tlaxcantla, on the very mountain slope, there are three teteles. To these we shall recur later. On the south-eastern edge of the plateau, and in the north-eastern section, most of the teteles are found, and in addition there are some north-east of Aljojuca. After having repeatedly walked over the ground, we arrived at the conclusion that the teteles numbered 23. One or more may perhaps be added to this figure, though it was considered to be correct by our constant guide, a native of Aljojuca.

As already mentioned, there are two types: of circular base, or square, and it is probable that the latter were all originally cased in stone, but as this had generally been entirely removed — we never found any continuous portions of it — it is (with one exception) impossible to determine the original profile. Those with square bases appear, judging by everything, to have been built in steps, that is, in profile they were stepped up like the temple-pyramids of Mexico and Yucatan. It is hardly to be supposed that also the circular ones had corresponding, stepped-up sides. Self-evidently, the surface is considerably more apt to become smoothed out and the steps obliterated, if there is no stone covering and if the base plan is circular, than if it be square. It is probable that the sides of the steps sloped, which, as we know, is also the case with the great temple-pyramids. They (the teteles) represent a more primitive prototype of the large and well-built temple-pyramids that are such typical elements of the architecture of the Teotihuacan, and later of the Aztec, culture.

As the excavations claimed the main part of our time and interest, we did not make a detailed study of more than one tetele. This is situated on the eastern edge of the plateau, roughly on a straight line connecting Aljojuca and Hacienda Jalapaxco. Although badly damaged from earlier "excavation", there remained enough of the stone-covering of the sides to give a rough idea of the ground-plan. Portions of the northern side were in a state of preservation, and by the help of these it was possible approximately to reconstruct the original shape, fig. 8, cf.

24

Fig. 7. The mountain-range between hacienda Jalapaxco and San Jerónimo Aljojuca seen from the tetele.

Dupaix' picture, fig. 2. The spoilers of the tetele had cut a trench through it in an east-to-west direction. This trench had been made so wide as to remove practically all of the top surface, wherefore no exact estimate could be made as to elevation. Nevertheless we had here the opportunity of ascertaining the presence of a building-detail that was not elsewhere found. This does not of course mean that it does not exist, or has existed, also in some other locality. On the western face of the lower terrace the upper portion was vertical, while its foot sloped at the same angle as the rest of the terraces. The stone casing of the top part consisted of large and uneven stones, while the foot is covered with smaller, smooth-surfaced stones. Only in the latter case had mortar been used. There seems to have been nothing to prevent the presence of a stairway on this side, although too small a portion of the structure was left intact to say with certainty. There is, however, another circumstance speaking in favour of such a supposition.

Generally no coordination of arrangement as between adjoining teteles could be observed. But in some few cases they were arranged in symmetrical groups of three. At Tlaxcantla, some 200 m from the convent, there is a layout of this type. Here unfortunately all three teteles were completely destroyed. Their remains showed that they had formed a triangle. The mound at one of the points of the triangle, which was directed northward, was much the largest of the three, and appears to have been rectangular, because its southern side had a stone casing which was oriented east-to-west.

Such, too, is the case with the tetele described above, because in front of, and west of it, there are two entirely demolished mounds. Itself, it formed the eastern point of the triangle, and the space between them may be described as a plaza. As already has been mentioned, this group is situated on the edge of the east-to-west

25

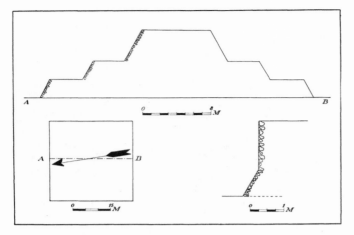

Fig. 8. Schematic sketch of a tetele between hacienda Jalapaxco and San Jerónimo Aljojuca. Shown in section at the top; below in plan, and section of the bottom terrace of the western face. Scale only approximate, nor was it possible to determine the exact shape. (Variation about 8° East.)

oriented, steeply falling, border-line of the plateau. On the sloping ground, some distance from the large tetele there was a stone-figure, fig. 10. This frog-like figure may in all certainty be supposed to have been rolled down from the tetele or its immediate surroundings, seeing that the settlement had never left the plateau nor extended down to, or towards, the plain. As can be seen, the frog has been given the face of Tlaloc, the Rain God. That the Lord of the Rains was an object of worship in ancient times in these regions which were so extremely waterless in the olden days before the introduction of the aqueducts from Citlaltépetl, is not to be wondered at. Even the frog himself, in his life and habits so intimately connected with water and rain, was no doubt credited with power to produce this commodity upon which the crops depended.[8]

Two figures of similar type, though of considerably smaller size and of poorer craftmanship, figs. 79 and 80, we acquired at Aljojuca. According to the vender's statement, which appears credible, they came from the tetele group at Tlaxcantla, referred to above. As they stylistically conform to the rest of the stone figures of the district which, in their extremely primitiveness, altogether differ from the sculptural art of the Teotihuacan culture, it shows that considerable antiquity must be ascribed to Tlaloc. For practical reasons the tetele group was after this figure christened "Tlaloc's teteles". It is not impossible that the pyramid that Dupaix — more artistically than exactly — reproduces, may be the very tetele that was

[8] "The frog was the emblem of the goddess of water, and she was worshipped under this form" (Nuttall 1926: 66). Cf. Wassén 1934: 634 seq.

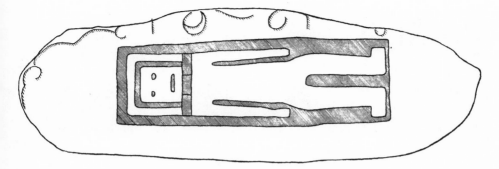

Fig. 9. Stone figure found by the side of "Tlaloc's teteles", between Jalapaxco and San Jerónimo Aljojuca. Was in 1935 lying at hacienda Jalapaxco. The sections delineated in graffito are sunk in the stone. Scale 1:18.

examined by us. If, as is taken for granted in "Atlas Arqueológico",[9] the locality stated by him, "the country-house called San Antonio", is identical with hacienda San Antonio Los Arcos, distance and direction would appear to agree fairly well. Los Arcos lies about 1,800 m south-west of Ocotenco (fig. 3), and the pyramid was situated "two miles further to the north of the country-house".

At a spot some 50—75 m west of the above mentioned tetele group, Sr. Carrasco had discovered a fairly large block of stone carrying a figure in "negative relief", fig. 9. In shape, it is somewhat suggestive of a clumsy boat, as will be seen from fig. 11. The place was pointed out to us by an old man who had assisted Carrasco in his severe toll-taking of the district's stock of antiquities. This object, measuring 2.8 m in length and of exceeding heaviness, he had carted to hacienda Jalapaxco, an undertaking which, in view of the character of the country, must have cost a great deal of toil and trouble. Unfortunately its progress stopped short at the hacienda, where it now runs the greatest risk of being exposed to wilful damage. Whether this monolith was originally set upright — a primitive analogy of the Maya stelae — or had been lying in the same position as now, one gathers, however, from the character of the terrain that it was not found in its original site. From the hollow in which it lay, the ground rises most steeply towards Tlaloc's teteles. This gives reason to suppose that it once formed part of that structure. If dislodged from it, it may quite well have landed in the spot where it was eventually found. If for some reason its removal had been begun in the colonial era, with Aljojuca, Jalapaxco, or some other place for a destination, its route ought to have lain via the spot where it was found. There is of course always the possibility that it was intended for Tlaloc's temple, but never reached its destination.

A bit of a way off, some 200 m distant from Tlaloc's teteles in the direction towards Aljojuca, in a maize field was found the stone depicted in fig. 12, which

[9] Marquina 1939: 186.

Fig. 10. Stone figure found near the tetele group referred to as "Tlaloc's teteles", between hacienda Jalapaxco and San Jerónimo Aljojuca (Museo Nacional, Mexico City). Length 60 cm.
Fig. 11. The stone figure seen in fig. 9.
Fig. 12. Sculptured stone found west of "Tlaloc's teteles".

is of parallelopiped form and provided with a bowl-shaped depression. That its site was not the original one was self-evident, and in its immediate neighbourhood existed neither teteles nor any notable accumulation of artifacts. The individual of whom we bought the stone only knew that it had been there in Sr. Carrasco's time and that the father of its present owner was unwilling to sell it.

EXCAVATION OF A "TETELE" AT ALJOJUCA

Only two or three of the 23 teteles found in the region north of Tlaxcantla and east of Aljojuca have escaped despoliation. On account of the strained relations that prevailed between the haciendas on the one part and certain villages on the other, as well as between the different villages themselves — the "agraristas" against one and all — we were constrained to devote our excavating operations to a tetele situated near the village of Aljojuca. To be exact, 1.5 km north-east of it. An imaginary line drawn from the tetele to the peak of Citlaltépetl would run through hacienda Jalapaxco. From the tetele are also visible Cofre de Perote, Malinche, Popocatépetl and Ixtaccíhuatl. Round about it were found artifacts in considerable numbers. The ground that most abounded in artifacts was, however, that round Tlaloc's teteles.

The tetele we are here concerned with consists, as seen from figs. 13 and 14, of a rounded mound, symmetrical in shape and with fairly smooth sides. It is about 7.5 m high, and its comparatively circular base measures 32 m in diameter. There is hardly any reason to suppose that the tetele originally had some different shape but lost it in the course of time, that is to say, if it once had a stone casing, and that had been removed, its height may from exposure to wind and rain, as well as other damage, maguey-planting included, have been decreased. Quite a lot of unworked stone had been piled up on one side, and part of it had been

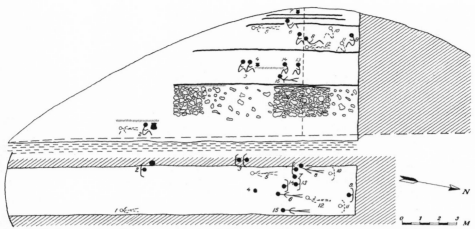

Fig. 13. Section and plan of the excavated part of the tetele. The numbers denote graves and finds referred to in the letterpress, and are given in the adjoined table.

1. Child skeleton, perished; an earthenware ear-plug, fig. 25.
2. Child skeleton; two ear-plugs, figs. 16—17; a shell ornament, fig. 18 and a plain earthenware pot, fig. 19; obsidian point, fig. 20.
3. Two skeletons, grave furniture absent.
4. Earthenware vessel, fig. 23.
5. Skeleton, much decayed; grave furniture absent.
6. Skeleton; small stone cup, fig. 26.
7. Earthenware vessel, fig. 22.
8. Two skeletons; trumpet-like bone object, fig. 27.

9. Skeleton; grave furniture absent.
10. Child skeleton, perished; thin, elongated bone object, fig. 24.
11. Skeleton, perished; grave furniture absent.
12. »   »   ; »   »   » .
13. »   »   ; »   »   » ; small earthenware idol, fig. 38 (?).
14. »   »   ; 16 obsidian knives and an unworked piece of the same material, figs. 28—30.
15. Skeleton; stone bead, fig. 21.

used as building material for a small hut, by now demolished, that stood at the foot of the tetele. Whether this stone material had originally covered the tetele could not be determined.

By kind courtesy of the precidente municipal of Aljojuca we were able to engage capable and reliable workmen. Their number included one who had taken part in Sr. Carrasco's pillaging excavations. Unfortunately he stubbornly refused to divulge the results that thereby had been gained. The only logical reason for his reticence on this point that we could think of seemed to be that Carrasco's excavations must have been somewhat poor of return. Had the fellow let this out, he might have feared that our ardour would cool down and he would risk — as the men themselves admitted — the loss of an exceptionally fine opportunity for himself and his mates of earning money. Mutual good will was further maintained by means of cheap though highly acceptable presents. Thus we were anything but unwelcome visitors, and all sorts of inducements were tried on us to prolong our stay, not knowing that our already fixed programme only allowed us a very restricted time for these researches. It also must strike one as rather strange that, although Sr. Trespalacios of Jalapaxco had a number of older men questioned, who had been there in Carrasco's time, no information whatever could be got regarding his finds, nor even as to what teteles he had excavated.

29

Fig. 14. The tetele at San Jerónimo Aljojuca; Citlaltépetl in the background.

For our foreman we had from the hacienda obtained a young and intelligent man and also a number of workmen. When work started, we had besides 9 men from Aljojuca, but added every day to the number of our working gang. In the end we had 22 men at work. The entire excavation was carried out in 12 working days, and was concluded on January 22nd. As always, the time expended in preliminaries was much out of proportion to the effective working hours. Abundance of patience is a commodity an archaeologist must carry in his luggage. The days taken up with actual excavation are few, but those spent in waiting, making applications, and in discussions, are so much the more numerous.

The tetele was overgrown with grass and a heatherlike plant, a few small trees had taken root, and a certain quantity of maguey had been planted. Our first step was to clear a strip about 3.5 m wide right across the mound, somewhat wider than the projected cutting. This ran in a roughly south-to-north direction. Excavation was begun at the mound's foot on the south side and sunk down to, and a little below, the true ground level. There was a slight northward rise in the ground. In consequence of masses of earth that had crumbled or been washed down, the area next to the tetele was somewhat raised above the original ground level. As the trench approached the centre, it was dug step-wise, fig. 15. With two of our assistants who showed the most aptitude for archaeological work, we took up our station farthest inside. The remainder formed a double chain, and the earth, after having been examined, was thrown from each man to his neighbour so as to land outside the tetele, on the south side. The work was not an unalloyed pleasure, the earth being fine as flour and the wind blowing all the time so bitingly cold that even the most glowing enthusiasm might have been chilled. Particularly irksome was the excavation of the graves, as skeletons and broken-up artifacts were difficult to uncover in the loose, ever-crumbling soil. Hence "fine-digging" was a

Fig. 15. Trenching through the tetele.

standing source of much vexation. Our excavation work finished, we handed to its owner the wherewithal to restore the mound as nearly as possible to the state in which it existed prior to our arrival. That this actually would be done, the precidente municipal promised to see to.

Graves and grave deposit.

The direct results of the excavation will appear from fig. 13, which shows the trench in section and in plan, and from the synoptical table adjoined to the illustration. Like all the rest of the teteles of this district, the one examined by us mainly consisted of sandy soil. It must have been erected after the region having been inhabited for some considerable time by the ancestors of the builders of the tetele, because large numbers of potsherds and other artifacts were found in the earth. A remarkable thing is that fragments from different levels are from vessels of similar types, and that the surface finds from all parts of the Chalchicomula district visited by us are alike. Objects recovered from graves did not either differ from the surface finds, although of a more simple character as regards the pottery. It should, however, be mentioned that the soil was not of the same character throughout. In places it consisted almost purely of sand, in which cases it was practically devoid of artifacts.

The section immediately within the edge only consisted of loose, sandy earth. About 6 m farther inside, and at a height of 1 m above the ground, we came upon a horizontal stratum of ashes, 10—15 cm thick. In this stratum, which had a

Figs. 16—21. Articles found with the burials of the tetele. (¹/₂) 16: 35. 10. 7 a; 17: 7 b; 18: 27; (¹/₄) 19: 6; 20: 8; 21: 29.

length of nearly 2.₅ m, there were also large quantities of charcoal, together with fragments of pottery, mainly of simple, spherical vessels encrusted with soot, no doubt cooking pots. Below this bed of ashes were found hard pieces of some clay-like material as well as stones, the size of a man's fist, which were thickly covered with soot. As an underlay for the hearth from which the charcoal and the ashes in all probability originate, it thus appears that a layer of clay had been laid, and the shape and size of the stones indicate that they had been used as supports for the cooking pots. Also below this stratum of ashes and at a distance of 6.₅ m from the edge were found the almost completely disintegrated skeletal remains of a very young infant. Close by it lay an unornamented ear-plug of fired clay, fig. 25. One meter inside of this, but along the opposite side of the trench, was the skeleton of a second child. This, judging by the teeth, appeared to have been 6—10 years old. In. association with it were found two ear-plugs of grey-white earthenware, figs. 16—17; a shell ornament, fig. 18, an intact cooking pot, fig. 19; (fragments of another?); and a large obsidian point, fig. 20.

As will be seen from fig. 13, the tetele had a core of stone. At a distance of about 4 m it was surrounded by a roughly 1.₅ m wide wall, or ring, of stone, equalling it in height. As the trench was not carried right through the tetele, it was of course not possible to determine whether this outer stone construction continued all the way round the core, but test cuttings on the northern and western sides suggested that such was the case. All the stones were unworked, and of exceedingly varying sizes: from being smaller than a man's fist to stones that only with difficulty could be shifted by a single man.

In the centre, among the stones, were discovered some skeletal fragments and also a few teeth. From the much-worn state of the masticating surfaces, they evidently had belonged to an elderly person. Further was found a fragment of a

Figs. 22—27. Articles found with the burials of the tetele. (¹/₄) 22: 35. 10. 13; 23: 26;
(¹/₂) 24: 18; 25: 5; 26: 16; (¹/₄) 27: 17.

not very large metate, grinding stone, without legs. Below this stone stratum, and down to the sandy, virgin soil, there was a layer of sand without any remains. The stratum next below the stone layer was much mixed with charcoal. Among the lowermost stones, and in the earth below them, a great deal of pottery was found, both painted, and decorated in carved ornamentation. The main part of it, however, consisted of fragments of cooking pots. Some of these were sooted also on the inner side.

On top of the central stone stratum had been spread a 2—3 cm thick layer of lime, with a slightly convex surface. Close above it was a second layer, which extended even above the outer stone section. This lime was of a darker, somewhat greyer colour than the other strata. Between this and the "stone wall" there was a thick layer of ashes which contained charcoal but not potsherds. The layers of ashes are in fig. 13 denoted by thin, obliquely drawn lines.

Above this were encountered 4 lime strata, the topmost three being fairly close together. They were all of a similar character, 2—3 cm thick, with a slightly convex surface, and of small resistance. By reason of the earth having in certain places, as above the graves, settled down, there were here and there considerable downward curves in the yielding lime strata. The lime was not mixed with sand, so there was no question of the strata consisting of mortar. As floors, or coverings, of an ever-growing mound they cannot have served on account of their fragility. In spite of being thus fragile, they were in a fairly good state of preservation. Having been deposited, they appear to have been covered over with earth. The only practical purpose they could have served would be that of keeping the loose earth together. It is not altogether impossible that religious conceptions may have had something to do with them. Supposing that the teteles were burial places pure and simple,

Figs. 28—30. Obsidian knives and an unworked piece of obsidian, from a grave in the tetele. ($^3/_4$) 28: 35. 10. 28 a; 29: 28 b; ($^1/_3$) 30: 28 c.

and as such were overlaid with a gleaming white covering of lime, this would constitute a parallel, so to speak, of the eternally snow-capped volcanoes, a miniature representation of Citlaltépetl, which though nowadays dormant wholly dominates the landscape.

The topmost lime stratum lay about 0.5 m below the summit of the tetele. On it stood an unornamented jar with egg-shaped body, fig. 22, and one-half of a metate, originally provided with legs, fig. 74. Part of the third layer counted from above, had been removed in connection with a burial. Strangely enough, the corpse had not been interred below the lime stratum, the skeleton lying partly above and partly below it. The deceased had been placed in "Hockerstellung", i. e. in a sitting posture with knees drawn up, the thighs pressed against the body and the arms crossed over the chest, although lying on his left side. By the head was found a small stone cup of good workmanship, fig. 26. The dead man had been covered over with a large flat stone, with a number of smaller stones around it.

Between the third and fourth layers were encountered seven skeletons in all. Most of them were in a very bad state of preservation. Near the north end of the trench and roughly in the middle of it, was found a skeleton which, as most frequently was the case, was doubled up in a sitting posture, with face turned towards the south. Just beneath the lime stratum, in the north-eastern corner of the trench, there were some exceedingly decayed remains of an infant. Next to this skeleton lay a thin, elongated object of bone, much of the appearance of a polishing bone, fig. 24. In the centre of the tetele and in the western side of the trench, the remains of two human bodies were found close together. One of them was in a sitting posture, though not in "Hockerstellung". In front of this skeleton lay another, with knees slightly drawn up, and its head had evidently been resting against the former. That both of them originally might have been deposited in the usual "Hocker-stellung", but later, as the soft parts of the bodies disintegrated, had assumed the positions described above, does not appear very probable. Everything seems to point to the bodies originally having been placed in quite the same position as we found them. Otherwise considerably heavier subsidences of the unsubstantial and friable lime strata would have taken place. Unfortunately the skeletons were so far gone in decay as to be impossible of preservation. The only thing that could be ascertained about them was that they were of adult persons. Neither age nor sex were determinable. A funerary offering consisted of a bone object, resembling a trumpet, fig. 27.

Beneath the fourth lime stratum were found five skeletons. One of them was lying stretched out full length, two were seated facing north and two facing south. The northernmost of the two last-mentioned had, — although a grown individual — possibly as a funeral offering, been provided with a clay figure, fig. 38. It is more probable, however, that this had inadvertantly been thrown down along with the earth. With the one sitting next in front, 16 obsidian knives, 11 long and 5 shorter, and a large piece of unworked obsidian had been deposited, figs. 28—30. The skull was strongly deformed, fig. 96. Such deformation was produced by tight bandaging in earliest childhood. Why the "obsidian man" had his skull deformed and thereby distinguished himself from the rest, is a question that cannot be solved, but one which invites to a variety of speculations. An exaggeratedly fronto-occipital cranial compression was very popular among the Maya and the Huaxtecs but also occurred in the central parts of Mexico, as e. g. at Teotihuacan.[1]

Farther away from the centre, two skeletons were found in the western side of the trench. They had been placed closely together, seated in "Hockerstellung" position, one behind the other. As in most cases, the bones were much decayed. Funeral offerings were absent.

Beneath the "obsidian man" were found the remains of an individual who had been buried in an almost outstretched position, his knees slightly drawn up and, as was generally the case, with the head towards the south.[2] Along with this skeleton was a bead, fig. 21, of some lightgreenish kind of rock. Its position was such as to suggest that it had been placed in the deceased's mouth, but as earth

[1] Dr. S. Lagercrantz has kindly directed my attention to Dingwall's excellent work "Artificial cranial deformation". With a wealth of authenticated instances drawn from the literature, Dingwall deals with artificial cranial deformation in America (pp. 151—225).

[2] The trench extended practically due south-to-north, and the interred were always placed parallel to each other. It is, however, more probable that the position of the dead related to the centre of the tetele and had nothing to do with the points of the compass.

pressure had reduced the cranium to fragments, this was not with full certainty ascertainable. If, however, the bead had been placed in the mouth of the buried individual, it would be a matter of considerable interest. For this was a Maya custom, and the beads, which among them were manufactured of the highly prized material jade, were also used as money.[3] In all parts of the Peruvian coastland mummies have been recovered with small metal disks in the mouth,[4] and the same burial custom is also known from the Inca Empire.[5] This would thus constitute an American analogy of Charon's obol in ancient Greece, the coin that was placed in the mouth of the deceased as his fare to the ferryman for carrying his soul across the Acheron to the realms of the dead.

ARTIFACTS FROM THE TETELE AND FROM THE ALJOJUCA DISTRICT

A comparative study of the pottery material from 17 sections of the excavated tetele, from the topmost surface layer to the one right at the bottom beneath the central stone layer, and from the perimeter of the base to its centre, shows — even if not absolutely similar ceramics throughout — no divergent pottery types in any section. In the foregoing has already been mentioned that the grave deposits and other artifacts found in the tetele are of the same character as the surface finds from the Aljojuca district. The best plan has therefore seemed to be that of dealing with the material as a whole and also to include with it the objects purchased at the village of Aljojuca. This also provides an opportunity to substantiate the assertion regarding the close kinship between the surface finds and the grave deposits.

As the excavation yielded a somewhat alarmingly poor return of archaeological objects, especially from an exhibition point of view — a matter we always had to bear in mind on behalf of our Museum — we did what we could to add to our collections by purchases of finds collected by the local population. Certain objects were also acquired at the village of Aljojuca. The latter originated from different localities in the neighbourhood, but only in two cases could the exact locality be pointed out, as also has been mentioned in the foregoing. In spite of our workpeople being instructed to keep a look-out for and report even the simplest antiquities, the resulting harvest was remarkably meagre. And this notwithstanding our remunerating both informants and owners very free-handedly indeed. We even offered cash rewards for the mere report of once recovered but subsequently lost

[3] Blom 1934 a. Thompson (1939: 283—284) reproduces an account given by Father Roman y Zamora of the funeral customs in Alta Verapaz. The latter's work, based on first-hand information, first appeared in 1575. He states that "a precious stone (jade?) was placed by one of the highest chiefs in the mouth of the deceased ruler, either at the moment he was breathing his last or immediately after his death ...." Thompson remarks that "in several cases jade has been found in the mouths of important individuals".

[4] Bennett 1939: 51—52; Kroeber 1937: 247.

[5] Cobo 1893: 237—238; Pomo de Ayala 1936: 292, 296.

objects. Not in one single instance did we have to redeem our promises in this respect to the poor but apparently honest inhabitants.

The object made of shell, and the two bone ones, have already been referred to in connection with the grave deposits. In the following only the pottery, obsidian, and stone material will be dealt with.

Pottery.

On our excursions in all directions through the width and breadth of the Aljojuca district we and our helpers picked up very considerable quantities of pottery fragments from the ground. This harvest having been gathered in, on the spot a rough-sorting of them was proceeded with. At the hacienda a further proportion was rejected, and a similar procedure was repeated at the final packing-up in Mexico City. The residual material eventually brought home nevertheless totals some 1,000 units. To anyone who has previously worked at Teotihuacan, the material is confusing on account of its multiplicity of types.

The pottery recovered in the earth of the tetele does not differ from the surface finds, and this also applies to the simple clay vessels that were found in the graves. Among the surface finds are, however, represented types that were not found in the graves, namely fragments of vessels of later periods.

In the southernmost section of the district, for example, were recovered a number of fragments which possibly may originate from Aztec clay vessels. Comparatively numerous are on the other hand fragments of vessels that had been manufactured in Cholula, or at any rate made by potters working in Cholula style, figs. 48—49. Finds belonging to this category were made throughout the area. Of the pottery material from the tetele, three small and undecorated fragments may — though with the greatest possible hesitation — be described as being of Teotihuacan type, but this only provided one is bent upon finding pottery of that kind. Many thousands of fragments and several dozens of intact vessels passed through my hands in the course of the excavations at Teotihuacan in 1932 and 1935 and it was with a certain degree of zest that I hunted for traces of this typical pottery here at Aljojuca. Among the surface finds, four might possibly be referred to it. Not one of them can, however, be definitely authenticated, and as regards the tetele finds I will change my reservation into negation. On the other hand, among the surface finds there were considerable numbers of fragments of the thin, yellowish-red pottery that is also so abundantly represented in Teotihuacan. In ware, as well as in ornamentation, it differs entirely from the classic Teotihuacan pottery, and analyses prove that consistence of the ware is of an entirely different character. There is no doubt about its having been imported into Teotihuacan, although where from, is still an open question. Before I had acquired familiarity with the Chalchicomula

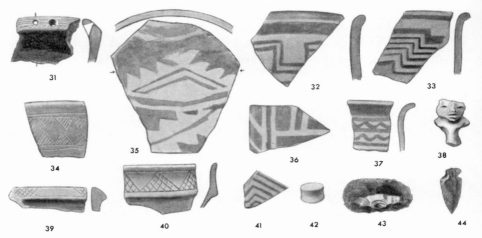

Figs. 31—44. Pottery fragments, etc., from the excavated tetele. ($^3/_8$) 31: 35. 10. 21; 32: 21 a; 33: 3; 34: 2; 35: 2 a; 36: 9; 37: 21 b; 38: 14; 39: 21 c; 40: 11; 41: 3 a; 42: 3 c; 43: 19; 44: 19 a.

area I supposed, on the basis of Sr. Carrasco's collections in the Museum für Völker-kunde at Berlin, that this type of pottery was manufactured in these parts.[1] That such a supposition is in error is evident.

Of the earthenware vessels acquired by purchase, only two are of any special interest. One of them, fig. 69, is of clear Teotihuacan type, a so-called candelero. What purpose these objects served remains an unsolved problem, but in Teotihuacan they are particularly numerously occurring. Among the many hundred candeleros included in our collections, none is so badly formed as this one. It has the appearance of having been manufactured by some local potter from a notion imported from Teotihuacan. Earthenware jars of the type seen in fig. 71, with three handles, of which one is placed lower than the others, also occur in Teotihuacan.[2] The type is also represented in an earlier collection from the Chalchicomula region, among "vasijas de tipo teotihuacano". The degree of certainty to which the provenance of that collection has been determined is not apparent from the accompanying letterpress. Of the other 17 clay vessels there illustrated, no counterpart exists in our collections from Teotihuacan.[3]

A vessel found in the tetele which could not be connected with any of the graves is the one shown in fig. 23. It is ornamented by the negative method. Pottery fragments prove its not having been the only one of its kind. This technique has a long ancestry in Mexico, but it is not impossible that it was imported from Central America. Its practice extended from the states of Jalisco and Michoacan in the north, over Central America, down to the Peruvian coast and to the mouth of the

[1] Linné 1934: 101—103, 213—214.   [2] Linné 1934: 94—95.   [3] Gamio 1922, tomo 1, vol. 1: pl. 128; p. 267.

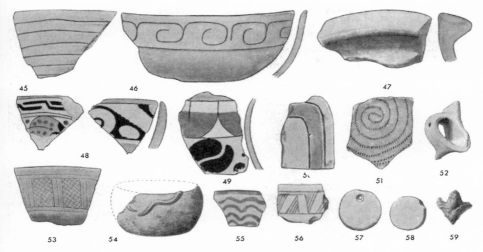

Figs. 45—59. Pottery fragments etc., collected in the Aljojuca district. (³/₈) 45: 35. 10. 37; 46: 37 a; 47: 32; 48: 37 b; 49: 33; 50: 32 a; 51: 32 b; 52: 22; 53: 35; (¹/₅) 54: 42; (³/₈) 55: 41; 56: 39; 57: 32 c; 58: 39 a; 59: 33 a.

Amazon river.[4] Lothrop holds that the technical process known as negative painting constitutes a contribution to the ceramic art of ancient America which originated in north-western South America.[5]

Figs. 31—42 and 45—58 show examples of pottery recovered, respectively, in the earth of the tetele and as surface finds in the Aljojuca region. They are, however, far from representative of all the types, the material being, as already pointed out, exceedingly heterogeneous. Among the most important absentees are: the spindle-whorl, not a single one being found, and also fragments of roasting dishes, comales (Mexican *comalli*), for baking cakes of maize flour, tortillas. The tortilla would thus seem to be a culinary invention of a late date. In earlier times maize was probably mostly eaten in the form of porridge and the like, and perhaps, as among tribes of the primeval forests of Central America, the paste was made into cakes and baked in the ashes. Roasting plates or griddles, nowadays indispensable in every Indian kitchen, appear to have come into use not earlier than with the later Teotihuacan culture.

The entire absence of spindle-whorls, or even their fragments, are more difficult of explanation. To conclude therefrom that spinning was not practised, and textiles consequently unknown, would probably be going too far. During our visit, the temperature fell to 0° C. every night, so it would have been impossible for the ancients to have managed without overclothing. Whether they possessed textiles or not, they would no doubt have had use for skin mantles and the like. The Early

[4] Linné 1934: 162—167; Lothrop 1936: 9 seq.   [5] Lothrop 1926: 410, 1936: 13. Cf. Butler 1936: 452 seq.

Figs. 60—67. Pottery heads, picked up from the ground in sundry localities in the Aljojuca district. (³/₄) 60: 35. 10. 40 a; 61: 40 b; 62: 44; 63: 40 c; 64: 35. 10. 40 d; 65: 43; 66: 46; 67: 47.

Cultures in the Valley of Mexico have left behind them only few spindle-whorls, but nevertheless the leading expert on that epoch, Vaillant, finds justification for stating that "textiles were probably extensively used".[6]

Plain cooking pots and unornamented brown bowls were definitely in preponderance. The cooking pots frequently have strongly out-curving brims, but there are also such as are necked and narrow-mouthed. A proportion of the bowls of dark-coloured ware have a rather flat bottom and, in point of form, come very near to the black flat-bottomed bowls with out-curving sides that are typical of Teotihuacan. Figural vessels and other more developed forms were absent. Handles were of fairly rare occurrence. Such as were found were vertical, flat, and often provided with a perforation bored in the manufacturing process, fig. 52. Of feet, there were both ordinary and annular, though more sparsely of the latter. The former were usually conical, not much developed, but occasionally hollow and provided with a rattle, and often turned inwards. The ornamentation was either incised, figs. 31, 34, 39, 40, 45—46, 53, punched, fig. 51, or painted. Other vessels had appliqué ornamentation consisting of spines and more or less definitely shaped rolls, fig. 54. Some few fragments were decorated with shallow grooves. An earplug of a type identical with those recovered in the child graves was found in the earth of the tetele, fig. 42.

Neither the painted nor the incised decoration, excepting that of the Cholula pottery, formed any particularly advanced designs. The incised ornamentation occurred on vessels of various shapes, often markedly profiled edges, figs. 31, 39

[6] Vaillant 1930: 38.

Figs. 68—72. Pottery vessels, acquired by purchase at the village of Aljojuca. (²/s) 68: 35. 10. 50; 69: 53; 70: 52; 71: 51; 72: 49.

and 40. Something resembling this has been depicted by Strebel from the neighbourhood of Misantla, in the Totonac territory.[7] The vessels bearing incised ornamentation present a highly variegated range of colours, from yellow-white, different shades of brown and red, to grey-black. Of painted ornamentation, yellow on a brown ground, and reddish-brown on greyish-yellow, are predominant, but here, too, the range of colouring is very wide. Strebel[8] shows ornamentation that is to some degree similar on vessels from the Ranchito de las Animas culture, and certain general resemblances can be seen in a pottery collection in our Museum from the Jalapa district.

Figures made of pottery were but sparsely represented. All of them, with the exception of a few fragments of human bodies of the type seen in fig. 65 are here reproduced, figs. 38, 60—67. If it may be said of this pottery that — apart from the additions from Cholula and the fragments that may possible derive from the Teotihuacan culture and the Aztecs — it chiefly conforms to the so-called Early Cultures, to some extent influenced from the Totonac area and this also applies to the clay figures. But both the pottery taken as a whole, and the anthropomorphic

[7] Strebel 1889: pl. 9.   [8] Strebel 1885: pl. 6.

41

section of it, have each their specific character, i. e. are typical of their place of origin. As for the rest of the artifacts, these possess no peculiarities that would argue against their being referred to the Early Cultures. The figures — like most of the pottery — fall, however, far below the by no means primitive modelling and technical skill that characterize the so far known earliest epochs of the Valley of Mexico.

The Indians of Mexico were, and still are, great traders. Thus, for example, to the great market-place at Tlaltelolco, the northern section of Tenochtitlán-Mexico, Indians travelled from distant parts in order to offer the specialities of their home villages for sale. The Aztec merchants even had their own tutelary god. Of him, and of commerce generally, excellent accounts are found in Sahagun.[9] There can be no doubt that from various places in this country, where the art of pottery had reached such a high level, ceramics were through chains of intermediaries transported to far distant parts. To this matter recurrence, as regards Teotihuacan, will be made below. Bernal Díaz del Castillo, the incomparable chronicler, who accompanied Cortés and took an active part in the Conquest, writes of the inhabitants of Cholula that "they make very good pottery in the city of red and black and white clay with various designs, and with it supply Mexico and all the neighbouring provinces as, so to say, do Talavera or Placencia in Spain".[10] Clavijero puts on record that the potters of Cholula took their products to the market-place at Tlaltelolco.[11]

In her work on the pottery of Culhuacan, Anita Brenner writes: "The conditions under which pottery is made and sold in the plateau region today seem similar in many ways to those reported in operation at the time of the Conquest".[12] This also applies to the Chalchicomula district. The art of the potter is there unknown and, so far as we were able to ascertain, no traditions to the contrary are surviving. The reason for this is probably to seek in the absence of suitable clay, this at any rate being the opinion of the natives. Pottery fragments show that importation had taken place from Cholula or its surrounding district. Cholula has lost its position as Mexico's "Talavera or Placencia", but the importation still partly follows the same route. Amozoc and San Jerónimo in the district of Tepeaca, and Molcajac in the district of Tepexi, all being localities some distance south of Puebla, are the principal exporters. From the last-mentioned place were mainly bought water jars and molcajetes (Mexican *molcaxitl*), grinding-pans used in the preparation of mole (Mexican *molli*). It is undeniably interesting to note that this place is still living up to its name, Molcajac or Molcaxac, which in Aztec means precisely "lugar de molcajetes".

That the Aljojuca region is and always has been reduced to obtaining their pottery — those absolutely indispensable household utensils — by importation, is

[9] Sahagun 1938, vol. 1: 42—45.   [10] Díaz del Castillo 1910, vol. 2: 18.   [11] Valle-Arizpe 1939: 72.
[12] Brenner 1931: 15.

an established fact. That this is a povery-stricken neighbourhood cannot be disputed, that it is becoming poorer still through the present "agrarian reforms" is not likely to be placed in doubt, and that in ancient times it was badly off is, among other things, apparent from the "crack-lacing" of the clay vessels. On either side of a crack holes were bored, and by means of strings threaded through the holes the crack was drawn together in the same way as the lacing of a boot. This method is exceedingly common in America.[18] In all parts of the area numerous fragments were found, even from the simplest vessels — the meanest workday ware — with mending-holes of this kind. This shows that clay vessels were costly and the people poor.

Stone and obsidian objects.

Stone objects were sparsely represented among the artifacts recovered in the tetele. Among the grave deposit were knives of obsidian, splintered off from a core and with fine-flaked edges, a large obsidian point, a small cup, and a bead. In the top stratum was also found a fragment of a metate of the legged kind. It is often difficult to determine whether a "point" has been that of an arrow. Attempts at defining the boundary line between arrow-heads and spear-heads have been made, both theoretically[1] and by practical experiments.[2] Its weight alone, 15.5 g, in the present case argues against its being classifiable as an arrow-point, and its shape and width at the base, 3.3 cm, rules out its employment that way. But it may also have been hafted as a knife.

The knives, which are of a peculiar type unknown to me from any other archaeological site,[3] bear witness — as regards their edging — of great skill in working the brittle material. The ends are pointed and the edges flaked. The flaked-off chips are exceedingly small, and the process bears witness of very advanced skill. An ordinary knife, obtained from a core by flaking, easily loses its edge. This has been established from practical experiments and by Torquemada's account, which is based on actual experience.[4] A finely flaked edge makes for a knife of less sharpness but on the other hand longer life. In the working of obsidian, the Indians of Mexico showed great expertness, and the so-called "eccentric flints" of the Maya are veritable masterpieces.[5] Fragments of knives of this type were encountered here and there throughout the district. Almost ubiquitous were small obsidian chips, waste matter left over from the manufacture of objects. In addition were found splinters of quartz and flint, and what possibly was a small fragment of a Totonac "yoke". The remainder of the obsidian objects consist of two arrow-heads, figs. 44 and 59, and a scraper, fig. 43.

[18] Linné 1925: 156—159, 1929: 207—209, 1934: 210—211.
[1] Cf. Fowke 1896: 142; Kidder 1932, 1938: 156—157.   [2] Browne 1938: 358—359, 1940: 209—213.   [3] Breker 1888: 214, depicts a lanceolate knife with a similar edge.   [4] Linné 1934: 145.   [5] Cf. Linné 1934: 152—153, 218.

Figs. 73—78. Objects of stone, bought in the district of Aljojuca. ($^1/_3$) 73: 35. 10. 57; 74: 10; 75: 62; 76: 54; 77: 72; 78: 60.

It is not improbable that the obsidian material itself might provide valuable hints as to the trade routes by which this important article of commerce travelled. It seems to be a fact that the lava of any particular quarry has a distinct character of its own, and the question of its origin is therefore solvable by petrographically analysing material from lava beds compared with objects that have been archaeologically recovered. From California instances are known of obsidian having served as a medium of exchange and passed from tribe to tribe.[6]

A few simple stone beads of the same type as that in fig. 21 we saw at Aljojuca. But as their owner was away from home, we could not come to terms about them. As to the implements, these consist of fairly well shaped stone balls, which were much worn and probably had served as grinding instruments; a fragment of the long handstone (Mexican *metlapilli*) of a metate and a pistil-shaped object, decorated with a chiselled animal head, fig. 75. At Aljojuca was acquired a large and heavy ball of unknown use, fig. 77, and a large axe, fig. 76. Of similar type is a find from the tetele.

In the foregoing mention has been made of a large stone figure in the form of a frog, with a face bearing certain features characteristic of the Rain God — the Aztecs' Tlaloc. Two figures of similar type, but smaller and of inferior workmanship, figs. 79 and 80, were obtained by purchase in Aljojuca. With these, fig. 83 is supposedly to be grouped. From the Huaxtec territory comes a froglike stone figure which undoubtedly presents strong points of contact.[7] A seated figure

[6] Pope 1918: 116.   [7] Seler 1904: fig. 14, p. 175; Staub 1921: fig. 14.

44

Figs. 79—84. Objects of stone, bought in the district of Aljojuca. (¹/₅) 79: 35. 10. 70; 80: 69; 81: 71; 82: 58; 83: 61; 84: 59.

and a number of heads were also acquired, figs. 78, 73, 81—82, 84. A stranger among this in the real sense of the word archaic collection is seen in fig. 97. It is an example of the glimpses of strikingly superior refinement that now and then may come into view in this artistically poor culture. Unfortunately we had no opportunity of ascertaining whether such high quality works as the one just referred to are ascribable to a different culture or to some local artist of outstanding ability.

Primitive stone figures and heads of particularly marked kinship with the above, are depicted by Strebel from the Totonac region, but above all from Atotonilco and Quimistlán.[8] Our sculptures are, however, throughout not quite so well carved if the head seen in fig. 97 be excepted. Their being connected with the archaeological finds from Atotonilco and Quimistlán is not very remarkable, seeing that these places are only 50 km away, and situated south of Cofre de Perote. What is of greater interest, however, is that the finds from those localities in their turn are allied to the Totonac culture. This indicates the route by which the influence from the lowlands in the east arrived. A strange thing is the almost complete absence of Aztec ceramics in the Aljojuca region, seeing that at all events Quimistlán was occupied by Aztec military forces.[9]

[8] Strebel 1889: pls. 2—4, 20, 23—26.   [9] Krickeberg 1918—22: 21.

Fig. 85. Tetele, near Tepetitlán; Citlaltépetl in the background.

RECONNAISSANCES AT TEPETITLÁN

As mentioned in the foregoing, we extended our explorations northwards as far as the hacienda Santa Cecilia Tepetitlán, where 15 or 16 teteles are situated. These have probably not been touched by the spades of treasure-seekers or amateur archaeologists. In appearance they, in other respects, resemble the mounds of other sections of the region. The hacienda stands at the foot of a small mountain with steep sides. On its opposite side, the north side, there are 4 large and 11 or 12 smaller teteles, fig. 85. The owner of the hacienda had picked up a number of minor archaeological objects from the ground, and these he handed over to us as a gift.

The greater part consists of earthenware heads, and some of these differ in character from the finds of Aljojuca, figs. 86—91. Only one object can be connected with the Teotihuacan culture, fig. 86. This is a whistle, formed in representation of the Fat God, a congenially human god. He occurs in association with the Teotihuacan culture, but is also found in the Totonac region.[1] Where his cradle stood, is for future research to discover, but even among the Maya he did not appear very frequently. His having showed up at Tepetitlán does therefore not clear up any problems. Possibly fig. 90, if anything at all can be deduced from this badly damaged head, represents a simplified version of the Fat God. As at

[1] Beyer 1930: 82.

46

Figs. 86—95. Surface finds from Tepetitlán. (⁴/₅) 86: 35. 10. 79; 87: 80; 88: 82; 89: 83; 90: 84;
91: 35. 10. 85; 92: 89; 93: 77; 94: 91; 95: 90.

Aljojuca, these heads appear for the most part to belong to the early type that Vaillant calls Eii.[2] In the gift collection is included a small cylindrical stamp, fig. 92.

This stamp is, as will be seen, very small and was most probably used in body-painting. Cylindrical stamps have a far more restricted area of distribution than the plane ones. They only occur in Mexico, Central America and north-western South America.[3]

Among the objects collected by us are obsidian knives of the type that was found in the excavated mound at Aljojuca, figs. 28—29. One whole and one broken point of light grey obsidian were also recovered. The former is of the same type as that found in the excavated tetele, cf. figs. 20 and 95. The points from Tepetitlán were undoubtedly arrow-points if one may judge by their weight, those in figs. 94 and 95 weighing, respectively, 4.₅ and 5.₅ grammes. One finds it difficult, however, to take for granted that the latter served such a purpose, in view of its broadness at the base, 2.₆ cm.

The ceramics were of the same kind as those from the Aljojuca district, viz. unpainted vessels with profiled brims, linear ornamentation in red on a greyish-yellow ground, and vessels imported from the Cholula area, fig. 93. On the other hand, none of fragments are connectable with the ceramics of the Teotihuacan culture.

[2] Vaillant 1931: 346—347.   [3] Linné 1929: 45 seq.

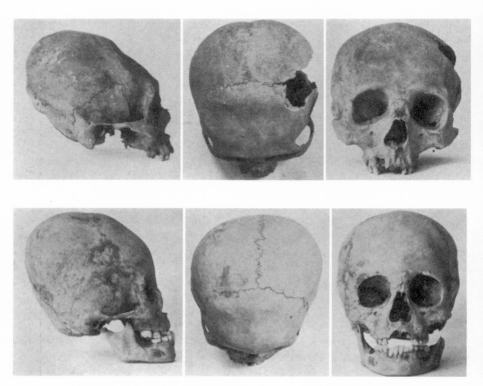

Fig. 96. Deformed skulls from the excavated tetele, Aljojuca. Nos. 14 (top row) and 9, fig. 13.

COMPARATIVE NOTES AND STUDIES.

Mexico offers an exceedingly rich field for archaeological research and no district, nor any single ancient city has been finally explored. By degrees the "white spots" of the map are being filled in, but it will take generations before the mosaic crystallizes into a fairly definite form. Our operations in the Chalchicomula district can only be described as a reconnaissance which should be followed up by further excavations at Tepetitlán. Connections might be obtained with such areas as, by means of stratigraphic excavations and co-ordination with the dateable Maya culture, are capable of being chronologically defined, relatively as well as absolutely. North of the area of our activities, Palacios has made cursory examination of some ancient remains of a culture closely related to that of the Chalchicomula district.

On the slopes of Cofre de Perote and in the surrounding country Henri de Saussure[1] and Palacios[2] have discovered important ancient monuments, certain of which, such as Cantona, Hueyaltépetl and others, may be described as cities. Unfortunately the latter's exceedingly important reports are suffering from a lack of illustrative material to meet even the most moderate pretensions. The building remains chiefly consist of teteles that in size and construction appear to agree with those of the Chalchicomula district, at all events with such of them as, like "Tlaloc's teteles", were temple foundations. As in the case of the latter complex, three teteles occasionally formed a symmetrical group about a levelled space. As regards the artifacts it is exceedingly difficult to arrive at any conclusion, but judging by the stone figures that are discernible in the illustrations, even in this case the agreement with our finds is obvious.

Palacios supposes from the points of resemblance that the ruins discovered by him have in common, that they are ascribable to one and the same culture. It is probable that this extended over large areas and that Chalchicomula fell within its compass. As the passes at Cofre de Perote probably afforded communication between the cultures of the coastland and the plateau, it is remarkable that not even the above-mentioned localities show any infiltration from either direction. These passes were used as ports of invasion by the Aztecs who maintained an outpost garrison at Xico Viejo, between Cofre de Perote and Jalapa, and by way of them Cortés led his army up to the tableland. Here must therefore, it would seem, have existed a culture of greater antiquity than the epoch of the Teotihuacan civilization.

Our work in the Chalchicomula district in one respect turned out disappointing, in that we did not find what we were looking for. The large collection in Berlin that Sr. Carrasco had maintained at Jalapaxco, and part of which Seler has published in his work on the Teotihuacan culture contained, as already mentioned, besides very fine specimens of pottery vessels, etc., also objects from the high cultures of the coast peoples. Of this, we found nothing at all. At first we were rather puzzled, then we began to suspect that the good luck that had attended our earlier work had forsaken us, but in the end we became doubtful of Sr. Carrasco. As pointed out in the foregoing, traces of Teotihuacan influence were extremely faint: statistically they would at best amount to a fraction of one-thousandth part, as only one of the objects bought at Aljojuca was of undoubted Teotihuacan type. At our interview with Sr. Carrasco he was exceedingly vague in his statements, although we had before us both a map of the district and Seler's treatise. If it be really true that he had got this collection together in his pillaging excavations, then the graves he opened must have been those of pilgrims or travellers, merchants or priests, that had visited the great city in the Valley of Mexico, or else the objects had been therefrom imported in some other way. And so it must have been also

[1] Saussure 1858.   [2] Palacios 1922: 179—192, 1923: 21—35.

with the art products of the coastal civilizations. If Teotihuacan had an outpost in these regions, then, among the tens of thousands of pottery fragments that passed through our hands, at least some must have been authentically derivable from one of those clay vessels that are so characteristic of that culture. To continued excavations, above all from Tepetitlán, must be left the solution of this problem. For the present one can only remain sceptical, and even take into account the possibility of Sr. Carrasco having himself imported his collection from Teotihuacan and other places.

In this connection it may be pointed out that in the Museum für Völkerkunde in München there is a skull whose front teeth are ornamented with small, round plates of jadeite.[3] Dental decoration of this type was common among the Maya people, but except from Oaxaca, Teotihuacan, Medellín in Vera Cruz, and Tacamarca in Jalisco — from each of the three latter places we have only one instance — there are no data so far as Mexico is concerned.[4] Exactly where the München skull was found is not stated, but it comes from a private collection.[5] In studying the distribution of a culture or of individual culture elements, one must of course not construct theories upon their absence within certain areas, as lacunae may easily be filled up through renewed researches. In this case, however, an attitude of rejection would appear more appropriate than an expectant one. This all the more as the archaeological sites at Perote, which appear to have carried the same, or a very similar, culture as the Chalchicomula region, are also derived of elements of higher cultures.

What we did find was remains of the earlier culture referred to above, the principal manifestations of which are mounds of two types: those with a square base and stepped sides, like "Tlaloc's teteles", and those with a circular base and probably of rounded contours, of which the one we explored is an example. The former were to a certainty covered with a casing of stone, while the latter — though to a lesser degree of certainty — were not provided with such a protective stone mantle. The former were temple foundations, the latter served as burial places. A few comparative notes on the origin of mounds and their occurrence in other parts of Mexico may in the present connection be of interest.

The practice of erecting mounds may be supposed to have been originally introduced from reasons of utility. As to this, a good deal of armchair research has only led to some rather pointless results.[6] But it is, however, not altogether impossible that utility-serving mounds and such as were only designed as burial places, independently came into being and developed, and that subsequently they occasionally amalgamated. In regions with regularly occurring inundation periods, Indians of certain parts of South America protected both dwellings and graves by

[3] Lehmann 1912: fig. 28.   [4] Linné 1940: 19.
[5] Letter from Professor Dr. Heinrich Doering, director of the Museum für Völkerkunde, München, of April 27th 1940.   [6] Greenman 1932: 286—295.

the erection of mounds that rose above the annual deluge. But such erections also served as a protection for certain cultivated plants, such as manioc, cotton and the sweet-potato, which do not thrive in ground that is for some time annually inundated.[7] It may indeed be that the original motive is to seek in the solving of agricultural problems. Their use as burial places followed as a consequence of the settlement of the land,[8] seeing that hut-burial is a by no means uncommon practice.[9] Whether there be a genetic connection between mounds in different parts of America is not clear. Of particularly great interest would be if connection could be established between mounds on the Atlantic coast of Mexico and those in the Mississippi valley.

The Indians of Mexico have devoted great interest to the erection of mounds in the form of foundations for temples. These supply undeniable proof that already in early epochs social organization was highly developed. Considerable forces under a powerful direction are required for erecting such imposing structures as the well-known "pyramid" of Cuicuilco.[10] But there also occur mounds that have only been used for burials.

"From Vera Cruz to the mouth of the Panuco river and beyond, the country is thickly strewn with mounds."[11] A proportion of these mounds are, as regards construction, very much akin to those of the Chalchicomula district. Beyer describes one that has been examined by him in the neighbourhood of Tlacotalpan, on Rio Papaloapan. It consisted of nothing beyond earth mixed with numerous pottery fragments.[12] If we turn to the northern part of the coastland, we find that mounds are of common occurrence in the Huaxtec country. Seler holds that they were foundations for dwelling houses, but also that they served as burial places.[13] Staub, who has also published a map of their distribution in the Huaxtec country, subscribes to that opinion.[14] Muellerried, too, states that some mounds were used for burials, and gives an account of mounds at Tampico.[15] These bear the closest resemblance to the one examined by us and to the remainder in this area, and consist of earth and horizontal, parallel layers of "cemento blanco". As a motive for their erection he chiefly places their being protective against inundations in the rainy season, because on them the houses had been built. Seeing that the Huaxtecs practised hut-burial, a custom that has survived into our days,[16] the parallel with South America is complete. Muellerried also advances a theory as to the origin of those layers of "cemento blanco" that are so difficult to explain. The floors of the houses, he suggests, were in course of time covered with sweepings and garbage of every kind. When this accumulation had grown to an inconvenient thickness, a second floor was laid down which in its turn was similarly defiled, and so on. In this way the mound increased in height and acquired its parallel strata of a more or less calcareous mass. Without supposing that the Huaxtecs were fanatics or even

[7] Nordenskiöld 1913: 215 seq., 1916: 148 seq.   [8] von den Steinen 1904: 101 seq.   [9] Preuss 1894: 17, 28 seq.
[10] Cummings 1933.   [11] Fewkes 1907: 272 seq.   [12] Beyer 1927: 321.   [13] Seler 1904: 122, 172.
[14] Staub 1921: 43.   [15] Muellerried 1924: 20—29.   [16] Staub 1919: 53.

enthusiasts, as regards cleanliness, I cannot but regard this explanation as being — at best — rather a subjective one. Muir has published some most extraordinary paintings, possibly some sort of complicated gaming-table, on the floors in a mound close to Tampico.[17] This shared the fate of its fellows of being cut down by order of the municipal authorities.

In Oaxaca, in the valleys of Oaxaca, Etla, Zaachila and Tlacolula, there occur two kinds of mounds: such as have been the foundations of temples, and burial mounds.[18] In this case the mounds are stone chambers but in other respects resemble those of Chalchicomula and are reinforced with horizontal "cement layers".

The Maya Indians buried their dead in different ways. Here will only be given some data concerning mounds that were used for such a purpose. From various parts of their territory true burial mounds are known, mounds that had not been designed as substructures for buildings.[19] Others had been built upon and burials had taken place beneath the floors, a custom also practised in Yucatan, as stated by Landa,[20] and is still surviving in other parts of the Maya country.[21] Some mounds had — after having for some reason or other been abandoned — "been converted into burial mounds".[22] Presumably due to the social position of the deceased, certain mounds contain grave chambers built of stone, and conform in the main to the burial mounds of Oaxaca, while other grave chambers are found beneath more complex structures and therefore fall beyond the scope here laid down.[23]

It is therefore evident that the mounds of the coastland served as dwellings, and that hut-burial was practised beneath the house floors. This does not seem to have been the case with the teteles of Chalchicomula, at any rate as regards the one we examined. They conform to the Oaxacan system with two kinds of mounds, and to the Maya, who had special burial mounds. Circular mounds, in so far as they served as dwellings, presuppose circular huts. Circular houses are not known from these parts. Pollock, who has devoted exceedingly close studies to circular buildings in Mexico, supposes that this type had its origin in "the upland region about Orizaba and Córdoba", and that in the days of the tetele builders there is no absolute certainty that circular houses did not exist.[24] The layers of ashes prove that our tetele possibly had occasionally been inhabited, fires had certainly been made, but there can have been no established residence.

In this connection it should be recalled that certain Indians had, and — in one case at least — still have, special grave houses of the same type as those used for dwellings. The former are grouped together into a village of the dead. Among the Cuna Indians, in 1927, I had the opportunity of visiting a village of that kind, in

[17] Muir 1926: 231—238.   [18] Saville 1899: 351 seq., 1909: 152—153.   [19] Cf. Blackiston 1910: 195—201; Ricketson 1925: 395, 1931; Wauchope 1934: 142 seq.; Yde 1938: 29, 67.   [20] Landa 1928, vol. 1: 228.   [21] Blom-La Farge 1927, vol. 2: 361—362.   [22] Cf. Gann 1918: 49 seq.; Wauchope 1934: 132 seq., 159.   [23] Cf. Thompson 1931: 290 seq.; Kidder 1935: 109—117; Lothrop 1936: 6—7.   [24] Pollock 1936: 156 seq.

which burials took place beneath the floor in huts of a type similar to those used by the living.[25]

The great abundance of pottery fragments in the area in which we were specially interested, in particular the ridgy ground extending between hacienda Jalapaxco and Aljojuca, bears witness of protracted settlement, or else considerable density of population. Arguing against the latter alternative are the climatic and physical conditions. But under no circumstances could the grave teteles have received all the dead. Therefore other kinds of burial, probably direct inhumation in the open or beneath the hut floor, must have occurred, although of this we found no direct evidence. Supposing that the distribution of the interred in the tetele as a whole equals in density that of the excavated portion, their total number would only amount to about 60 individuals.

The interred — as will be apparent from fig. 13 — were not posed according to any definite system. In their case did therefore not apply the rule obtaining in at least certain parts of the Maya region that "persons of rank were usually buried in a horizontal position".[26] In many cases, however, they were found in a doubled-up position. In his study of this mode of burial, "Hockerbestattung", Andree came to the conclusion that the limbs of the dead were tied together in this position in order to protect the living against the dead — against malevolent ghosts walking.[27] Greenman, on the other hand, attaches a purely practical significance to the burial mode in question, in that it "was practised as a labour-saving device".[28] As far as our tetele is concerned, so very little care seems to have been bestowed upon the interment of the dead that the labour-saving explanation in this case would appear the more acceptable.

The archaeological finds, both those excavated from the tetele and those made outside it or acquired by purchase at Aljojuca, have, as will be apparent from sections in the foregoing, given rise to a great deal of discussions and comparative studies. There remains, however, to touch with a few words on the age of the tetele-building culture in Chalchicomula.

It has already been mentioned that the pottery exhibits certain points of resemblance to that of Strebel's primitive "Ranchito de las Animas" culture in the Totonac area. While the so far earliest known culture in the Valley of Mexico, "the Copilco-Zacatenco culture", which according to Vaillant falls between 200 B. C. and A. D. 400, geographically appears restricted to the Valley of Mexico and its nearest surroundings, the culture of the epoch next following can be traced over a larger area. This culture, which he calls "the Cuicuilco-Ticoman culture", A. D. 400—700, extended eastward as far as the Atlantic coast.[29] Stirling connects his discoveries at Tres Zapotes, in the canton of the Tuxtlas in the extreme south of Vera Cruz, with the earliest epoch at Gualupita (Gualupita I).[30] This is by

[25] Linné 1929: 247—252.   [26] Thompson 1939: 283.   [27] Andree 1907: 307.   [28] Greenman 1932: 291.
[29] Vaillant 1936: 325.   [30] Stirling 1940: 4.

Fig. 97. Head carved in stone, acquired by purchase at Aljojuca. (¹/₂) 35. 10. 56.

Vaillant shifted farther back in time, as next preceding "Early Ticoman",[31] and in a later work of his he relegates it to an even lower place chronologically, earlier than the Copilco-Zacatenco period.[32] Concerning the Chalchicomula finds, Vaillant writes that "Linné's excavations at Chalchicomula, Puebla, Noguera's at Cholula, and collections purchased in the same state, which is east of the Valley, indicate that the Cuicuilco-Ticoman culture flourished there, and a few examples from near Medellin, Vera Cruz, give an even wider eastern distribution. Thus there are good grounds for postulating that the Cuicuilco-Ticoman culture was developed in the Puebla region at the same time that Copilco-Zacatenco existed in the Valley of Mexico. At a later date, tribes with specialized aspects of the same culture, like the existent Cuicuilco-Ticoman, penetrated into the Valley and supplanted the makers of the Copilco-Zacatenco culture."[33] Whether Stirling's finds can be connected with those of Chalchicomula is a question that cannot be determined as the material has not yet been published. If such a connection really can be proved to exist, the period assigned to the development of that culture would be extended, which undeniably is a matter to be desired. Far be it from me to question the chronology of the leading expert on the Early Cultures, and to plump for the higher dates asserted by previous researchers,[34] but it appears to me as if he had shortened the length of the periods to a somewhat excessive degree. Of great interest, too, is that he finds that "elements of the Cuicuilco-Ticoman ceramic occur in the first Teotihuacan horizon".[35] This, however, would hardly explain the occurrence of fragments of what may turn out to be Teotihuacan pottery in Chalchicomula, and still less the alleged rich finds of Carrasco from the peak period of that culture.

[31] Vaillant 1935: the tables.   [32] Vaillant 1938: 554.   [33] Vaillant 1938: 538.
[34] Krickeberg 1935: 359; Cummings 1933: 55.   [35] Vaillant 1938: 539.

54

RESULTS OF THE RESEARCHES

In the Chalchicomula district, 75 mounds known as "teteles" have so far been discovered. Their actual number no doubt exceeds this figure. Most of them have been looted.

Of these mounds two types occur: one of square ground plan and with stepped sides, cased in stone — substructures of temples — and another of circular ground plan, with rounded contour and (possibly) without stone covering — burial mounds. Their construction is in all cases the same: earth and stones, held together by strata consisting of calcareous matter.

Now and then the mounds occur in symmetrically triangular groups of three, one being larger than the other two.

One of the teteles of circular ground plan was partly excavated. 15 skeletons were found but the grave equipment was remarkable poor. One of the skulls was strongly deformed, fig. 96.

The artifacts collected mainly consist of pottery, stone and obsidian. Grave deposits, objects recovered in the earth of which the excavated mound is constructed, and the surface finds were all of a similar character. There was an abundance of pottery types, some of which were allied to those of the coastland. Of Teotihuacan ceramics — apart from a purchased "candelero" — no undubitable trace was found. The thin, orange-coloured type of ware that occurs in Teotihuacan although not manufactured there, was on the other hand represented. A few of the potsherds may possibly be of Aztec origin, and some are of Cholula type. Into this country, pottery was probably at all times imported, as it is to this day.

In this border region of the tableland there developed a specific culture which possibly received impulses from the coast. Its geographical boundaries are still unknown, but the ancient remains around Cofre de Perote it certainly included.

In order of time, the mound-building culture of Chalchicomula falls within the Early Cultures, being approximately coincident with the Cuicuilco-Ticoman culture in the Valley of Mexico, which, according to Vaillant, flourished during the period A. D. 400—700, with a certain retrograde margin.

PART II

ARCHAEOLOGICAL RECONNAISSANCES IN THE REGION OF CALPULALPAN, STATE OF TLAXCALA

The small town of Calpulalpan is situated in the northwestern corner of the State of Tlaxcala. In the month of March 1935, accompanied by Mrs. Helga Larsen and Miss Bodil Christensen, I carried out archaeological excursions to places east of the said town. In the meantime Dr. Montell had sole supervision of our excavation work at Teotihuacan. The idea of exploring these parts originated from Dr. George C. Vaillant, who had previously visited two of the localities referred to in the following, viz. Las Colinas and Zoquiapan. One day in November 1934 Dr. Montell and I were accorded the very great privilege of travelling from Mexico City with him and his wife in their motor car on a visit to these parts.

This region has never before been archaeologically explored, but even the superficial operations that have now been carried out, are enough to show that in these parts further investigation offers a rich field of possibilities. In pre-Spanish times, here must have lived a numerous population, perhaps larger than the present one. In the days of the Teotihuacan culture there were many important centres within this area. Next to Teotihuacan itself, Cholula and Azcapotzalco, it may be, that — so far as can be judged from the standpoint of our present knowledge — from here will be recovered finds that will rank among the most important from this cultural epoch.[1] That Calpulalpan continued as an important place is shown by the fact that Nezahualcoyotl, the great ruler of Texcoco, from here organized the war against the usurper that during his minority had murdered his father and seized his ancestral throne.[2] Strangely enough, the antiquities that we acquired originated, with some few exceptions, from the Teotihuacan culture.

Investigations were carried out at the following three localities: Las Colinas, San José Zoquiapan and San Nicolás el Grande. All of them are situated east of the town. The distances are, as the crow flies, respectively 2.5, 10 and 15 km, see map, fig. 98. In this neighbourhood further archaeological sites can with certainty

[1] In "Atlas arqueológico de la República Mexicana", published in 1939, no reference is made to our results. On the other hand is mentioned, on p. 243, the hacienda San Antonio Mazapa, 5 km south of Calpulalpan (cf. fig. 98), of which it is said: "Montículos. Estructuras arquitectónicas. Cerámica. En el cerro de Yehualica se encuentran cerámica y obsidiana así como restos de edificios de forma octogonal. En toda esa región existen numerosos montículos."

[2] Aragón 1931: 20.

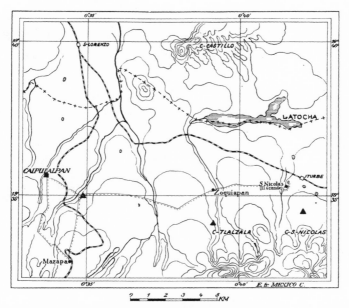

Fig. 98. Sketch map of the region east of the town of Calpulalpan, State of Tlaxcala. The ruin places here dealt with are marked with triangles.

be found. As to that, we bought from the inhabitants of the town figurines and other pottery objects that had been found in land cultivation in various places south of Calpulalpan. In the ground below the present town are also hidden relics of ancient inhabitation. Considerable quantities of potsherds are also said to have been observed on elevated portions of the ground west and north of the town.

OBJECTS FROM THE TOWN OF CALPULALPAN

The collection of objects recovered in the town of Calpulalpan and at a place just south of it, that we acquired by purchase, mainly consists of clay heads, some of which are here reproduced, figs. 99—105. The most noteworthy is perhaps the erect figure, which unfortunately is minus head, one leg and one hand. The figure is dressed in either a cape, *quechquemitl,* or a small mantle, *ayate.* A good many of both these kinds of garment, which are still being worn in places, are included in our ethnographical collections. The former are used by women, while ayates are worn by men. The body of the figure is hollow and made into a rattle. It might therefore have served as a toy, but against this speaks that it was only designed for being viewed from the front, seeing that its back part is rough and uneven.

57

Figs. 99—105. Figurine and heads found in the town of Calpulalpan. (¹/₂)
99: 35. 9. 1; 100: 2; 101: 9;
102: 25; 103: 17; 104: 11; 105: 4.

A head of the so-called "portrait type" is interesting inasmuch as it is provided with a vertically bored hole. It evidently rested on a peg fixed in the figure and serving for a neck. The usual description of "portrait head" is, besides, most inapt. In such a case individuality in its modelling should above all form the distinguishing feature. This type is anything but individual: it is instead as conventional as that of the deity most frequently represented — and most standardized — of all, the Buddha. Among the other heads may be noted one of primitive type and another — the only one in our collections from the Calpulalpan region — an Aztec one. Of the vessel fragments only one has seemed worth reproducing, viz. a portion of the side of a tripod vessel, with rectangular, hollow feet, fig. 106. It is adorned with the head of the Fat God, apparently made in a mould and then attached to the vessel. It is surrounded by three plumes in relief. The rest of the potsherds are simple, but of unmistakable Teotihuacan type.

The collection also includes three beads of dark-green, hard rock, and exceedingly finely polished. We also acquired an object of tecali, or onyx marble. It consists of a fragment of a plate, accurately planed by grinding.

LAS COLINAS

Our operations, which only purposed a preliminary reconnaissance, were mainly confined to the first-mentioned, nearest the town situated locality, Las Colinas. It must be most emphatically stated that time did not permit of any exact

Figs. 106—107. Potsherds from Calpulalpan and Las Colinas with moulded, respectively impressed ornamentation. (¹/₂) 106: 35. 9. 28; 107: 191.

measurements. While the excavated building details are in their essentials correctly reproduced, the plan of their situation cannot claim to be anything but a hastily constructed sketch.

Through the kind offices of the secretary to the Presidente Municipal of Calpulalpan we engaged 10 peons, or native labourers, from the town, and by the courtesy of Sr. José Andrade, manager of the hacienda San Antonio Mazapa, we were enabled to increase our working strength by a similar number locally. The greater part of the area occupied by the archaeological site of Las Colinas, the terrain south of the road Calpulalpan-Zòquiapan, belongs to Mazapa. Those 20 helpers of ours were exclusively employed at Las Colinas, the only locality where we carried out excavations in this neighbourhood.

This formerly settled area is traversed by the main road Calpulalpan—Zoquiapan—San Nicolás, and is situated east-southeast of the first-mentioned of the above places, on the northern and western slopes of a low ridge of ground. Some hundred of meters to the west of it there is a deep ravine with a brook, which in the rainy season is relatively water-bearing, running northeastward.

The road divides, as will be seen from the plan sketch, fig. 108, the area in a northern and a southern portion. The artifacts, chiefly heads and fragments of clay figures, potsherds, clay pellets and stone implements are found within an area many times larger than that occupied by the building remains visible above the ground, A—H on the plan. In the corn fields, occurring on the northward slopes down towards the ravine referred to above, quantities of ancient relics of the kinds just mentioned had been collected by the local inhabitants. By purchases from them we added to our collections. North of the road, starting from a point 40 m away from it, a trench was opened in a northerly direction, roughly on a level with Mound G on the plan. At this spot the ground had not been laid under cultivation, except for a few maguey plants. Contrary to our expectations, we here found the archaeological stratum very thin, and potsherds, etc., to any considerable quantity

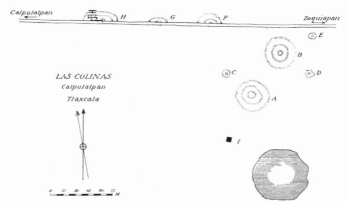

Fig. 108. Sketch plan of Las Colinas ruin area. At the top, the road Calpulalpan—Zoquiapan. Bottom right, the small lake. The letters denote mounds, and (I) the excavated building. (Variation was stated to be 9° 29′ East.)

only occurred quite superficially. Even at a depth of a few centimeters, all artifacts ceased.

The road constructors have dealt sad havoc with the ancient remains that are left above the surface level. These consist of two rather large hillocks, A and B, three smaller ones ·next to them, C, D and E, and three more at the side of the road, F, G and H. The last-mentioned have all been cut by the road, and for no conceivable reason whatever. As the road, even when judged by local conditions, was extremely wretched, it would hardly have been necessary to cut through these mounds in order to straighten it. The one that had been most extensively damaged is F, fig. 109. In the roadway are seen two walls of stone and mortar, cut down to its level, with plastered south sides. Probably, judging from their situation, these have constituted the south side of the building, which has been deformed into a mound. If this be correct, it must have had a square base. If the two walls that are laid bare in the roadway formed part of the F construction, this must have been enlarged at some time or other. The building material generally seems to have been adobe. As to the shape of the others, nothing can be determined without excavation. Today they look like rather irregular, rounded mounds of earth, fig. 110. A and B are certain to have been temple foundations, and F may be supposed to have served the same purpose. The three small ones have also carried buildings, as minor remains of floors can be observed on their highest parts.

While G is a small, low, and apparently uninteresting mound, the road has uncovered building remains in H. Working along the walls and floors that had thus been laid bare, through a hastily carried out excavation, we ascertained the form and size of a number of rooms, fig. 111. It appears that H must have been a tall building or, more likely, a pyramid or other massive foundation, on the western side of which dwelling rooms had been constructed. For east of these the

60

Fig. 109. Mound F, partly cut by the road. Las Colinas.

mound is higher, and solid, and 7 m farther east a thick adobe wall runs in a north-to-south direction. This wall does not appear to have anything to do with rooms, and may therefore be supposed to constitute a constructional element of a solid building. In the west the layer of earth is very thin, and the walls to a large extent so crumbled that here and there only remain traces of them and of the floors, which are also badly damaged. It is interesting to note that at least two building periods are definable. In the northern and eastern portions of the excavated area the remains of two floors can be seen, one above the other. A strangē thing is that the western face of the northernmost north-to-south running wall slopes and is plastered, carefully smoothed and painted white. This gives the impression of having been an outer wall during some period of the history of the building, probably the earlier. It may also be noted that the floors as a rule have a slight western slope. Practically no artifacts, at any rate of any particular importance, were discovered either above or below the floors. In spite of the complete absence of architectural decoration and distinctive constructional details, the uncovered building remains agree with those whose acquaintance we made at Teotihuacan. The walls, as will be seen, are not exactly orientated to the four cardinal points of the compass. Those running in a south-to-north direction have an easterly deviation of 9°.

Some distance south or southwest of this settlement, remains of some buildings could be seen. Time did not allow of any detailed studies of this apparently less important group.

Fig. 110. Mound A; western aspect. Las Colinas.

The main portion of the settlement seems to have lain between the present road and a miniature lake, figs. 108 and 112. It is here we find the two large mounds, A and B, and the three smaller ones, C, D and E. A line drawn through the centres of A and B strikes the top of Cerro Castillo, fig. 113, the nearest mountain in the north. It does not seem improbable that closer investigation would reveal that also the rest of the mounds are, so to speak, orientated according to the terrain. Another circumstance worth being again emphasized is that neither the walls of Mound H nor the sides of Platform I — referred to in the following — are orientated north and south but have an easterly deviation from the astronomical north. In the last-mentioned case the deviation roughly amounts to the same angle as in Teotihuacan.

Mounds A and B are of about the same size, with a diameter of ca. 45 m and height ca. 8 m. Naturally, the original height must have been greater and the diameter smaller, because the action of wind and weather has joined with man's tendency to destroy in working their ruin. They are overgrown with maguey, and no constructional details are discernible on the surface. Adjoining them there are, as seen from the general plan, three small hillocks. These are much ruined, but, as already mentioned, fragments of floors indicate that they probable were foundations of buildings.

The only reason now evident why this spot was selected for habitation is the presence of the miniature lake already referred to. Its shores are flat and boggy,

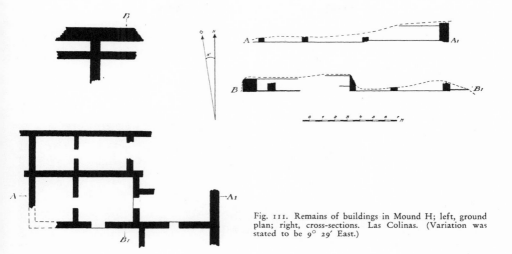

Fig. 111. Remains of buildings in Mound H; left, ground plan; right, cross-sections. Las Colinas. (Variation was stated to be 9° 29′ East.)

only the southern one consisting of a short stretch of a rock, in consequence of which its surface varies greatly in extent from dry season to rainy season. It is round in shape, and its diameter apparently some 70 m. Notwithstanding the modesty of its size, this little lake — if its shores were kept in order and its waters preserved from pollution — might well prove a satisfactory reservoir during the dry season, sufficient for the requirements of a considerable number of people. That it also played some part in the cult, particularly that of the Rain God, Tlaloc of the Aztecs, is very probable.

Everywhere round the ruins and in the surrounding ground potsherds and other artifacts are to be found. Some little distance southwest of Mound A there seemed to be an unusual abundance of fragments, so I decided to cut a trench at a venture at this spot, where the ground is level. But even here the artifacts were confined to the surface layer, and my hopes of stratigraphical studies were baffled. The trenches appear to indicate that the place probably had not been inhabited for some considerable time, which tallies well with the fact that only two building periods could be made out in Mound H (and possibly also in F). Even if we were disappointed in our hopes of successful stratigraphical researches, we, however, here made a find of the very greatest importance. In the digging of the trench we came upon remains of walls, and were almost from the start able to establish the hidden presence of the remains of a small square building, fig. 114.

Under the direction of Mrs. Larsen, the 10 peons from Hacienda Mazapa were here at work. The excavation proceeded at a brisk pace, and soon the outer walls of the construction could be followed to their full extent. Their lowermost portions are at a depth of ca. 1.80 m. The sides are carefully smoothed, white-painted, and

Fig. 112. The lake seen from the top of Mound A. Las Colinas.

inward-sloping. A trench cut right across this little ruin revealed that these remains were not those of a house, but of a solid, almost square platform, measuring about 8 by 9 metres. In the places where the sides are best preserved, the walls are squared at the top, and even the upper, horizontal portion is smoothed and white-painted. As, however, there are no remains of any "floor" farther in, it is probable that the platform carried a superstructure, perhaps one with stepped sides. The original appearance of this is impossible of determination. Neither were we able to ascertain what purpose it had served, so we simply referred to it as "the platform". It may possibly have been used as an altar. Here, as almost universally in Las Colinas, the building material consists of sun-baked brick, adobe. Regarding its shape it should, among other things, be pointed out that the western portion of the northern side is perpendicular, and that three of the corners are somewhat drawn-out. The upper edge of the projecting portions are in exact line with the base of the rest. From the northern and eastern sides, one and two walls issue at right angles, respectively. The latter are vertical, with their outer sides plastered and white-painted, gleaming white like the faces of the platform. Their inner sides do not appear to have been plastered, but, as unfortunately this section has been damaged through cultivation of the ground, this cannot be definitely ascertained. It is probable that they flanked a staircase. In the space between them there is no trace either of a slanting wall or plastered surface. The orientation of the construction is identical with that of Teotihuacan, i. e. the easterly deviation of the sides running south-to-north from true north amounts to 16—17°.

64

Fig. 113. Mound B seen from the top of A. In the background Cerro Castillo. Las Colinas.

The graves below the platform.

Between the walls projecting from the eastern side, just within the contour line of the platform — which must be imaginary, in the absence of mural remains at this point — a grave was discovered, GRAVE I. The body lay stretched out with its head towards the north, at a shallow depth below the original ground level. Whether here had existed a staircase or other construction connected with the platform, or not, the grave had been well protected. The skeleton was, however, for the most part disintegrated, and so brittle that nothing of it could be preserved. By the head of the body lay a bowl, fig. 115, a double vessel, fig. 116, and a pot, fig. 117. The bowl contained an obsidian knife of the "flake" type, and by the right shoulder of the body there was a small, unevenly shaped but finely polished bead of some greenish kind of rock.

About 1 m to the east, outside the platform, a second grave was found, GRAVE II. Unfortunately, this had been badly damaged by cultivators. Only fragments of the skeleton remained, but they sufficed to show that the person here inhumed had lain parallel with the former. He was equipped with a good deal of pottery vessels. Close to the left shoulder of the skeleton stood two jars, figs. 118 and 119, and level with its knees the rest of the funerary deposits, figs. 120—129, had been clustered together without any apparent system. In addition to the above, there were a number of clay vessels which had been particularly badly damaged in the cultivating of the ground, i. e. digging planting-holes for maguey. In association with the deposits were ashes, pieces of charcoal and of unworked mother-of-pearl. In point of wares, the vessels were only of two categories, and variation in form was also slight. The greater part consisted of unornamented jars, clumsily shaped and with very thick walls, figs. 118—121, 123, and two broken ones, not illustrated, similar to fig. 121. Fig. 122 shows a variant form, which may conceivable have

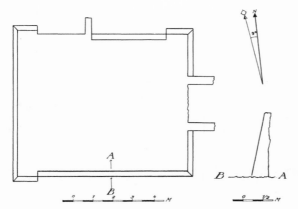

Fig. 114. Plan of "the platfor...", a small building discovered below ground, I on the plan. Las Colinas. (Variation was stated to be 9° 29′ East.)

carried painted ornamentation, applied after firing. While the mouth has both the inner and the outer surfaces polished, those of the body itself are rough and decorated with short incised lines. This surface treatment has not the appearance of owing its existence to esthetic reasons, but would certainly have provided a suitable ground for the application of a fine coating of plaster, on which decoration subsequently could have been painted. This in-fresco technique was popular in Teotihuacan,[3] where we have also collected fragments of vessels with the surface scored in the same way as in fig. 122, with traces of paint still remaining.

By way of the earthenware bowls, figs. 125, 126, we pass on to the second category as regards material: orange wares — light yellowish-red, hard, and of excellent quality in every respect. Vessels of this material are therefore generally thin-walled, and the beautiful and well-made specimen seen in fig. 127 only weighs about half as much as the smaller vessel, fig. 118. While the two similar bowls, one of which is seen in fig. 124, are common in Teotihuacan, there were recovered fragments of a thin-walled vessel of irregular shape which defied attempts at reconstruction, one complete and entirely undamaged bowl, figs. 128 and 170, and fragments of another, similar one, fig. 129. They are completely covered with figures in relief, and were possibly manufactured in moulds.[4] Their composition is excellent, and the individual details executed with elegance and sureness. It is extremely to be regretted that the maguey planter's tool struck just here, as it is not improbable that these two bowls — most likely complements of one another — might together have supplied still more interesting information

[3] Linné 1934: 168—171.
[4] Big pottery moulds probably for the manufacture of large bowls with relieved ornamentation are known from Guatemala. Ricketson 1935: figs. 1—4.

Figs. 115—117. Clay vessels found in Grave I, Las Colinas. (²/₅) 115: 35. 9. 198; 116: 200; 117: 199.

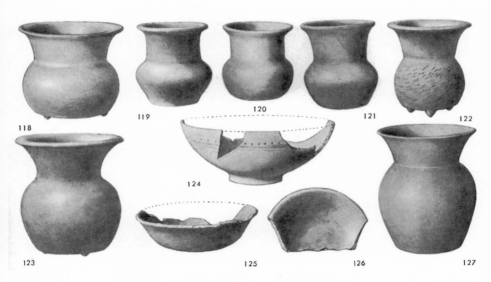

Figs. 118—127. Clay vessels found in Grave II, Las Colinas. (¹/₄) 118: 35. 9. 202; 119: 203; 120: 201; 121: 206; 122: 207; 123: 204; 124: 212; 125: 209; 126: 210; 127: 215.

regarding iconography, religious conceptions, mythology, rites and perhaps chronology from "prehistoric" times. We may, however, congratulate ourselves that at least one of them has been preserved, being, as it is, a bit of a codex in clay, from the days of the Teotihuacan culture.

Fig. 128. Clay bowl found in Grave I1, Las Colinas. (²/₃). Museo Nacional. Mexico City.

Fig. 129. Part of clay bowl of the same type as fig. 128. Grave II, Las Colinas. (²/₃) 35.9.214.

Surface finds from Las Colinas.

Our collection of incidental finds is fairly extensive and contains artifacts of various kinds. It was brought together by hunting for artifacts in the open grounds, by the purchase of such as had been picked up by the natives in the corn-fields, and those collected in the excavation of the platform. In the last-mentioned case they were found in the ground surface. No reason exists for discrimination between the groups of finds discovered in different ways and in different localities as the stratigraphical diggings, as mentioned, gave negative results.

Heads and other parts of clay figures dominate as to numbers. Typical representatives are reproduced in figs. 130—148. The majority belongs to the Teotihuacan III type, but even Period IV — Vaillant's classification — is represented. Vaillant is, however, not absolutely certain that Period IV may not merely have been "an interval in the development of Teotihuacan figurine technique". His statement that "seventy-five percent of the figurines picked up in the fields (at Las Colinas and to some extent perhaps also at Zoquiapan) were of this type" appears somewhat of an exaggeration.[5]

Remarkably numerous are heads of to some extent well-known deities — Tlaloc (the Rain God) and Ueueteotl (the Old God) of the Aztecs, figs. 139 and 147—148 — and of the peculiar un-Indian "Fat God", whose sphere of action is unknown. Of the last-mentioned there are no less than 8 representations, figs. 130—131, 133—138.

The largest of the heads, figs. 130 and 132, are hollow. Some of them are made in the same moulds and thus identical, as may be seen of figs. 136—137, 144—145. In addition there are heads of monkeys and jaguars.

Strangely enough, spindle-whorls were of exceedingly rare occurrence: only a small and plain one, a larger, fig. 146, and fragments of two more. These are of the same type as the last-mentioned.

A great abundance of potsherds were met with, mainly fragments of the same kinds of vessels as those depicted in figs. 118—127 and 149—168. To these may be added a number of other types common in Teotihuacan, and fragments in which the ware had a thickness of more than 2 cm, and of storing vessels of most respectable dimensions. The cylindrical tripod vases, of which a fair number of fragments were found, carry remarkably plain decorative designs. Moulded or freehand-manufactured ornamental details, such as were attached to the vessels while still wet, were collected. Even the method of impressing ornaments was practised, fig. 107. A sherd with an exactly identical ornament is reproduced by Tozzer from Azcapotzalco.[6] A few simple plane stamps and one candelero are also worth mentioning.

---

[5] Vaillant 1938: 542—543. [6] Tozzer 1921: fig. 8.

Figs. 130—148. Clay heads of figurines and one spindle whorl. Las Colinas. (¹/₂)
130: 35. 9. 167; 131: 168; 132: 178; 133: 169; 134: 221;
135: 35. 9. 51; 136: 62; 137: 170; 138: 63;
139: 35. 9. 174; 140: 172; 141: 34; 142: 56; 143: 92;
144: 35. 9. 74; 145: 177; 146: 190; 147: 64; 148: 171.

No less than 41 clay pellets are included in the collection from Las Colinas. The majority are of exact spherical form and the average diameter amounts to 15.₁ mm. Disregarding the two largest ones, the figure stops at 14.₈ mm. There is much that argues in favour of the pellets having been used as blow-gun projectils, a question that will be discussed in "Comparative notes and studies".

Among the objects of stone or obsidian may be noted parts of knives of the latter material, and lanceolate ones with flaked edges. Fragments of grinding stones, metates, and handstones, as well as stone balls of various sizes, were also recovered. There were further some objects of tecali. Among these may be mentioned a very finely shaped pellet (diam. 17.₅ mm) and a piece which evidently had done duty as a hone. Some beads of yellowish-white rock, or of various shades of green — including a long and cylindrical one of uncommon type — were purchased from the natives.

SAN JOSÉ ZOQUIAPAN

At a spot some 2.5 km south of hacienda San José Zoquiapan, in the course of agricultural work were discovered remains of ancient habitation which also derive from the era of the Teotihuacan culture. The position of this archaeological site is rather remarkable. The ground has a slight northward slope. The only explanation that now can be found as to why exactly this place was selected for habitation is that the settlers must have been peaceful agriculturists and therefore preferred living in the midst of their cultivations to occupying a dominating site, or a place that would have been easier to defend against an enemy. A little way to the east there runs a small brook in an almost due northerly direction, passes close to the hacienda and empties itself in Lago Atocha, whose edges are very swampy.[7]

The ground is flat, and practically no building remains are visible above its surface. Extremely few potsherds, far too few for an archaeological site of any importance to be revealed by their presence alone, were to be seen outside the small space that had been subjected to desultory excavation on a modest scale. In planting maguey, it appeared that walls had been encountered, and the hope of finding treasure had acted as a spur to further operations. In these, some remains of walls and sections of floor had been laid bare, as well as three wells sunk in the rocky ground. The depth of these wells or water-cisterns is unknown, because, when discovered, they were filled with earth and have not — so far as we could find — been completely emptied. At the time of our visit they were 3 to 4 m deep, and almost dry.

In the digging for treasure, a goodly quantity of coarse ceramics had been recovered, as also some finer vessels. At least part of the latter were, so far as we could ascertain from the vague description given us, funerary deposits. Even parts of skeletons had been found, and two skulls had been recovered. The latter and part of the pottery were preserved at the hacienda. Our offers to purchase these were declined. From what we hear, the pottery has since been destroyed. On this account it may be appropriate here to reproduce those clay vessels, which I photographed. The photos were taken in a hurry, and from a technical point of view the results were not altogether satisfactory. Therefore I have had drawings in watercolours made from those photographs, and these "translations" are as true to the originals as could reasonably be desired. To this little collection, which was the property of the hacienda-owner, Lic. Eduardo Tamariz, the following notes may be appended.

---

[7] Here, as always, the ancient name has a meaning. The Spaniards acted sensibly in allowing the Indian place-names to survive and only christianizing them by the tacking on of a saint's name. Peñafiel (1897, vol. 2: 335) resolves Zoquiapan as follows: zoqui-apan, río de agua fangosa, en lengua mexicana: *zoquitl*, lodo y *apan*, río.

Figs. 149—158. Pottery from the archaeological site at San José Zoquiapan. (¹/₄). The hacienda collection, 1935.

Tripod vessels.

There were three tripod vessels, which in the general character of the material and decoration, agree with finds made in Teotihuacan. Two of these were almost identical and had round the bottom an engraved frieze of a design largely corresponding to that on a specimen from Teotihuacan contained in our collection, fig. 151. The remaining tripod vase carried a more complicated design, thrice repeated, which supposedly belongs to the conventional representations of the Rain God, Tlaloc, figs. 149 and 150.

Pointed-bottomed vessels.

Of this unpainted and unornamented vessel type, not very common in Teotihuacan, there were two kinds: those which were large, elegant, carefully formed and with a smooth surface, and smaller ones, badly shaped, and with rough, uneven surface. Each category was represented by five specimens. These being among themselves very similar, only one representative of each category has here been depicted, figs. 162 and 163. This type of vessel, of rare occurrence in Mexico and all America, may well represent an excellent invention, a heat-saving vessel and quick-boiling cooking pot. If embedded in the heart of the fire, the large surface should have resulted in considerable heat economizing.

"Shoe-vessels" and "Foot-vessels".

This type of vessel, still less common in Teotihuacan, was represented by two different varieties. Of these, in fig. 166 we see a relatively naturalistic right foot, black ware, and in fig. 165 a stylized foot, a "shoe-vessel", provided with two very small feet under the "sole". Vessels of this type are still used in Oaxaca as fuel-economizers, and are inserted between the hearth-stones, e. g. underneath a griddle, Mexican *comalli*. In this way it is possible to bake tortillas and cook the food at the same time.

Figs. 159—168. Pottery from the archaeological site at San José Zoquiapan.
(³/₈) 159: 35. 9. 296; (¹/₄) 160: 295; 161—163: The hacienda collection, 1935.
(¹/₄) 164—168: The hacienda collection, 1935.

Vessels with undulate collar.

Of this type there were five specimens. They were all very much of the same shape, but in size they varied from 8.5 to 15 cm as to height. There were traces of decoration in red: a border with vertical lines, sparsely applied, and almost obliterated. The collar was sharply cut, that of the smallest one being of small waves, the others with 5 or 6 undulations; figs. 152 and 153.

Flat-bottomed and wide-mouthed vessels.

Of this type, which is closely allied to the foregoing, and no doubt a prototype of it, there were 36 specimens, 13 of them with rudimentary feet and 23 without. In height, they varied from 8 to 13.5 cm in the former case, and from 7.5 to 15.5 in the latter. In material, shape and execution they corresponded with Teotihuacan finds. Decoration absent; figs. 154—157.

Flat-bottomed bowls.

Both in type and material these were of pure Teotihuacan character. 12 in number. Diameter, 11—15.5 cm; fig. 164.

Household pottery.

Two of the vessels appeared to have been used as cooking pots. Both had bulging sides, were flat-bottomed, of course material, not shaped to any particular exactness, and with surfaces of indifferent smoothness, fig. 161. A third vessel, which may also be classed as utility pottery, was made of light-coloured material. In form, it resembled that in fig. 157, but its neck was shorter. Among the same category may also be counted 6 smaller vessels with rounded bottom and wide mouth. They had no distinguishing features. Their height varied between 5 and 8 cm.

Three-handled vessels.

Of this type of vessel, which also occurred in the Mazapan culture of Teotihuacan, there were two specimens, one with out-curving mouth, fig. 168, and another of the same size but less bulgy and with straighter mouth region. Diameter 6.5 and 7 cm, respectively.

Cup.

The material was dark, and the cup clumsily and unevenly shaped, fig. 167.

Bowl with annular foot.

In shape it corresponded with those of the thin, light yellowish-red ware, although made of ordinary clay. Diameter 14 cm.

Candeleros.

Parts of two 2-holed candeleros, one smooth and polished, the other ornamented with serried rows of vertical impressed lines.

Earthenware ball.

This was well shaped, and contained loose objects which rattled when the ball was shaken; diameter 6.2 cm, fig. 158. In some places, excisions had been made in the wall. That balls of this type were used as toys may be taken as fairly certain. In collections from Aztec times they are not infrequent, but this is the only specimen I have seen from the Teotihuacan era; it may be mentioned that no Aztec artifacts of any kind were found at Zoquiapan.

The collection in question also contained a number of other objects which either did not lend themselves to reproduction or else belonged to categories which have already been depicted from other archaeological sites. Of the former, there were nine clay pellets. Their average diameter was 14.9 mm, the difference between the largest and the smallest being 1.5 mm. In connection with the artifacts from Las Colinas, a suggestion has been advanced as to the employment of pellets of this description. This problem will closely be discussed in the chapter "Comparative notes and studies". Among minor objects may be mentioned four circular flat stamps with conical handles, one small lid of the kind numerously occurring in the cremation grave, Burial 1, at Tlamimilolpa, Teotihuacan, and rather uninteresting fragments of the complicated incense-burners that also will be dealt with in connection with the finds of that locality.

Lastly, it may be mentioned that the collection also contained heads and bodies of clay figurines. These, too, were of the types common in Teotihuacan. For example, there was a head representing Ueueteotl, the "Old God", with part of the sun's disk (according to Seler's interpretation) as head ornament. Among the bodies were two large (9.5 and 10.5 cm, respectively) hollow figures with movable arms and legs, together with arms and legs that possibly had belonged to them. They were of the same kind as some from Tlamimilolpa. Some heads belonged to early types, possibly Teotihuacan II, according to Vaillant's classification, but the majority to Period III. Any that might reasonably be referred to his hypothetic Period IV were, however, absent.

The modest little collection that we got together in two quite brief visits contains a number of interesting objects. Of the nine of figurine heads that it contains, three represented Ueueteotl, one approaches the so-called portrait type, two are

stylistically akin to those of the Early Cultures, while the remainder are zoo-
morphic. Besides a number of fragments of clay figures of minor interest, we found
a small, flat, circular stamp, two clay pellets with a diameter of 15.5 and 19.5 mm,
respectively, and a large number of potsherds. All are of more or less pronounced
Teotihuacan types. One of them, which is of light yellowish-red ware, carries a
decoration — (probably) made in a mould separately and then attached to the
newly made, still wet, vessel, fig. 160. Fig. 159 reproduces a fragment of a large
vessel decorated with engraved figures, somewhat carelessly filled in with red
paint. There are in addition fragments of a large number of bowls of the thin,
hard, yellowish-red ware, identical with the material of which many fine pieces
from Las Colinas are made.

SAN NICOLÁS EL GRANDE

About 2 km south-east of San Nicolás el Grande there are some considerable
remains of an ancient city. The site is on the lowest part of the northern slope of
Cerro San Nicolás, and covers an extensive area, cf. the sketch map, fig. 98.

The ruins consist of 3 larger and 40-odd smaller mounds, some of which were
pyramids and others foundations of buildings. The larger ones are of a character
similar to those of Las Colinas, although of more modest dimensions. Two of them
are not very far apart, fig. 169, and on the eastern one, on the right in the picture,
there are fairly extensive remains of floors quite close to the top. In front of the
westernmost of the three larger mounds, situated some distance away from the two
just referred to, seems to have lain a rectangular courtyard surrounded by buildings
and facing north, i. e. on to the plain. This courtyard was probably plastered or
"cemented", as the vegetation is here very sparse. It is fenced in with low, but fairly
regular walls, no doubt low foundations or platforms for buildings.

The larger mounds have probably had buildings on their summits, because in the
sides of all of them more or less extensive remains of floors could be observed. In
some cases these floors are of uncommonly heavy construction, frequently being as
thick as 20 cm. Even remains of walls are here and there to be seen. These are
wider at the base, their outer sides sloping inwards while the inner ones are vertical.
Whether the smaller mounds, too, had once been foundations of temples or profane
buildings is for the present impossible to determine, but their dimensions favour the
supposition that the former alternative is the more probable. In some places these
mounds stand strikingly close together, although not in any symmetrical arrangement. That the three larger ones were formerly surmounted by temples must be
considered as certain.

Fig. 169. Two of the larger mounds, San Nicolás el Grande. The man standing on top of the right-hand one serves to give an idea of their dimensions. In the background, though indistinct, is the hacienda and Lago Atocha.

On our lightning visit we had only time to collect a number of potsherds. With the exception of part of an Aztec bowl from an early period, they were all of pure Teotihuacan type. The thin, yellowish-red pottery was comparatively numerously represented, and in places the ground was tinted yellow from being thickly strewn with pulverized fragments of this kind. Unfortunately we had no opportunity to give any close study to this place, but our cursory inspection sufficed to convince us that we had here before us a site that should yield rich results in future excavations. Its general character was that of all the ruined sites from the Teotihuacan culture.

Fig. 170. Bottom of the clay bowl, fig. 128, found in Grave II, Las Colinas. Photo. Ola Apenes.

COMPARATIVE NOTES AND STUDIES

From a strategic point of view, nothing can be found in explanation of the situations of the ruins at Las Colinas, Zoquiapan or San Nicolás. Seldom did the peoples of ancient Mexico build their cities, settlements or villages on sites where they could easily be defended, or in such a way that they dominated mountain passes, river fords, etc. The Aztec capital, Tenochtitlán, forms a rare exception, while Xochicalco and Monte Albán — to give a couple of examples of places that might easily have been fortified — were not fortresses but cult centres. The high civilizations of Mexico must have existed and flourished under peaceful conditions, and this probably explains why, when warlike tribes from the North and, lastly, the Spaniards invaded them, they were so speedily subjugated and the fruits of peace looted and annihilated.

In choosing the sites for the places mentioned in the foregoing there must, as always in case of cities dating from the era of the Teotihuacan culture, have prevailed considerations other than strategic ones. If we were fully acquainted with these factors, a corner would be lifted of the veil concealing from us the religious conceptions of this culture. Religion must have dominated the life of the people, it must have penetrated into all departments: potters and stone-carvers fashioned images of the gods, and the architects designed plans for their dwellings. The gigantic erections at Teotihuacan and Cholula fill our minds with profound respect for the energy that was capable of being mustered, concentrated and

77

brought to bear upon the construction and decoration of these sacred edifices. Deities were wont to be imprisoned and confined in the temples of their worshippers, but the gods of this people must have been ethereal beings, who rode the rain-clouds and, themselves invisible, manifested their presence through the sprouting of the crops. There is something sublime about a religion that links the fortunes of men and gods together with the stars and the sun, with mountains and lakes.

As already stated, there was, however, a natural motive for a settlement to be established at Las Colinas, viz. the small lake. Mention has also been made as to correspondences concerning artifacts and architecture between the here discussed ruins and Teotihuacan, but in the case of Las Colinas there are also points in common as regards the orientation of the buildings. Camino de los Muertos, the main axis of Teotihuacan, if produced in a straight line would in its extension cut Cerro Gordo, and other mountain peaks, too, appear to have played a part in the planning of this city.[1] That in Las Colinas the sides of the platform have an easterly deviation from astronomical north identical with the buildings of Teotihuacan, seems to indicate that in both places the same astronomical observation was used in orientating the main axis of the groups of buildings. It would also appear as if certain geographical lines connected with the small lake had been taken into account for fixing the site. Palacios has explained why the north-to-south axis of the building aggregations of Teotihuacan has an easterly deviation amounting to roughly $17°$ E. He writes as follows:

"Los tránsitos anuales del sol por el zenit local (evento cuya significación señalaba, a su vez, el comienzo del año) determinan la dirección de las aristas de los edificios, las cuales resultan paralelas y perpendiculares — son plantas en rectángulo — a la línea ideal dirigida desde aquéllos al ocaso del astro en tales días. La importancia que tales fechas revisten engloba varios hechos: a) momento en que el sol culmina en el lugar, apreciable con pozos y gnomones; b) ocaso del astro en línea recta de los frentes y escaleras de los adoratorios ... Las investigaciones respectivas (1930—33) en sus varios aspectos, son obra de Marquina o el autor."[2]

As regards the artifacts found by us in the Calpulalpan district, a certain amount of divergences are noticeable as against the Teotihuacan finds. Thus, for example, there was an almost complete absence of even fragments of tripod vessels typical of Teotihuacan, with decoration scratched out after firing, often figural motives, filled with red paint (cinnabar). Plainly decorated tripod vessels, also occurring in Teotihuacan, were on the other hand included in the hacienda Zoquiapan collection, and further fragments were found at Las Colinas. These are, however, in no way remarkable. This, on the other hand, is the case with the yellowish-red, thin-walled pottery, which was omnipresent. Most numerously represented are bowls with or without decoration and provided with annular foot.

[1] Linné 1934: 32—33. [2] Palacios 1937: 54.

The decoration is throughout the same: punched dots and incised lines, always simple but applied with sureness and elegance. But beside this standardized form, there are numerous other types. No pottery in the highlands of central Mexico presents such a variety of forms. The specialized material, the plastic treatment, and the exceedingly scanty decoration, are instead the type-forming elements. Thus in 1932 we found in Teotihuacan, among other things, huge bowls and diminutive pots, a rectangular box and a fruit with a monkey sitting on it.[3] But the ware was the same, all other differences notwithstanding. The same monkey appears on the intercommunicating, double-bodied or twin vessel, fig. 116, and a pot depicted by Noguera from Huejotzingo, very closely akin to it, probably carries the same figure. Here, as in fig. 116, the head has been knocked off before the vessels ended up in their respective graves. Both the monkeys have had whistles in their heads. In the case of another double jar of the same material from Tepeaca, the monkey figure also plays a prominent part.[4] The monkey figure may possibly indicate that the place of manufacture is to seek in the low country,[5] and this supposition is supported by the micro-analysis of the ware cited in the foregoing. The forms are besides all too diversified for providing a clue to their place of origin.

The geographical distribution of the above-mentioned vessels — vessels consisting of two bodies in the same horizontal plane and connected by a tube — is among the more interesting problems. Rydén has published data concerning the occurrence of intercommunicating vessels in South America, where they have a decided westerly distribution.[6] Archaeological vessels of this type, generally provided with a whistling contrivance in the closed half, were exceedingly common on the Peruvian coast, particularly during the Middle and Late Chimu periods, i. e. the centuries next preceding the era of the Conquest (900—1500 A. D.?). They are also found in Chile, Argentina, Bolivia, on the coast of Ecuador, and a few are reported from Colombia. Modern double-bodied intercommunicating vessels are known from some Indian tribes in South America: the Chocó of north-western Colombia, Chebero of western Brazil, Palikur of Brazilian Guiana, Chiriguano of Bolivia and also a few from Caribs in Guiana. Going north they recur in Costa Rica and in Guatemala, but foremost in Mexico they reappear in the Peruvian type, often provided with a whistle. As a rule one half of the vessel resembles an ordinary pot, and is connected by means of a horizontal tube with the other half, which is frequently shaped like an animal, e. g. a bird or a monkey, with the whistle in its head. Lack of published material from Mexico and Central America makes it difficult to draw up a map of the geographical distribution. As to this, Noguera

[3] Linné 1934: figs. 131—135.   [4] Noguera 1937: figs. 22—23.
[5] As a positive proof of the tropical situation of the locality of its manufacture, the monkey will not do, seeing that it also played an important part in the mythology of the Aztecs. Cf. Beyer 1913: 140—154.
[6] Rydén 1936: 169—172.

says: "Vasos silbadores sencillos son también muy abundantes en las colecciones del Museo Nacional ... y proceden de varias regiones culturales".[7] A preliminary collocation of double-bodied vessels — a cross marking those fitted with a whistle — has, however, the following interesting appearance:

Zacualpa, Guatemala	....	Lothrop 1936: figs. 13, 17.	
Salcajá-Momostenango distr., Guatemala +	....	» » fig. 92.	
Chalchitan, Huehuetenango, Guatemala +(?)	....	Lehmann 1912: 103.	
Ulua River, Honduras	....	Popenoe 1934: 74; fig. 12.	
Corozal Distr., British Honduras	....	Gann and Gann 1939: 48; pl. 4.	
Cerro de las Mesas, Veracruz +	....	Stirling 1941: 282.	
Monte Albán, Oaxaca	....	Museo Nacional, Mexico.	
Ixtlán, »	....	» » »	
Ejutla, »	....	» » »	
Zimatlán, » +	....	Lehmann 1912: 103.	
Ocotlán, · » +	....	» » » ; fig. 31.	
Yetlán, » +	....	Noguera 1937: fig. 17.	
Miahuatlán, » +	....	» » fig. 18.	
Tepeaca, Puebla +	....	» » figs. 21, 22.	
Cholula, » +	....	» » figs. 14—16.	
Huejotzingo, Puebla +	....	» » fig. 23.	
Calpulalpan, Tlaxcala +	....	fig. 116.	
Teotihuacan	....	Museo Nacional, Mexico.	
Zamora, Michoacán +	....	Noguera 1937: fig. 20.	

The drawing of any conclusions from a table like the above, i. e. from the geographical distribution, is a difficult matter. The pessimist may be justified in maintaining that it is by no means a "culture element" but a form of clay vessel that, by different routes and in different localities, has developed into a uniform type. That's easy enough to point out the close agreement between the whistle vessels of Peru and Mexico-Guatemala, but Lothrop was the first to venture drawing the conclusions to their full extent. He says: "The double whistling jar is not the kind of apparatus apt to be repeatedly invented, yet it is just the sort of novelty to be easily copied if once seen. We believe that this specimen (Lothrop 1936: fig. 92) could have been made only as the result of the journey of some unknown individual from Guatemala to Peru or vice versa."[8] This is exactly the conclusion my travelling companion and I arrived at when in 1934 in Museo Nacional, Mexico City, we saw a double jar found by Caso in a grave at Monte Alban.

In an earlier work I have collocated a certain amount of material lending colour to communications of some sort having existed between Oaxaca and Peru, and

[7] Noguera 1937: 17. Seler (1915: fig. 147) reproduces a double-bodied vessel of the hard, thin-walled, yellowish-red ware. Its provenance is stated to be Huauchinango, but as this vessel was part of the Carrasco collection (now in Berlin), the place where it was found may not be so very certain.

[8] Lothrop 1936: 89.

then also cited Lothrop's statement that golden objects from Tomb 7 at Monte Alban are of Peruvian manufacture.[9] Such an assertion might seem fantastic and be received by doubt, had it not been made by an authority of Lothrop's standing. But in Oaxaca there are other, enigmatical, elements that can only be explained by far-distant connections. As an example of this, Seler depicts pattern on clay vessels from Cuicatlán, in Museo Nacional, Mexico City, purely Peruvian in style.[10] The clay vessel type is alien to Peru, but identical to other vessels in the same collection, which have the rich decoration characteristic of the Mixtecs.[11] The designs consist of geometrical heads of a type alien to Mexico, divided by fields also consisting of heads of the same kind, but in a different colour, and turned upside down. Merely looking at a reproduction of the decoration might lead to the conclusion that it referred to Peru, and that it represented a textile design. The only explanation that for the present seems possible — even though it may seem fantastic and contrary to etiquette in the circumspect science of archaeology — is that that textiles from the Peruvian coast have found their way here, and that their pattern motives were transferred to the clay vessels.

The collections from Las Colinas and Zoquiapan include 43 small clay pellets, generally of very fairly exact spherical shape and with smooth, occasionally polished surface. These, and their counterparts from Teotihuacan, together more than one hundred in number, have been dealt with in a separate paper.[12] In this I have endeavoured to show that they were used as ammunition for blow-guns, and on the basis of that hypothesis also suggested the possibility of our being able to determine the lengths of the blow-guns used. Blow-guns with clay pellet ammunition were hunting weapons among the Aztecs, and are still being used here and there in Guatemala, by the Jicaque Indians in Honduras and Talamanca Indians in Costa Rica. Among those which are still in use, the projectiles are slightly smaller than our finds, viz. 12—14 mm as against 14.7—14.8, the mean diameter of the recovered pellets. Computation of the volume of a large number of American blow-guns, and also that of some from the Indo-Malayan archipelago, makes it apparent that this volume — the length of the blow-gun multiplied by $\pi \left(\dfrac{\text{caliber}}{2} \right)^2$ —

varies only between very narrow limits. This is due to the limited capacity of human lungs of suddenly expelling, by compression, a certain volume of air. Should this line of reasoning prove to be correct, the weapons of the blow-gun marksmen of the Teotihuacan period must have had a length of not less than 150, and not exceeding 170 centimeters. These figures naturally only apply to blow-guns with

[9] Linné 1938: 169; Lothrop 1936: 72.   [10] Seler 1908: 530—531; Joyce 1914: 192.

[11] Marquina 1928 reproduces these and other clay vessels of the same collection in colour on unnumbered plates between pp. 78 and 79.

[12] Linné 1939. Further to the instances there cited may be mentioned a blow-gun in the Department of Middle American Research, Tulane University of Louisiana, New Orleans. It originates from the Jacalteca Indians, Guatemala, and has a length of 191 cm, while its caliber is 13—14 mm.

a caliber corresponding to the mean diameter of the recovered clay pellets. For smaller pellets, the most suitable tubes would have been longer, and vice versa in the case of larger projectiles.

The relief-ornamented bowl, figs. 128, 170—174, is in itself a most valuable result of our Calpulalpan excursion.[13] Anything in the way of an unassailable interpretation of its decoration is beyond my capacity of providing. For this would be required a profound knowledge of mythology, technical skill in iconography, bold powers of combination, imagination, and a capacity for "thinking Indian". The problem is undoubtedly by no means simple, being, as it were, set by a people not even known by name and who have only left part of their wisdom — their world of conceptions — to the Aztecs. The latter possessed a symbolism of a richness hardly surpassed by any people unacquainted with phonetic writing. But whether the same key would open the door of their predecessors' world of ideas, their thoughts behind the symbols, is perhaps less certain. Some of the signs on the bowl are ideographic in their character: the symbols of speech or song — curving lines before the faces of the figures — and the representation of water streaming from the hands.

It would seem as if every detail of the decoration of the bowl was connected with complex problems in the world of conceptions of the Teotihuacan culture. In the centre of the decoration, i. e. the bottom of the bowl, is seen the Rain God, Tlaloc of the Aztecs, surrounded by rivers of water and possibly equipped with insignia, later characterizing other gods, such as a breast ornament resembling that of Quetzalcoatl. The deity is framed within a border consisting of two circular lines between which a wavy line, usually symbolizing water, has been worked in.

Round the circuit of the bowl four human figures are seen walking in procession, with animal figures and a symbolic sign interposed. The Rain God is a deity of very ancient standing, for even the earliest agriculturists must in years of drought despairingly have extended suppliant hands towards the power behind the veil that alone could bestow upon them the life-giving rain. Even the existence of the small lake, or pond, predestined Las Colinas to the special cult-place of the Rain God. The God of Rain, with minor variations, occurs on Mexican clay vessels from the Early Cultures to the Aztec era, as well as in central and southern Mexico, Salvador and Guatemala. Doering holds that he has even discovered a definite connection between Tlaloc and figures on pottery on the Peruvian coast.[14] Tlaloc still survives to this day in certain parts, in the Indian world of conceptions.[15] I cannot resist mentioning that one day, when rain-clouds were gathering above Cerro Gordo, one of our workers at Teotihuacan — the actual mother-tongue of whose oldest

---

[13] It has already been reproduced, so far as I know, on four different occasions. I have myself reproduced it twice (1936: fig. 3, 1937: fig. 22). Caso (1937: fig. 18) has included it as a — technically indifferent — illustration in a very interesting paper, but only refers to it in passing. Palacios (1937: fig. 25) reproduces a technically not wholly satisfactory drawing of its decoration, without analysing it in detail.

[14] Doering 1931: 3 seq.   [15] Redfield 1930: 121—122; Parsons 1936: 211 seq.

82

family members was Aztec — let fall the observation "here is Tlaloc coming!" In the Huichol Indian pantheon, too, there are — as among the Maya — four Rain Gods, one for each of the cardinal points of the compass. The god known as "B" in the Mayan codices, appears more than twice as often as any other deity. It is possible that he had several spheres of activity, but that of a rain god seems to have been his most important one. All the civilized peoples of Mexico and Central America have undoubtedly in common a primary cultural stratum out of which specific developments have subsequently taken place. Not least in religion and science, above all in their chronology — these peoples' most important manifestation in the realm of abstract reasoning — can this be traced. The number 4 plays an important part in the construction of their calendar. The Zapotecs, for example, divided their year of 260 days into four periods of 65 days. But the number 4 is also of great importance in the longer cycles of time, such as the one that contains 4 times 13, i. e. 52, solar years. With the abstract number the four points of the compass were also linked together.

Tlaloc had a room in each quarter, and the Maya even reckoned with four Rain Gods, "god B is represented with all the four cardinal points ... he appears as ruler of all the points of the compass; north, south, east and west as well as air, fire, water and earth are subject to him".[16] According to the Aztecs, Tlaloc had four assistants, one in each of the four rooms, and also four large casks of water.

"The water in one of these was said to be very good, and the rain came from it at the right time, when the grain and the corn were growing. In the next the water was said to be bad, and the rain which came from it produced fungous growths in the corn, which turned black. It came from the third when it rained and froze; from the fourth, when it rained and no corn came up or when it came up and dried." [17]

It does not appear improbable that the four figures perambulating the bowl on cloud-symbolizing signs are Tlaloc's servants, who distributed different kinds of rain. They are attired in rich dresses of fairly similar appearance, and the head-dresses of three of them are very much alike.

One of them has the "spectacled" face of Tlaloc, and water is raining down from his right hand, figs. 128 and 173. In front of him, in the centre of fig. 128, appears a large, symmetrical figure of the same kind as his head-dress. It is surrounded by maize grains(?). Consequently, this one should be the dispenser of the beneficial water.

On his right is seen a figure which does not appear to be a purveyor of water, and in front of him is a dog or a coyote, figs. 128 and 173—174. The dog generally symbolizes death, is in the Maya codices associated with the god of death, and plays a prominent part in rites connected with burials. In him we may

[16] Schellhas 1904: 16—19.
[17] Seler 1895: 18, 1904 a: 267—268 (Historia de los mexicanos por sus pinturas. Joaquín García Icazbalceta. Nueva colección de documentos para la historia de México, tomo 3, p. 230, México 1891).

Figs. 171—172. The clay bowl, fig. 128, found in Grave II, Las Colinas. Diameter 13.7 cm. Photo. Ola Apenes.

perhaps have before us the one of Tlaloc's servants that dispenses rain accompanied by frost, that is to say, kills off the growing crops.

The figure, left centre, who has a bird (an owl or an eagle) in front of him, may possibly be the servant that causes the maize to turn black, figs. 128 and 171—172. In Codex Vaticanus 3773 or B, pp. 13—14, 15—16, dwells an owl in the house of drought.

The figure on the extreme left, lastly, close to whom is the sun's disk together with a serpent, represents the last-mentioned of the Rain God's servants referred to above, figs. 128 and 171, 174. In Aztec picture-writing, varying functions are ascribed to the serpent: there are water-, rain-, and lightning-serpents; among the Maya it was mythologically allied to water. The combination sun and serpent appositely symbolizes this not very congenial ministering spirit who distributes rain that either stifles vegetable growth, or allows the corn to shoot forth, only to parch it up afterwards.

A peculiar fact is — or perhaps it is only a mere chance — that the mythological Moan-bird, the Maya cloud spirit, appears in the codices as a combination of the above-mentioned animals: serpent, owl and dog or jaguar. According to Seler the nineteenth day sign, Cauac, is partly an abbreviation of the Moan-bird's head. Cauac as well as Quiauitl, the nineteenth of the Aztec day signs, express in some way or other rain-clouds, thunderstorm or, simply, rain.[18]

As regards the points of the compass — provided that the above interpretation of the functions of the figures is correct — and in accordance with Seler's studies cited in the foregoing, the figures represent, counted from the right in fig. 128: north, east, west and south. The correctness of these speculations may perhaps be

[18] Seler 1900: 15, 1902: 414—415, 496—497, 1923: 613—616.

Figs. 173—174. The clay bowl, fig. 128, found in Grave II, Las Colinas. Diameter 13.7 cm. Photo. Ola Apenes.

called in question, but they constitute an attempted interpretation. If they should give rise to discussion, they will have served as a useful purpose.

A counterpart of the carved or mould-made representation in relief on the bowl occurs on p. 28 of Codex Borgia (and another on p. 69 of Codex Vaticanus B.) with the difference, however, that both the central figure and those in each corner are but different representations of the Rain God. In their right hand they hold a vessel containing the varieties of rain mentioned above, and in their left, a serpent. With one exception the figures on the bowl lack the typical attributes of the god, and all of them carry a satchel (presumably containing incense) in their left hand. The four corner figures of the codices are provided with the numerals and signs of the initial days of the four divisions of the tonalamatl (tonalpohualli), as well as of the initial years of the four sections of the cycle of 52 years. The figures represent north, west, south and east. The central figure has nothing to do with the divisions of the calendar as he represents the fifth direction: the perpendicular.

No numerals, at any rate clearly expressed, are to be found either in connection with the animal figures or the central symbol sign in fig. 128. On the other hand it is possible that these figures correspond to certain day signs of the Mayas, Zapotecs and Aztecs. They occur among the last-mentioned people: snake, dog, eagle, flower. On the bowl they do not, it will be noted, occur in that order, but as snake, dog, flower, eagle. If at that time the calendar had been fully developed, this does not tally with the sequence of the Year Bearers, unless the daysigns occurred in a different order. Otherwise it must be an error and two signs, flower and eagle, have to change places. If the figures represent the points of the compass it comes, as above stated to the same thing: north, east, west, south. Whether they are symbols of the cardinal points associated with Tlaloc, or Year Bearers in a 365-day calendar, they consequently cannot be read in direct sequence, but one

85

has to read diametrically via the Tlaloc figure on the bottom of the bowl. On p. 26 in Codex Troano (= p. 31 in Codex Tro-Cortesianus) such an arrangement occurs: in the centre Chac, the God of Rain, and in each corner the Chac of the different cardinal points in the following order: north, south, west, east, as is apparent from the directional hieroglyph each has by his side. In the passage above quoted from "Historia de los mexicanos por sus pinturas" the four Rain Gods, or the four servants of Tlaloc, represent according to Seler: east, west, north, south. This sequence is corresponding to that of the figures on the bowl from Calpulalpan or the Chacs in the Maya codex.

How far speculations may be carried depends on whether a fully developed calendar was actually in use. If the bowl belongs to the epoch Teotihuacan III, the Maya must for centuries have had their famous calendar in function. Even the Zapotecs of the period Monte Albán III — when intercommunications with the civilized people of the Mexico Valley and the surrounding region were very lively — probably possessed an elaborate, perhaps even fully worked out, calendar. Caso has pointed out that the 260-day period was known as tonalpohualli, and not tonalamatl, which means "papel de los días". In the same work he presents good reasons for supposing that this time-period was known to the peoples of Teoti-huacan, and that the numeral signs were identical with those of the Mayas and Zapotecs, i. e. that the number five was expressed by a line and not by dots, as in the case of the Mixtecs and Aztecs. His arguments would be convincing if only the supporting material he adduces from Teotihuacan were wholly convincing.[19] Personally, I am rather sceptical about the "hieroglyphs" that yet have been discovered at Teotihuacan, but all the same I do not entirely adhere to the tradition according to which the peoples of the Valley of Mexico became, by way of the Mixtecs, acquainted with the knowledge of writing in 1328.

During the fifth working season, 1935—1936, at Monte Albán was discovered a stone slab inscribed with hieroglyphs, partly corresponding to the Teotihuacan material, and two figures.[20] One of these is of pure Zapotec type, and the other is almost identical with the figures on the badly damaged frescoes in Teopancaxco, at Teotihuacan.[21] Somewhat cruder of workmanship but of the same type is a figure on a potsherd found by Tozzer at Santiago Ahuitzotla, in Azcapotzalco.[22] These figures reappear on the bowl from Calpulalpan, and as further evidence of the intimate cultural connections, the latter is of great importance. Of the Monte Albán find Caso says: "La escritura de Monte Albán durante su tercera época, parece haber recibido la influencia de Teotihuacán".[23] Or it may have been the other way about!

The next working season, 1936—1937, was likewise productive of remarkable

[19] Caso 1937: 131—143.   [20] Caso 1937: fig. 17, 1938: figs. 25—26.
[21] Starr 1894: figs. 2—10; Peñafiel 1900: pls. 81—87; Seler 1915: fig. 8, pls. 10—12; Gamio 1922, tomo 1, vol. 1: pls. 34—35.   [22] Tozzer 1921: fig. 5.   [23] Caso 1937: 138.

finds at Monte Albán. In the present connection the frescoes in Tomb 104 are of interest.[24] Here again is found an Ahuitzotla-Teotihuacan-Calpulalpan figure in association with Zapotec hieroglyphs and a figure of pure Zapotec character. This in many respects exceedingly interesting grave chamber dates from the period Monte Albán III. Even in Tomb 105, which belongs to the same period, there are rich wall paintings including figures, 9 male and as many female deities. They show close affinity in particular to those of the Teotihuacan locality just referred to, but are connected by Zapotec hieroglyphs.[25] In his résumé of the discoveries made during the season of 1936—1937, among other things, Caso writes: "Las pinturas también demuestran conexión de la Epoca III de Monte Albán, con Teotihuacán, y confirman que existió un estilo antiguo de escritura y pintura que se usó en estas ciudades" . . .[26]

As mentioned in the foregoing, the bowl is intimately connected with the Zapotec culture as it appears in the period that Caso calls Monte Albán III. In the section which deals with Teotihuacan we shall have occasion to dwell upon clay vessels that likewise possess direct counterparts among the finds from Monte Albán during the third period. The double-bodied whistling vessel, fig. 116, also points to Oaxaca without, however, providing any fixed point chronologically.

Thanks to Noguera's study on the earliest period at Teotihuacan and Vaillant's stratigraphical excavations at Teotihuacan and San Miguel Amantla in Azcapotzalco, Vaillant is able to distinguish between five different stages dating from epochs following the Early Cultures — Teotihuacan I—V — "some of which have the fullness of definition of a period, while others represent intervals in the development of technical processes". Figurines and ceramic wares of Teotihuacan I—III are closely connected with the monuments and structures of the ceremonial site. In addition to these stages there is yet another, whose material, especially the figurines, surpass everything hitherto known from Teotihuacan. This he calls Period V. As already mentioned in connection with the figurines — the period-indicators par préférence — Vaillant considers that at Calpulalpan there was a transition period, Period IV, between Period III, i. e. classical Teotihuacan type, and the highest developed one from San Miguel Amantla. "It would seem as if the zone of Teotihuacan were abandoned at the end of Teotihuacan III or early IV, with the population residing in the neighbourhood. By early V times this population had left the vicinity of Teotihuacan, but there developed an elaboration of the Teotihuacan culture at Azcapotzalco expressed in the prevalence of Teotihuacan V types."[27]

That the clay figures, at all events the majority of them, possessed significance in connection with religious conceptions, is surely beyond doubt. I am afraid that the student that measures ritual objects with the foot-rule of typology and weighs them on the scale of logic, is running risks of miscalculation. As to this, there is no

[24] Caso 1938: pl. 1.   [25] Caso 1938: pls. 2—5.   [26] Caso 1938: 96.   [27] Vaillant 1938: 539—543.

appealing against the results of the stratigraphic excavations, but it would indeed be strange if particularly in ancient Mexico ceramic artists of different localities would have been incapable of reaching varying heights in the art of modelling the images of time-honoured gods.

Whether the ancient relics of the Calpulalpan district refer to Teotihuacan III or IV is, besides, of minor importance. What is more to the point in the present case is their connection with Monte Albán III. Caso and his assistants have since 1931 every year been at work in the Monte Albán ruins and in that time examined more than 100 graves, by means of which they have been able to put on record five successive periods. A chronological system, pivoting on the Maya calendar and the correlation of our own chronology, is beginning to take shape. Vaillant has compiled some exceedingly interesting chronological tables, regarding the results of which he modestly says: "the writer feels that none of them should be used as a positive working hypothesis".[28] According to these, the third periods of Monte Albán and Teotihuacan, respectively, correspond well with one another. As to their dating, by the table corresponding to the Maya correlation nowadays generally used, they would fall roughly between A. D. 900—1000.

The unreliability of the data concerning the correlation between Maya and Christian chronology that we are working with, will best be seen from the following. The correlation launched by Spinden is by Vaillant altogether left out of account as it renders extremely unfavourable chronological relations as between the different cultures. Most specialists on the thorny subject of Maya chronological research follow the Thompson-Martínez-Goodman-Teeple-Beyer correlation which advances the Long Count dates approximately 260 years. Against this, the eminent astronomer and head of the astrophysical observatory of Potsdam, Professor Hans Ludendorff, however, writes:

"Die Umrechnung der Maya-Daten in unsere Zeitrechnung geschah bei der vorliegenden Untersuchung auf Grund der sogenannten Spindenschen Korrelation. Die Ergebnisse bilden wiederum einen zwingenden Beweis für die Richtigkeit dieser Korrelation, denn wenn sie falsch wäre, so würden alle die erwähnten Koinzidenzen der Daten mit astronomischen Erscheinungen ja rein dem Zufall zuzuschreiben sein, und dies widerspricht in schroffster Weise den angeführten Wahrscheinlichkeitszahlen sowie auch der Tatsache, dass in der Auswahl der Daten, wie erwähnt, deutliche Gedankengänge hervortreten. Ich habe nun aber neuerdings die Daten auch nach der Goodmanschen Korrelation, die von manchen Mayaforschern immer noch der Spindenschen vorgezogen wird, umgerechnet und alsdann diskutiert. Ein astronomischer Sinn lässt sich dann, wie es zu erwarten war, für die Inschrift nicht mehr feststellen." [29]

[28] Vaillant 1935: 138.   [29] Ludendorff 1936: 18.

Fig. 175. Fragment of clay vessel from Teotihuacan, probably representing a blow-gun hunter. Musée de l'Homme, Paris. (Désiré Charnay's collection, no. 82. 17. 72.) Height 11 cm.

RECAPITULATION OF RESULTS

From the era of the Teotihuacan culture, building remains and artifacts, as well as graves, were discovered in three places east of the present town of Calpulalpan. Other archaeological sites exist to a certainty in the environs of the town. Below the houses of the town remains of earlier settlements are found. Artifacts here obtained by purchase provide evidence of a cultural connection with Teotihuacan.

The present studies were altogether in the nature of reconnaissances, and only one place was more thoroughly examined but even these researches were merely of a superficial kind. At the site here dealt with, Las Colinas, the buildings were orientated in relation to certain mountain peaks, and the axis of the excavated ruin has the same deviation from astronomical north as those of Teotihuacan, i. e. about 17° East. Two successive stages in the construction of some of the buildings would seem to be discernible. Lack of suitable building material had necessitated an extensive use of adobe.

Within and alongside a platform at Las Colinas, two graves were discovered. Among the grave deposit, which is of pure Teotihuacan character, may be noted a double-bodied whistling vessel and a bowl with rich figural decoration, representing the Rain God, Tlaloc of the Aztecs, and his four satellites. Double vessels

89

may possibly belong to the Mexican elements that have been imported from Peru. The bowl, with its excellent composition and details executed with sureness and elegance, is incomparably the most interesting of the finds that were made, and altogether one of the most interesting clay vessels from the Teotihuacan culture. It may be described as a codex fragment in clay.

All the artifacts, whether recovered by us or acquired by purchase, belong to the Teotihuacan culture, with the exception of one earthenware head from the town of Calpulalpan and a potsherd from San Nicolás el Grande. These are of Aztec type.

As regards the pottery, the dominant part consists of crude pots and other vessels of utility character, and imported ceramics of thin-walled, yellowish-red ware. Cylindrical tripod vessels with incised decoration are not very numerous, and those with decoration scratched out after firing — the parts of the surface thus removed being usually replaced by cinnabar — are almost entirely absent. Mould-made or impressed ornamentation is more numerously represented. The clay heads, too, are of types characteristic of Teotihuacan, and often representing the Rain God, the Old God and the Fat God. Some of them were manufactured in the same moulds. Clay pellets are relatively common. Their dimensions favour the supposition that they must have served as blow-gun munition.

The ruin sites, at any rate Las Colinas, appear to have been daughter cities of Teotihuacan. The artifacts belong mainly to the Teotihuacan III period, and also indicate connection with Monte Albán during the latter's third period.

PART III

EXCAVATIONS AT TEOTIHUACAN

Very shortly after our arrival in Mexico City we left for Teotihuacan to inspect the excavations that had been carried out there since our departure in August 1932. The Mexican archaeologists, it is true, had in the meantime chiefly been engaged in other parts of the country, but, under the guidance of Señor Eduardo Noguera, Señor José Pérez, the local superintendent (Administrador del Campamento), had in 1933 directed the digging of a 116 m long tunnel into the Pyramid of the Sun from the west.[1] Among the results of this exceedingly important work may be mentioned that inside the pyramid no remains were found of any earlier architectural work. In other words, this project — a gigantic one even if measured by modern standards — was not realized by stages. In contrast with this, the pyramid at Tenayuca was built in a series of seven stages, each succeeding one being built about and upon its next precedent,[2] and that of Cholula comprises a multitude of constructions from several predecessors.[3] In the digging of the tunnel, an abundance of artifacts were collected, found in the adobes from which the pyramid is constructed. This material has been worked up by Noguera, and his interesting work above all throws light on the earlier periods of the history of Teotihuacan and of the origin and development of the Teotihuacan culture.

At the same time we also looked up our Indian helpers at the excavations of 1932, who, from the interest in the antiquities of their native country they then acquired, might be expected to have made some useful observations. This, too, proved to be the case. The most alert of them, Joaquín Oliva, had in fact noticed that in a field belonging to a kinsman of his, potsherds occurred in large numbers. On trial, he had dug holes in the ground here and there, and come upon both walls and floors of an ancient building complex. We there and then arranged with him and the owner of the field that, pending our securing the requisite permit, we should together excavate the place. But in our working programme we had, as mentioned in the foregoing, given preference to researches in the Chalchicomula district, and for various reasons we thought it inadvisable to change our plans. Then, when we had finished our work at that place, while waiting for the new permit, we made all preparations for this second excavation, planned it in detail and engaged our workpeople. Joaquín who had shown himself to possess both understanding of,

[1] Noguera 1935: 5—6; Pérez 1935: 91—95.   [2] Tenayuca 1935.   [3] Marquina 1939 a.

91

Fig. 176. Part of Teotihuacan seen from the air, looking east. In the foreground the Pyramid of the Sun. The arrow indicates the position of the excavated ruin, Tlamimilolpa in San Francisco Mazapan. Photograph by Fairchild Aerial Surveys de Mexico, S. A.

and aptitude for, archaeological work, was entrusted with the selection of suitable assistants, both at the start and later on as the number of workmen successively increased. In this way we steered clear of such squabbles as might easily have arisen on account of the inhabitants of different sections of the village not being on the best of terms with each other. Thus he became in a certain degree the foreman of the work-gang, with higher wages and a responsible position. He never abused our trust in him, and the relations between ourselves and our workpeople, and mutually among the latter, were throughout of the happiest nature. They were not only industrious and willing, but Joaquín always saw to it that they did their allotted tasks with exactitude and care. No sooner had we received our license to excavate, than spades were put into the ground. This was on February 11.

To begin with, we had twelve men in action. Of these, apart from Joaquín, two were "veterans" from our 1932 excavations, viz. Porfirio Reyes and Tomás Mendoza. As it, however, soon became apparent that the building complex was considerably larger in extent than we had expected, we increased our working strength as far as our means allowed. Before long it totalled 21 men and an errand-boy. Our plan for the excavation was as follows: first we intended to uncover the central section of the ruin — the gently undulating field was roughly in the centre somewhat raised, and sloped from there on all sides — and from it trenches would be cut to the four points of the compass. By means of these trenches the extent of the ruin would in the main be ascertained. This operation completed, we should be able to plan the continuation of the work. Those working in the central section, for example, would then sink vertical shafts down to the bedrock, for we had at once realized that beneath the floors were hidden remains of earlier buildings.

This plan had, however, to be partly modified as none of the trenches reached any outer wall. Consequently the ruin was of considerably larger area than we had estimated. While the building remains in the central portion were hidden beneath rather deep masses of earth — some of the walls measured over 2 meters in height (e. g. those of the alley between rooms 33, 4, 35, 49, 48 and 5, 2, 27, 3) — the protective earth cover became increasingly thinner the farther we got away from the centre. Here not only the walls but also, in part, the floors had been totally destroyed by earlier agricultural operations.

Our helpers were divided into groups, some of whom worked at or about the spot where Joaquín had made his discovery, and others in various parts of the field. It is because of this that rooms at a distance from those first excavated, 1—3 on the plan, pl. 1, may have low numbers and others, in between, higher. For technical reasons — the finds, studies of architectural details, photographs, etc., were catalogued directly on the spot according to the numeration in the field sketch — no change was made in this respect when, on our return home, the plan was fair-copied. For the removal of the large accumulations of earth that collected about the uncovered places, and which overlay rooms that could not be excavated until considerably later than the adjoining ones, we used a drag-scoop to which two mules were harnessed. So as to make the fullest use of our precious time, working hours were usually lengthened until darkness fell, and towards the end we even worked on Sundays.

Dr. Montell's time was largely occupied in taking care of and cataloguing the collections, while to my lot fell the personal direction and supervision of the field work, keeping register of the excavation, the drawing of plans, excavations of graves, and other details of the work. In spite of our working pace — much speeded up towards the latter part — we had not, when on April 22 we had to bring the excavation to an end, in any spot reached the outer walls of the extensive building complex. This embraced, so far as our excavation went, 176 rooms, 4 or 5 court-yards and a number of large and small passages. Besides this, we ascertained the presence of about 50 rooms which were contiguous to, or by means of doorways communicated with the excavated portion, cf. plan, pl. 1. Judging by the extent of the field, the nature of the terrain, samplings of the ground outside the uncovered section, etc., I am inclined to believe that the total number of rooms in the building complex would rather exceed than fall below 300.

Fig. 177. Pottery vase, carved yellow ware, purchased at Teotihuacan. ($^1/_3$) 35. 8. 2358.

THE TLAMIMILOLPA HOUSE RUIN

We turned out to have been fortunate in the selection of this new working site. As in all archaeological work, accident or luck — in our case personified by Joaquín — plays an important part. The ruin is situated about 200 m east of the church of San Francisco Mazapan. A line drawn from the top of the Pyramid of the Sun to that of the church tower would cut right almost through the centre of the ruin, the north-western corner of room 6, cf. fig. 176. The place itself is a maize-field, with a dwelling-house and a cactusgarden farthest west. Its eastern boundary consists of one of the forks of Río San Juan, which flows gently along at the bottom of a deep ravine and is at a distance of about 40 m from the easternmost wall of the, by us, uncovered section of the ruin complex. Here it runs in a nearly due north-to-south direction, and appears to have practically coincided with the eastern limit of the ancient town. As, however, this river according to what we were told by old local inhabitants had in their lifetime worn itself down to a very great extent, it is by no means certain that this line of demarcation, now so obvious, also played the same role, or even existed, in former days. The Methuselah-old grandmother of Joaquín, our chief workman, one of the few in San Francisco Mazapan that also spoke Aztec, and whom I already in 1932 had questioned about place-names at Teotihuacan, told us before we began excavating that the name of this place was Tlamimilolpa, or Tlamimilolpan. This name is particularly descriptive, as it means "on (or above) the ruins".[4]

[4] José María Arreola (Gamio 1922, tomo 2: 666) writes: "Tlamimilolpa. De *tlamimilolli*, altozano o cuesta pequeña, y la terminación *pa*, encima: sobre el paredón". Peñafiel (1897, vol. 2: 286) on the other hand says:

The ruin that we uncovered at Xolalpan in 1932 — also situated in San Francisco Mazapan, but between the village church and the Pyramid of the Sun — had a clear and regular plan.[5] In the centre of the settlement was a courtyard bordered by four platforms, and round this were grouped 45 rooms and 7 forecourts. The ruin at Tlamimilolpa, on the other hand, with a medley of courtyards and rooms, produces a chaotic impression. It was not at all like a single building, but more in the nature of a small village. If it had stood on the crest of a hill, or on an island, or for some other reason had had a restricted space at its disposal, then its compressed character would have been quite natural. We, at any rate, can see no intelligible reason for adding room to room instead of building separate houses. In Xolalpan there was a central section: a courtyard surrounded by platforms, and there it seemed quite natural that outside the central — sacral — section, living rooms should be grouped. As it is, one stands perplexed in the face of this from every point of view misbegotten architectonic creation. If a fire broke out, it would at once have set ablaze all the rooms and houses, and under the cloud-bursts of the rainy season the alleys, all the drains notwithstanding, must have turned into torrential rivers, so that a large part of the rooms would probably have been made uninhabitable. Occasionally the alleys served as drains, as, e. g., is apparent from the conduits from rooms 9 and 10, and from 1 and 2, ending in one of them which was also one of the "high streets". This alley begins at room 11, turns at right angles southward at the corner of room 27, then again at right angles westward at 33 and then continues straight on past 21.

In addition to 21 forecourts there were 4 or rather 5 courtyards and complicated systems of the above mentioned alleys, which in places widen out and assume fairly large proportions. As they were open to the sky and divided the settlement into separate quarters, they might almost be called streets. From these streets, and from courtyards and forecourts, the rooms obtained light and air, as window apertures almost certainly did not exist. The window, as we understand it, was, so far as can be judged from such buildings as have escaped destruction, an unknown element in the architecture of ancient Mexico. Indian huts, on the whole, lack windows, and those actually to be seen in the Indian houses of Teotihuacan are few and far between. In the model houses that the authorities have built in some villages in the Valley of Mexico, the window-openings were always carefully bricked up after a time. Rooms with forecourts exactly resemble the *atrium*, the chief apartment of the ancient Roman house. Light was admitted through an opening in the roof which sloped inwards, and through this the rainwater fell into a shallow basin.

As already mentioned, for lack of time — our leave of absence from the museum could not be extended — we had to discontinue excavating before the whole of the

"Tlamimilolpa. Tlalmimilolpan, Tlamimilulpan, Tla-mimilol-pa, nombre mexicano: *tlalli*, tierra, *mimiloa*, rodar, *pa*, final del lugar."

[5] Linné 1934: 40 seq.

ruin had been uncovered. But yet another serious defect attaches to our excavation work, viz. that time only allowed a vertical examination of certain portions of the ruin. A complete examination of that kind would have taken very long time. The force of these two self-accusations is, however, lessened by the fact that we paid the owner of the ground to the full for him to restore, as near as possible, his field to the state in which it was prior to our starting work on it. In this way we occasioned very little damage to the building remains, especially as he received compensation for the loss of one year's harvest and consequently would have an abundance of time for carrying out that work. Apart from this, we certainly gained many valuable results, which not only have enriched Mexican and Swedish museums but also, through their publication, have been made accessible to international research. In the present connection it should be pointed out that Teotihuacan is abounding in ruins awaiting the spade of the archaeologist, and it is hardly fit that they should be left to be destroyed by the natives to the extent it is now being done. The scattered finds made in that process, if at all retrieved, generally go into the pockets of the tourists.

A general tour of the ruin.

A mere glance at the plan, pl. 1, suffices to show that this building complex was not erected all at the same time, or by any definite system. In certain portions of it the rooms are of greatly different sizes and shapes, and the thickness of the walls varies in a seemingly capricious manner. To reach some of the rooms, the visitor must have needed a highly developed bump of locality. Getting to rooms 16, 27, 66 or 86, to give a few instances, could not have been very easy. By opening up a doorway here and there, traffic within the labyrinth would have been considerably simplified, but for reasons unknown to us this was considered unnecessary or unsuitable. Cuttings through the floors showed that particularly those blocks which are confusedly arranged, are superimposed on earlier building remains. While in certain parts the ruin was so badly damaged that it was difficult to distinguish between the different building stages, all the earlier remains were well preserved in the central section, the greater part of which falls within a square described by rooms 27, 18, 36 and 11. Exception must, however, be made for damage caused in connection with superimposed building operations. To this I shall recur later.

The north-western section is distinguishable by the markedly large size of its rooms, many of which have a floor area exceeding 25 m², which are symmetrically arranged and all of a utilitarian character. Here everything is strictly practical, there is no break in the uniformity, no decorative details. These rooms are besides almost on the same level. Only between 114 and 107, and between 120 and 108, is there a difference of level amounting to 15 cm. The floors of rooms 107 and 108 are at a lower level than those of the other two, these being on a level with 109—113. The

Fig. 178. Rooms 27 and 2 seen from room 35.

floor of the last-mentioned is also 15 cm lower than that of 117. In this case the threshold has been "wrongly" placed. Otherwise it is the universal rule that the threshold is, so to speak, on the outside. Below the floors of these rooms there were, as revealed by test cuttings, remains of earlier periods, the walls of 117 continuing downwards to a depth of 0.80 m, and underneath the upper floor another one was discovered. The sites of the rooms did not correspond with those of the latter, which were larger. It is therefore not impossible that these rooms, all built almost on the same level, were added at a later date when other parts of the complex had been demolished. Some building material may then very likely have been taken from the older and ruined portions. That this took place in Aztec times is possible, but however that may be, there is much that argues in favour of their having been inhabited during this later epoch, seeing that here were found large numbers of fragments of Aztec clay vessels. As the westernmost walls were being uncovered, we again encountered walls at right angles, which showed that the building extended farther on, and that the style of architecture entirely corresponded with that of the adjacent excavated portions.

The south-western section differs, as will be apparent, in a very high degree from that to the north of it. Unfortunately its excavation took place at such a late date that there was no time for examining the constructions below the floors. One of its rooms, no. 21, was however included in the first part of the excavation plan, i. e. the test diggings outside the central area. At the expressed wish of the workman detached, Tomás Mendoza, he was allowed to do the job thoroughly, so he dug down to the bedrock, 2.8 m below the ground surface. Just below this he came upon a floor, partly destroyed by cultivators, and 0.60 m below this there was an earlier floor which was entirely undamaged. From here the walls continued down to a depth of 1.90 m, but they had most probably not been the walls of a room but merely

7

substructures. Beneath this second floor were found potsherds which, according to Vaillant, who had an opportunity of studying them, originated from the Maya. An account of these finds will be given later. In this way Tomás' insistence turned out far more profitable than if he had worked strictly according to plan in a horizontal direction and thereby enriched our map with a certain number of rooms, for of such we anyhow got more than enough.

On either side of room 21 run alleys leading into different parts of the complex, both taking at first an easterly direction. If we choose the northern one it takes us past rooms 113, 111 and 112; then it turns in a northerly direction and continues to room 118. Door-openings in 112 and 110 lead into rooms of the north-western section. Room 118 is for the most part a forecourt, and from that we could either enter the "suite" that consists of rooms 130, 34 (with forecourt), 45 and 35, and then the single rooms 119 and 128, or continue eastwards. The congested planning and the uncalled-for thickness of some of the walls indicate that this section was erected on top of earlier house ruins. Strangely enough, this alley ends in a cul-de-sac. The first doorway on the left leads into rooms 70—73. Of these, 71 and 73 are on a somewhat higher level, the thresholds in both cases being 10 cm high. Close to the former are two circular holes in the floor, about 15 cm in diameter. Evidently columns of wood have here contributed to the support of the lintel. Sockets of this kind also occur in 89, 132 and 151, as well as in the masonry columns in room 18. The next door admits us to a most irregular "suite of apartments", rooms 61—62, 77, 64—69. The forecourt found here would appear to have no drain, but as this section was covered by a very thin layer of earth and therefore badly damaged, that fact could not be ascertained definitely. It may be supposed that this court, too, had a drain, and that it led northward. The last doorway in this alley, this time on the right, had been closed up, not accidentally blocked but bricked up with great care, and subsequently the wall had been replastered. If not for this, one could have passed through to the other alley or street, that also begins at room 21.

Near the beginning of this second alley we find a constructional detail consisting of two masonry projections, opposite one another, which jut out 10 cm from the walls and have a length of 80 cm. They are rather loosely connected with the walls and thus of a relatively not very solid construction. Projections of this type are found here and there, singly or, as in this case, in pairs. What purpose they served is doubtful. At room 144 is a doorway leading, apart from this room, into 143, 142, and a room which by an oversight (certain rooms were only later given their numbers and during the excavation referred to as, e. g., "East 21") has not been numbered on the plan. From here the alley leads to a small courtyard or forecourt which gives access to two "suites", of which the southern consists of rooms 156, 30, 133, 24 and 155. The northern is rather complicated. Room 132 has a wide doorway with sockets from wooden columns. The roof of 131 was partly supported by a free-standing wall, measuring 120 × 50 cm. The northern portion of 31 is slightly elevated, but only at the sides, the middle portion having the same level all the way. Its northern wall has two pilasters. From the south-eastern corner of 33 runs a wall, 125 cm thick, which continues into part of 32, thus giving the latter a somewhat irregular shape. And room 129, too, is irregular in shape. The door between 33 and 4 is, contrary to the general rule, not placed in the middle of the wall.

From the courtyard or forecourt just referred to the alley continues eastward, but at 33 it takes a northerly direction. Two pairs of wall-projections of the mentioned kind have then been passed. At this point is a narrowing of the passage owing to the wall of room 2 having, for a distance, been reinforced on its outer side so as to measure 95 cm in thickness. The corner itself is besides provided with projections set at right angles, cf. fig. 192. This alley, which is paved with large slabs of stone, in the north ends up against the above mentioned closed up doorway. A little before this, on the left side, there is another walled up doorway which had given access to rooms 81 and 82, cf. fig. 193. The only remarkable thing about these small rooms is that in the northern portion of 81 the floor lies 20 cm below the level of the entrance, while in the western it is at the same elevation above it. Besides this, in the "treshold" of the former, there is a recess for which no reasons is apparent.

Before terminating at the closed up doorway, the alley makes an eastward turn and continues to 10—12. Room 10 is probably a forecourt and not a room. A step leads up to room 11 and a door-opening to 9, which in its western part also has a forecourt. For some unknown reason the door between 10 and 15 had been closed up. It is possible that the latter room, from which steps lead east and west, also is a forecourt and that the water had simply flowed out over the threshold, which is raised 15 cm above level of the alley. Against this argues the carefully built draining arrangement found both in the alley and in 9 and 10. This will be described later. Possibly certain reconstructions north of this section at some later date may have necessitated this forecourt, in consequence of which the doorway, which until then had admitted the light, had become superfluous. How the "suite" 49, 87, 48, 15, 59 and 54 could ever have been fit to live in without a forecourt, is difficult to understand. The whole of this intricate building complex resembles a living organism that is ever changing its form; any alteration or dislocation results in another.

North of the suite of apartments just referred to is situated the most peculiar and irregular section of the settlement. Its only communication with the outer world is found in the top right corner of the plan. Here two alleys cross. The one running in an east-to-west direction first passes the entrance to 89—90, which lies on the left. These two rooms have exceptionally massive walls, and the former has a forecourt whose drain carries the water outside into the alley. The roof was supported by four wooden posts, as is evident from the round holes in the floor. From the alley, a step leads up to a rather strange architectonic creation, a courtyard flanked in the north by a single room, 43, and in the south of a platform partly built over. At the back of 43 is another room, 93, the roof of which was carried by two masonry columns

99

of rectangular section. The architects of Teotihuacan never seem to have been able to get hold of roof beams of any considerable length, so the roof of 93 must have been regarded as a daring piece of construction. In order to relieve the load on the north wall, it had been partly reinforced with an extra wall. Rooms 92—91, the former with a forecourt of which the drain leads to the alley we have just passed through, more or less conform to the average except for the wall between them. It is remarkably thick, and at the doorway provided with a jutting out projection.

The courtyard, which is drained through the alley, has in its southern portion a platform. As has already been mentioned, there is an absence of the architectonic designing that, in spite of its modest size, lent a certain degree of monumentality to the central section of the courtyard of Xolalpan.[6] This moderate extravagance or clearance had been carried out at the cost of two rooms. 85 cm beneath the platform there are floors which are a little above the level of the courtyard and have belonged to two rooms separated by an east-to-west running wall. This wall had a door, not placed in the middle of it. This because the rooms had originally been larger but cut down by a north-to-south running wall so as to form a passage from the courtyard to the alley running south of rooms 56 and 60, and thus corresponding to the one found on the western side of the latter room. The rooms and the passage had been demolished and built over with the platform, and on the latter room 88 was built. This alcove, the floor of which is raised 10 cm above the platform, is, as will be noticed, quite narrow, probably with a view to obtain some sort of symmetry in relation to the stairway leading up from the courtyard. Room 86 had not been affected by the reconstruction, but north of it was formed a space which was filled in with a miniature room, like 88 quite open to the platform. A stairway now leads from the platform down to the alley south of 56 and 60.

If this alley had not been blocked at the corner between 60 and 49 it would have been possible to traverse the full extent of the settlement. Evidently there was no need for doing this, there having been as little intercommunication as between the flats in the modern tenement house. Close examination revealed that here had never been any passage. Between 56 and 60 is a small courtyard, sunk 30 cm below the level of the alley. Room 56 is a cross between a room and a platform. It is raised about 1 m above the level of the courtyard, has a stairway and a façade corresponding to that of the above mentioned platform, but from the top of the stairs had risen pillars of quadratic section, and in the centre of the room were remains of yet another masonry column. These columns had undoubtedly served as supports for the roof. The floor of room 60 is on a slightly higher level, and its eastern wall rests on a platform façade corresponding to that of 56. For the rest, its character was entirely that of a room. From the courtyard a stairway leads up to it, but these stairs, as will be seen, are not detached but let into the platform. This is simply because of insufficient space for the ordinary type of stairway. Why

[6] Linné 1934: figs. 8, 9, 15.

Fig. 179. Room 2 seen from room 27. The remains of two columns are seen near the basin of the forecourt. Here was collected the rainwater that came through the opening in the roof.

it should have been necessary to extend room 60 so far eastward, one is at a loss to understand, as in this case there has been no question of underlying constructions. The platform of 60, it may be noted, is partly built on the upper floor of the courtyard, while the earlier floor which is just below it was laid after the stairs leading to 56 had already been built. Light and air meant nothing to the architect and builder of this erection, neither were even the most moderate aesthetic excesses permitted. One might feel inclined to let one's thoughts wander to the "functional" architecture of modern times — only that the erection we are here concerned with must, so far as we can understand, have functioned very indifferently.

If we leave this dwarfed courtyard and follow the alley round the corner of room 60, we arrive at the room numbered 100. It was for the most part open to the sky, probably only the southern portion of it having been covered by a roof, which was supported by two columns standing near the sunk portion of the room-forecourt. It is on an unusually low level, viz. 30 cm, and from here the rainwater was drawn off northward. No less than eight rooms are more or less directly connected with this intake for light and air: 96—99, 63 and 102—104. From 99 it is possible, by way of 94, again to reach the above mentioned courtyard with the platform. Just one detail of some interest in this part of the compound remains to be pointed out, viz. the space, only 60 cm wide but nearly 4 m long, which is found in the eastern portion of room 80. What purpose it served is difficult to understand. The eastern wall of room 80 is a main wall which continued downwards below the floor-level, but the other wall had been built for the particular purpose of this absurdly narrow room. This brings to an end our tour of the north-eastern section of the ruin, and we return by the alley we came, the only entrance to this part of the building complex. Let us now pay a short visit to its eastern section, and from the north-eastern corner of room 90 take the alley leading south.

The architects of Teotihuacan conceived in terms of right angles, and so all rooms and courtyards must be rectangular. At times they were obliged to abate their demands to some extent. When the "suite" 83—86 was built, use could be made of certain earlier walls which still are easily distinguishable from the newly built ones, but space had to be economized. The width of the alley was reduced to a minimum, and in the south-eastern corner of 83 a recess was made so that it could continue to a wholly walled in courtyard. What purpose this served is not easy to understand. Its walls are in part unplastered, entirely without ornamentation, and no room opens into this comparatively large courtyard. As will be apparent from the plan all the adjoining rooms were, with one exception, without light and here, if ever, windows or other intakes for light and air would have been called for. Through an opening in the south wall we arrive, after having passed through two small rooms, 159 and 160, at a point where the alley divides. It is possible that from here one might pass into the easternmost sections of the house, which we had only partly uncovered. There was only a thin layer of earth covering these building remains, but no outer wall was encountered, probably because the ground was here sloping slightly towards the adjoining, deep ravine. During past ages the rain has washed the earth down into it, and earlier occupiers had presumably shifted stones and other debris the same way.

Through the west-leading alley we enter another open space of "backyard" character. Close by, on the right-hand side, is the entrance to a large suite of irregular rooms. Room 57 has been given a forecourt which stretches right across the room and is on a level with the threshold. The rainwater would thus run off into the courtyard but not flow into the alley by way of which we have come, because this is on a higher level than the yard, the difference in both cases amounting to 30 cm. There is no drain by which the water could be carried off from the courtyard, which during rainy days must have been turned into a small lake. The entrance to 78 is flanked by two projections from the walls. A flight of two steps, each 20 cm high, connects 78 with 79, and room 52 is raised another 40 cm above this. The reason for this elevation from the level of the yard, amounting in all to 110 cm, is that the upper rooms are older and have been overlaid with, respectively, one and two floors on top of the original floor, which is roughly on a level with the courtyard. Room 79 is provided with a small depression suggesting a forecourt, although lacking an outlet. The remainder of the rooms are of later date, except 28 which has been fitted with a new floor laid directly on top of the old one.

But the courtyard receives rainwater not only from 57 but also from 50. The floor of this large room has a threshold 22 cm high, underneath which the outlet from the forecourt passes. Originally the courtyard was on a still lower level, for underneath the present floor, which is 15 cm thick, there is another which also extends to all the walls surrounding the courtyard. On the outside wall of 55 occurs

Fig. 180. Part of the excavated ruin seen from the eastern wall of room 81.

a pilaster resembling the projections described in the foregoing. It differs from its fellows in that it stands on a broad fundament.

Having made the above hasty round, only the central section remains for us to visit. Access to it is not so easy. At the bottom of the plan and to the left of the middle, an alley coming from the south enters between rooms 14 and 141. From here we pass through 141, 140, 22 and 19, and then find ourselves in a courtyard, towards which room 19 slopes sharply. The western part of it, which is on a 25 cm higher level but farthest north slopes down to the level of the courtyard, has had a roof which was supported by a masonry pillar. The south side of the courtyard is formed by a dead wall, the monotony of which is broken by wall-paintings and by two pilasters, each marking a wall in the room behind it. On the east side is an unusually wide door-opening, and on the north side an open "veranda" or portico. Two steps lead up to the latter, and these, like the courtyard, show remains of thick, white paint. Here the roof was supported by two masonry pillars of quadratic section, each of which sheathed a wooden column. Of the latter nothing remained, but impressions were left in the casing. From this portico we next pass on to 17, the single room in the background and then a doorway on our right leads towards the central section of the house. But let us first look in at the rooms bordering on the courtyard. Room 37 is on a level with the latter, and it was therefore surprising that we could find no drain. It is, however, not absolutely certain that none had existed, as the south side of the courtyard, like the adjoining rooms in this direction, had suffered sadly through agricultural operations carried on here for centuries. In the back part of room 38 is a boxlike contrivance, sunk 180 cm below the level of the floor. Its walls and bottom are neatly plastered. The use it was put to is unknown. If it had been more solidly constructed, one might have been tempted to guess at a water-cistern, but the part of it projecting above the floor was markedly

103

Fig. 181. Stone let into the wall of room 1. Possibly a simplified representation of the god Xipe.

fragile. But the purpose of the whole of this building section is a mystery. The constructions found between room 38 and the above mentioned "backyard" are unplastered, markedly crude walls, and floors are entirely absent. That they could have been dwelling-rooms is altogether out of the question; it is more likely that they were substructures of something that was considerable raised above the levels of the surrounding floors.

Through a narrow opening in the north-western corner of the courtyard we enter a short alley, raised 20 cm above the level of the court and leading to rooms 23, 26 and 5. At an earlier period room 23 was provided with a forecourt, sloping in a northerly direction and occupying its whole width from the columns to the west wall. Rainwater was carried off through the wall to the adjoining alley in the north. The walls extending north-to-south and also the columns have slanting sides. The doorway to room 26 was on its eastern side probably framed with wood, because 20 cm from the edge there had been made a 5 cm deep and 25 cm wide recess, and in the plaster, which unlike the wall had not been smoothed or painted, faint traces of woodwork are discernible. In the south wall of the alley, 30 cm from the courtyard entrance and 35 cm above the floor, a stone ring had been built into the wall. In one end of a stone slab a hole had been bored. Then a hollow had been made in the wall, and in the bottom of it the stone had been firmly built in with masonry in such a way that only its pierced end, set on edge, protruded. In the east sides of the columns and also 35 cm above the floor, similar rings occur. This explains the use of stone rings or holed stones of this type that have repeatedly been found lying about loose. There can be no doubt that draperies or hangings were kept in place by their means.

Through the doorway leading into room 6, access can be had to the rest of the rooms of this group, 7, 36, 1, 8, 3, 2 and 27, though it may be noted that the entrances to some of them have been walled up. In the foregoing has been mentioned that the entrance to 81—82 had been closed up in a similar way, and so had also been done to certain openings in the alleys. One might be inclined to suppose that this must have been done by people who had come to live here after the compound had been abandoned, or fallen into ruins. But this can hardly have been the case seeing that all of the walled up doorways had been plastered over, and that this operation extended over the entire surrounding wall, while in some cases all the walls, and the floor as well, had been replastered. This had everywhere been done on the outside, counting from the closed rooms, with the exception of the closed up entrance to room 15, which had been plastered on the inside, and the one in the alley at 81, which had been concealed from both sides. The rooms had not been blocked up because of their being defective, or in any other visible respect unsuitable for human habitation, and beneath them were no graves that might have played some part, e. g., by way of deterrents. The true solution of the riddle of the closed up rooms seems unattainable.[7]

Rooms 1 and 2 are very much alike: both have forecourts, and roofs supported by four masonry columns. The rain-water from 1 was carried to the basin in 2, and from there it passed beneath the floor and through the wall to the alley outside. The wall between 1 and 6 had been reinforced by an extra wall, and a corner of 28 encroaches upon 8. In other respects, however, they present nothing remarkable apart from a small stone which is let into the north wall of room 1, at a distance of 35 cm east of the closed up entrance to room 3. It has a flat surface, measures about 9 × 9 cm, and is placed 27 cm above the floor, fig. 181. Its shape is roughly that of a face, with eyes represented by two bored holes and the mouth by a round depression. It bears a great resemblance to a Xipe mask, and finds a direct counterpart in a certain type of small earthenware heads. Xipe, that bloodthirsty god of planting and harvesting, the worship of whom included such macabre rites as the flaying of sacrificed humans and the putting on of their skins by officiants, is a deity of ancient lineage.[8] Originally, he probably belongs to the Zapotecs of Oaxaca,

[7] An instance of sealing up rooms is known from the time of the Conquest. When on November 8, 1519, Cortés' troops entered Tenochtitlán-Mexico, the self-invited guests took up their quarters in Axayacatl's palace. A recently walled up door was then discovered, in spite of attempts made at hiding it behind a coating of plaster. The Spaniards broke the door open and found, to their great delight, a room filled with treasure that had belonged to Axayacatl, Moctezuma's father. Of this, Bernal Díaz del Castillo gives the following account: ... "two of our soldiers, one of whom was a carpenter, named Alonzo Yañes, noticed on one of the walls marks showing that there had been a door there, and that it had been closed up and carefully plastered over and burnished. Now as there was a rumour and we had heard the story that Montezuma kept the treasure of his father Axayaca in that building, it was suspected that it might be in this chamber which had been closed up and cemented only a few days before" (Díaz del Castillo 1910, vol. 2: 84). Another eye-witness, Andrés de Tápia, uses fewer words: ... "é vió una puerta que le pareció que estaba recien cerrada con piedra é cal, é hízola abrir" (Tápia 1866: 579). Father Diego Duran, too, makes mention of the discovery of the walled up door. Father Francisco de Aguilar, who was himself present, had told him of it, while the writer, who was the son of a Conquistador and an Indian woman, was born about 17 years later: ... "les hizo advertir que una puerta muy pequeña y baxa que estaba tapiada en un aposento secreto y recien encalada, no debia de ser sin misterio" (Duran 1880, vol. 2: 37).

[8] Cf. Linné 1934: 172 seq., 1938: 38—39. Krickeberg (1937: 215—216) is disinclined to accept the above-mentioned clay heads as Xipe representations. In Grave 58 at Monte Alban a large incense burner in the form of a Xipe figure has, however, been recovered, the face of which closely agrees with the heads in question (Caso 1935: 20; figs. 33—34). Human sacrifices, at all events on a large scale, did not come into practice until the Aztec era, while the traditions of the "Toltecs" (Teotihuacan period) indicate that to them such usages were unknown (Preuss 1938: 449).

but the clay heads and the simplified representation just described show that he had made himself at home also in Teotihuacan. He survived the Teotihuacan culture as well as its immediate successor, the Mazapan period, and was especially going strong in Aztec times until the day when the hardly less bloodthirsty divinities of Spain and the Inquisition drove the ancient gods away.

Early constructions below the floors of the ruin.

Where the building of their temples was concerned, the peoples of ancient Mexico possèssed very little sense of labour economy, as conceived by us. There was a total absence of mechanical apparatus, draught animals and beasts of burden, while stone-masons and sculptors had to do their work in stone with tools of the same material. The erection and decoration of immense temple-cities by primitive means points to a high degree of organization and strong-handed management, but also to toilsome labour, privation and hardship. But the gods must have willed it so, and as submissive religiosity seems to be an Indian racial trait, the will of the gods was complied with. Otherwise, it can hardly be said that any love of work, just for the sake of working, is an Indian characteristic. The Mexican temple pyramids are often imposing monuments, but as a rule they besides include earlier counterparts that have not been scrapped on account of dilapidation. Reasons other than that of creating fitting cult-places have been at work when a building in apparently excellent condition was buried within a new one, and solely came to serve as a foundation.

At the close of each 52-year cycle the Aztecs destroyed their goods and chattels, put out all fires, and awaited the coming of the end of the world. On the summit of the mountain Uixachtécatl, now known as Cerro de la Estrella, in the Valley of Mexico, a new fire was lit at midnight at each turn of the cycle. As this mountain was visible from almost every part of the valley, thence was speedily spread the good news that the earth was not to perish but that another 52 years were vouch-safed to mankind. In all directions runners were sent out with new fire from the altar on the mountain, new household goods and new images of gods were procured, temples and sacred buildings were given necessary repairs and renovation.

It is possible that this end-of-the-world conception, and all that was connected with it, took its rise from ideas, ceremonies and customs dating from the era of the Teotihuacan culture. In our tour of the ruin were mentioned sub-floor constructions that occasionally determined later partitionings of the rooms. The ruin, such as it appears on our plan, shows its final stage of construction. It is not altogether impossible that the north-western section was added at some later date, when the rest of the establishment had already been àbandoned. In the excavation of the Xolalpan ruin in 1932 it was found that the building had been pulled down, and sand and earth had transformed the entire site into a low mound — the mud of the adobe walls having again turned to earth. This ground was built upon by a fresh wave of settlers, who, if we may judge from their pottery, possessed a culture of a character wholly different from that of the classic Teotihuacan era. At Tlamimilolpa we found only sparse remains of this so-called Mazapan culture, while however the abundant occurrence of Aztec pottery, mainly potsherds, bears witness of prolonged or populous Aztec habitation of the place. The question is whether these people erected buildings of a perishable character, or whether — superimposed on earlier constructions forming part of the settlement as a whole — they built the north-western section, or again, whether they inhabited certain parts of the buildings that had been erected before their time. The planning of the northwestern section differs, it is true, from the rest of the ruin, but everything points to its having been built and occupied contemporaneously with the adjoining parts. If this block of buildings had not in its entirety been ravaged and left to fall into ruins, or been pulled down and covered by drifting sand, but taken into occupation by the Aztecs immediately upon the dislodgement of its original owners, then universally accepted chronological theses would be turned topsy-turvy. If the space of time between the collapse of the Teotihuacan culture and the Aztec settlement at this spot be shorter than our usual estimate, how then should the "Mazapan culture" be fitted in? There still remains one possibility, viz. that the Aztecs may have repaired certain parts of the building they had taken possession of as a ruin. But unless they worked in exactly the same manner as the earlier builders, no such repair operations are capable of verification. For the ruin presents uniformity of style, and clay vessels of pure Teotihuacan type were also found on the floors, fig. 189, while Aztec pottery fragments were markedly concentrated to certain places, namely in the earth overlaying rooms 107—117, 121—123, the courtyard south of 18 and the adjacent rooms. In a ruined state, a building of such unsubstantial construction as this could not have existed for any considerable time. It may be that the present population consists of a mixture of descendants of the bearers of the Teotihuacan and Mazapan cultures, and Aztecs. That with their sharply differing cultures preserved more or less intact, they could have simultaneously occupied the same place, must on the other hand be regarded as impossible.

As already mentioned, time did not allow any extensive examination of the ground below the floors. Rather than continuing to take a trial sample here and there, we decided to concentrate upon a limited area, a square described by rooms 27, 18, 36 and 11 for its corners. We had two reasons for making this choice, firstly because that section had at an early stage been completely uncovered, and secondly because it was the best preserved. In an examination of this kind, damage is bound to be done to the building remains. Greater heedfulness in going about the work would involve disproportionate expenses, not to mention time, and that in a district where the native population is ever destroying ancient monuments encountered below dwellings and fields. Wherever possible, we made our way through holes that had been broken up — in the course of agricultural operations — through floors. Through narrow tunnels running along the walls we examined details of minor interest. Unintentional subsidences occasionally took place. When more promising discoveries were made, we sometimes proceeded with a heavier hand. It appeared to us that in such cases the results thereby gained were of greater and more enduring value than walls and floors, which in any case would sooner or later be crumbling away to dust.

Extensive remains of earlier constructions — walls, floors, forecourts and drainage conduits — were hidden below the floors. Careful comparisons between these building remains, room by room — as in part they conformed to the plan of the final constructional stage — revealed that they had frequently been simultaneously constructed. A definite course of development began to be discernible, and eventually it was possible to make out certain distinct building periods. It may be that our results have been strained rather hard, but in the choice between a medley of walls and floors, or clearly detached building periods, the latter were selected. In either case, the only difference would be the hatchings and other denotations of the cross sections, figs. 182—187.

The building plan during the consecutive periods being largely the same, the course of development can be followed in the best and simplest way from the somewhat schematized cross sections that are here shown. In the successive alterations that were made, the walls were often left standing, the floors were raised by superimposing a layer of filling, on the top of which a fresh floor was laid. The fillings varied in character. Stones and rubbish predominated, but adobe — sunbaked brick — also occurred. "Rubbish" is not a particularly apt description with regard to this peculiar material which in some degree resembles the soil in the fields of Teotihuacan: earth, sand, stones and artifacts of various kinds. In larger or smaller proportions it formerly consisted of adobe mixed with artifacts. On account of this, objects from the Early Cultures may be found in association with artifacts from later epochs. As the level of the floors was raised, the walls were similarly dealt with. This done, floors and walls were plastered, and coated with white, or occasionally red, paint. The latter consists of red ochre (hematite, ferric oxide). For the sake of system and clarity, in the sections the walls have been laid in all black, and occasionally parts of them have, for the same reason, been "sectioned". In many cases it has not been possible with certainty to determine what portions of them had been built during this or that period. One and the same wall may have been left standing through several superstructures. If it has greater thickness below a floor than above it, this is no doubt due to its having been widened, or the superadded wall made thinner, in order to form a firmer support for the floor, as the edges of the latter would in that case rest on walls, and not solely on the loose filling. In certain cases it could, however, be clearly observed that the older walls had been cut off and the newer ones built directly on top of them. It should be noted that in the sections no discrimination has been made between walls that are smooth, plastered and painted, and those that are raw and unplastered. The thickness of the floors is not given to exact scale. For constructional reasons it may even vary in the same room. The thickness generally varies from 5 to 10 cm. In rooms with forecourts the floors slope down towards the basin in the centre of the room. Dimensions being too tiny as to be practically unnoticeable in the reproduction of the reduced diagrams, this has been disregarded. The sections run either from south to north or from east to west, and intersect at right angles. It should also be mentioned that, in order to include as many details as possible, in one case, fig. 184, the sections are not shown absolutely straight, but in parts moved to one side, as will be seen from fig. 188.

By differently marking the fillings between the floors, and by sectioning them in different ways, the different building periods have been made distinct. It must, however, be emphasized that these periods only guardedly should be used as working hypotheses, and that the results must therefore not unreservedly be given the rank of actual facts. Cases that are especially doubtful will in the following accordingly be emphasized. Although everything seemed to indicate that the superstructures had been carried out universally and simultaneously throughout the portion of the ruin examined by us, it must, however, be taken into account that certain "house-holders" may have accomplished alterations and repairs independently of their neighbours. This reservation only applies in cases where a party-wall occurs, because where rooms are directly connected, the simultaneousness of the alterations are with great certainty ascertainable. Bearing in mind the above-mentioned reservations, we shall now proceed to review the sections.

STAGE I.

The original layout covered very nearly the same area as that of the final stage. In plan, it was, however, somewhat different. Strangely enough, there were no earlier floors below the southern portion of room 2 (the numeration of the rooms in the plan, pl. 1, is in the following also used for indicating the situation of the rooms belonging to the earlier stages, i. e. of building remains underlying the rooms concerned). Already from the start, all the floors were laid at a certain elevation above the bedrock. In order to make room for the notable grave below room 16, its floor had to be raised, but this cannot explain the raising of the others, as part of them are at a higher level than the room just referred to. The rooms of the north-western portion, 2, 27 and 3, belonged to the parts of the building that lay to the north and west of them. These are not here dealt with, neither is this connection noted in figs. 182, 183 and 186. On the other hand, the rooms were on the whole roughly of the same size and grouping as during the later stages, although with radical alterations. There are, however, exceptions: room 3 and part of 27, and the remains of 27 and part of 2 formed two rooms; 17 and 18 formed one room; and 7 and 8 were each divided into two rooms.

The courtyard south of 18, here terminated in a profiled wall, fig. 182. Judging from the façade of its preserved substructure, it was of the same type as the façades of the platforms in Ciudadela, etc., and in the Xolalpan ruin. But, as already mentioned, it was not a platform

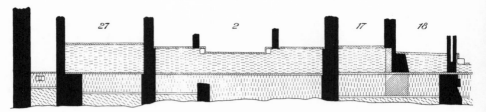

Fig. 182. Section through rooms 27, 2, 17 and 18; cf. fig. 188.

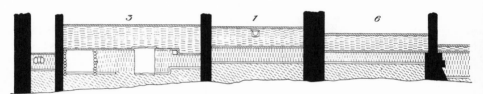

Fig. 183. Section through rooms 3, 1 and 6; cf. fig. 188.

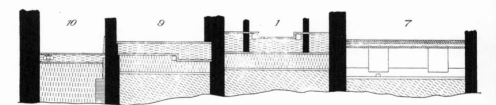

Fig. 184. Section through rooms 10, 9, 1 and 7; cf. fig. 188.

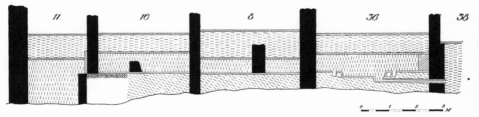

Fig. 185. Section through rooms 11, 16, 8 and 36; cf. fig. 188.

Figs. 182—185. Sections in a north-to-south direction through the central portion of the Tlamimilolpa ruin; cf. fig. 188.

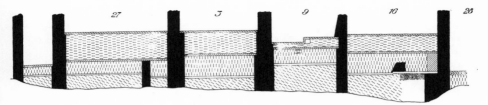

Fig. 186. Section through rooms 27, 3, 9 and 16; cf. fig. 188.

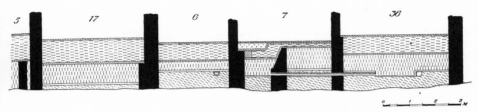

Fig. 187. Section through rooms 17, 6, 7 and 36; cf. fig. 188.

Figs. 186—187. West-to-east sections through the central portion of the Tlamimilolpa ruin; cf. fig. 188.

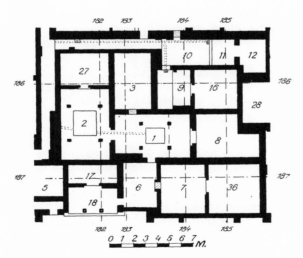

Fig. 188. Detail of plan, pl. 1, showing where the sections, figs. 182—187, were made.

As fully discussed in the text, the original building at Tlamimilolpa has twice been added to, in height as well as in extent. These alterations were not successively carried out, but, when the building was for some reason rejected, a new structure was superimposed the old one. Only the walls were partly taken into service for the new one. In this way the sections revealed three buildings, one on top of the other.

The contemporaneous floors and their appurtenant fillings are distinguished by similar hatchings to demonstrate the three building stages. Floors and fillings belonging to the same stage have, however, not been denoted by the same hatchings, as this would not have resulted in the desired clarity. If the different sections be compared with each other, the system will be readily seen.

At the cliché-printing office some of the sections were inadvertently more reduced in size than the rest. Hence their relative proportions do not wholly agree, as will be apparent from a reference to the plan, fig. 188.

façade but a wall, the southern wall of room 6 and of the room underlying 17 and 18. The last-mentioned room formed the central portion of the northern face of the courtyard — which was subsequently reduced in size by the hall of room 19 — and on both sides the profiled wall was slightly regressed.

Room 36 was provided with a forecourt, the roof aperture of which was supported by four wooden posts, a constructional element whose acquaintance we have made on our tour of the ruin. In the sockets along the edges of the basin, in which the posts had been planted, decayed remains of the latter were found. The basin was provided with a draining-well. This forms part of an interesting drainage system.

To room 16 there was a forecourt. By the roof-aperture, a broad wall-pier had been placed as a support, a rather unnecessary arrangement, seeing that the dimensions of the room were small. In figs. 185 and 186, remains can be seen of the wall-pier. From this basin a conduit ran obliquely below room 1, and thence due southward below 6. Here it was joined by another conduit coming from subsequently demolished rooms lying below the eastern part of the court-yard south of 18. From the junction, the conduit turned at right angles eastward to a forecourt in room 7. The wall between this and the room inside it sloped and was painted red, and two doorways gave into the narrow but elongated room. In fig. 184 this wall is sectioned longitudinally, but for the sake of clarity it is neither hatched nor wholly marked in black. Below one of the thresholds another conduit had been opened up, leading, into the basin in 36. From the well in its south-western corner, a rather wide conduit carried the rain-water collected from at least four forecourts outside the then existing outer wall (below what subsequently became room 38). This extended and rather complicated conduit system consisted of stone gutters, in lengths of up to 1 m, which were covered with thin slabs of stone. The conduits are partly traceable in figs. 185 and 187. In room 6, in the latter figure can also be seen the conduit leading from room 16.

STAGE II.

During Stage II, a number of fairly radical alterations took place. These included the partitioning off of rooms 2, 27 and 3 from western and northern adjoining rooms. Parallel walls formed the alley running outside of the rooms just referred to. This gave them their enclosed character — the north-western corner section — and the grouping of the rooms, with some few exceptions, being thereby settled also for Stage III. Room 27 had had a strongly built north wall, which was partly razed and made to serve as a foundation for the new floor, while the new wall was erected at its side, fig. 182. As a consequence of the construction of the alley, rooms 10 and 11 (figs. 184 and 185) were built. The north walls of these rooms, which earlier had been outer walls, were, as will be seen, reinforced by thin walls almost exclusively consisting of plaster, marked in oblique hatching in the figures just mentioned. That belonging to room 10 was placed on a socle of adobe.

The forecourts, too, were subjected to considerable alterations. That of room 3 was moved from the middle to the south side, and in 9, one was added in a corresponding place, figs. 183 and 184. The forecourt of room 36 was entirely done away with, and simplifications were also carried out in the case of room 7. The sloping wall was reduced in height, the level of the forecourt was raised, and the room thereby enlarged. The doorway of 36 was discarded and replaced by a new one, giving on room 8. The plan of room 16 was also simplified, and here a level floor was laid, supported in its eastern part by an adobe wall. Room 2 received its first floor simultaneously with the erection of a wall between it and 27. New floors corresponding to earlier ones were also laid in 1 and 8.

Fig. 189. Clay vessel found on the uppermost floor of room 57. (²/₅) 35. 8. 1486.

A new construction is found in room 17. The courtyard south of it, which during Stage I reached as far as the before-mentioned profiled wall, was enlarged. The wall was cut down, the level of the courtyard was raised and extended over part of the underlying room, which was scrapped. At this point the courtyard terminates in a smooth, redpainted slanting wall, and beyond this, room 17 is fixed up. As will be seen from fig. 182, this wall — which evidently was a fairly heavy one — was built upon a massive foundation. As to the position of the wall there appears to have been no hesitation whatever from the side of the architect, because at first the floor was laid over the foundation, and the wall thereafter was built, exactly on top of the latter. The foundation in question was constructed of adobe, which was the rule regarding auxiliary constructions of this kind. A wide doorway was opened up towards the courtyard, and through another wide opening giving on room 2, light and air were admitted to that room and to 27.

STAGE III.

The final superstructural stage sees few alterations as regards the apportioning of the rooms. All the rooms — but on the other hand not the alley west of 2 and 27, and that north of 27 and 3 — are given new floors, topping the earlier ones by up to 1 m. Some of the rooms wholly retain their old appearance, viz. 27, 10, 11, 16, 6, and 36. The remaining rooms were altered in the following ways: the forecourt of 3 was scrapped, but two new ones were added, viz. those of 1 and 2. In both cases the roof was supported by rectangular wall-piers. In room 2 these were standing directly on the floor, but in 1 a foundation was first constructed on the underlying floor, over this, filling was laid and the new floor moulded, and only then were erected the wall-piers, fig. 184. The forecourt of 9 was moved from the south to the west wall. In room 8 an east-to-west orientated wall was pulled down, and the forecourt of 7 was narrowed down. For some reason or other, its foundation was reinforced with a row of — judging from their small dimensions — specially made blocks of sun-dried brick. This substantial underlay notwithstanding, this forecourt was subsequently discarded — whether it ever functioned is uncertain, as it lacked a drain — and closed up, whereupon the room was provided with a new floor, laid directly upon those of earlier date, fig. 187. This, and not the final one, could with certainty be dated to the same period as the top ones in 6 and 36.

The courtyard south of 17 was raised, but again reduced in size, room 18 came into being. It was separated from the courtyard by two steps of well hewn stones, the upper one being, however, entirely embedded in the floor. Room 18, on the other hand, was left without a wall towards the courtyard, its roof being instead carried by two columns. The construction of the latter has been described in the foregoing: they consisted of wooden pillars, round which cement was moulded. The width of room 17 was slightly reduced, the old wall was cut down and, as was frequently the fate of discarded walls, degraded to a support of the new floor. The new wall was partly built up from what was left of the old one, and partly from an adobe-built wall behind it, fig. 182.

On the whole, the place has retained a uniform character during the different stages of its architectural history — three in number, as we mainly consider them to be. In size and grouping, the rooms show very little change, and the same technical methods have been employed throughout. A certain aiming at simplification — utility before decorativeness — is noticeable. It must be stressed that in no respect can here be discerned any progressive development, while instead there are indications of incipient decadence: quantity is gaining ascendancy over quality. It is possible that originally several building complexes here existed side by side, but that they subsequently grew into a whole through the alterations that were carried out during Stages II and III.

What purpose this building served is hardly possible to determine. That common people, and in that case one or more families or other fairly numerous community, would have lived at such a high standard, when compared with modern conditions, seems unlikely. Neither does it appear very probable that some personage of high rank resided here. If so, some detail or other would have been of more imposing character, of a certain monumentality and richer decoration. But this is not the case. In a warlike community, a building of this kind might have served as a barracks, or as a depot for weapons, armature, military standards, and the like. Not least its location in the outskirts of the city would be well suited for quarters to troops. But the city evidently flourished during an era of peace, and the finds we made indicate that its inhabitants were no worshippers of the gods of war, but of powers with beneficial and sensible spheres of interest. That a pilgrims' shrine and a religious centre must have possessed a considerable number of temple-servants of various kinds and degrees is obvious. But the distance from the temples within the present archaeological zone is too great, and there is no likely reason why a lodgment for priests should have been erected at this spot. It is true that Vaillant — as already pointed out — considers that it would seem as if the sacral section of Teotihuacan had been abandoned "at the end of Teotihuacan III, or early IV, with the population residing in the neighborhood". But this is hardly applicable to the erection of this building, but rather to its abandonment. It may not be altogether unthinkable that communities that were culturally, religiously, and perhaps even politically allied with and dependent on Teotihuacan, here maintained lodgings for pilgrims and delegations, or schools for their own priests, scientists and artists. Temporary habitation might explain the remarkable circumstance that the rooms hardly show any signs of having been occupied. Even soft sandals or bare feet ought

114

to have caused some wear on the by no means durable surfaces of the floors, and on fragile edges and corners.

Another strange thing is that no evidence of kitchens, or even of makeshift premises where food had been prepared, could be observed. The same was the case also in the Xolalpan ruin, which we excavated in 1932. Charcoal and ashes do not disappear without leaving a trace, and charcoal was only found in the so-called cremation tomb underneath the floor of Stage I in room 16. We searched intensely for charcoal and for traces of soot on walls and floors, but only achieved a negative result. Neither did we discover any clay vessels or potsherds that were soot-encrusted, and such pottery as might have been used in the preparation of food was exceedingly rare. The possibility of cooking having been carried on outside the house appears — on the ground of its impracticability — extremely remote. Its enclosed character might suggest a cloister or an institution of research, but monks and nuns, as well as scientists cannot ever be content with only satisfying their spiritual needs. That the population of Teotihuacan subsisted exclusively on uncooked vegetables does not strike one as very probable — maize, at any rate, having to be cooked. To use a modern conception: hotel or apartment house may perhaps not sound quite the thing, but would be a fairly apt description.

Each rebuilding or enlargement generally created an entirely new house. Certain walls were allowed to remain, but it is remarkable that architectural details, whose construction must have involved considerable labour, were not retained and made use of. Of this, the carefully hewn stone gutters are an example. From this it may be inferred that strict religious ordinances demanded the total abandonment of the house at certain periods. The tearing down and breaking up of large and complicated "incense burners" to form part of the filling on top of which the new floors were laid, point to the same thing. Whether the 52-years period, of such importance among the Aztecs, as mentioned earlier in this chapter, represents the intervals between the different building periods also in this case, cannot be determined. But it is possible, perhaps even probable. No very great stylistic difference between the artifacts of Teotihuacan type that were found below the undermost floor and those above the uppermost one could, however, be established.

Wall-paintings.

As already mentioned, the doorway between rooms 6 and 7 had been walled up, and both 7 and 36, which latter only communicates with the former, were thus for some reason isolated. That any practical motive lay at the bottom of this measure can hardly be supposed, as these two rooms were the exact counterparts of the majority, and in a good state of preservation. Faint traces indicated that the walls of rooms 36, 38, 48, 88, 90, 154 and the southern wall of the courtyard

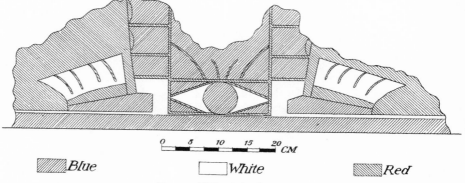

Blue   White   Red

Fig. 190. Wall-painting in room 7.

south of room 18 had been decorated with paintings, but beyond all comparison the best preserved were those in room 7. All the walls had been decorated in this way, but only on the north wall and the adjoining part of the east wall, sizable areas were found. As soon as the earth that covered the walls had been removed and the white layer of lime, 1.5—2 mm thick, had dried, it came away from the plaster that covered the wall. We succeeded, however, in saving the essential part of the best preserved painting, fig. 190. Both paintings were identical. Here, as well as in the fragments of paintings in the before mentioned rooms, the colours are red and blue. On the figure — though not in reality — all contours are drawn in black. The lowermost horizontal line coincides with the floor level, from which follows that in both cases only the very bottom portion was recovered. The height of the walls was less than one meter. The fragments from room 38 were unfortunately much too small to convey even a suggestion as to the motives. Composition would, however, seem to have been of a freer character and not so severely geometrical as in room 7. A certain dash and elegance of touch nevertheless revealed that a master had here been at work.

What the severely geometrical and symmetrical picture detail is designed to represent I do not know, and rather than forming conjectures I prefer to leave it to further discoveries to provide its explanation. Perhaps it may be deemed a waste of space to dwell upon this detail, but as so very little of wall-painting has been preserved from the ancient cultures of Mexico, the reproduction of also this unassuming fragment has seemed to me to be of some value.

Drainage system.

July is the rainiest month of the year, with almost one-fifth of the entire annual rainfall, or about 100 mm.[9] As the uncovered portion of the house ruin has an area

[9] Sapper 1928: 143.

Fig. 191. The entrance to room 9. The picture is taken from the forecourt, and shows the latter's well and the conduit beneath the uncovered floor of room 10.

of more than 3500 m², it follows that in the rainy season very considerable quantities of water must have had to be carried away from the 5 courtyards and 21 forecourts. In at least one case, that of the "backyard" in the south-eastern corner of the plan, the courtyard on the other hand seems to have acted as a water reservoir. On our circuit of the place it was pointed out that the alleys largely served as drains.

The forecourts are provided with drains, marked with dotted lines on the plan, carried below floors and walls and occasionally through the latter. All adjacent floors slope down towards these quadratic or rectangular basins, being themselves of course deepest next the drains. The basin of room 1, pl. 1 and fig. 179, is in its eastern part 13 cm deep, while in its western it sinks to 18 cm. That of room 2, also receiving the water from room 1, has a depth which from 17 cm increases towards the west to 24 cm. In room 9 the corresponding figures are 18 and 28. As a rule these basins are framed in neatly dressed stones set on edge, measuring, in the first-mentioned of the above cases, ca. 45 × 25 × 20 cm. In most cases the conduits start from the side of the basin, but in three instances, room 9, fig. 191, forecourt or room 10 and 118, from a water-collecting well at one end. These wells were covered with a stone plate with a hole in the centre. When rainwater was to be collected, the conduit could be closed by stopping up these holes with stone plugs. In room 9 this stopper, ground to an exact fit, was still in its place. The conduits from rooms 9 and 10 were joined, and the water carried westward, cf. plan. Strangely enough, it had been thought important that this section of the alley, which lies 5 cm higher than room 10 and 15 cm higher than its adjacent, south-to-north running part, be kept dry, for, as will be seen, there is even here a stone fitted with a hole. In either direction the alley slopes slightly towards this opening in the conduit. This little system of conduits is constructed with a great deal of exactitude. Its roof consists of stone slabs, the sides of dressed stone, and the bottom is concreted

117

and polished. Occasionally the conduits consist of carved stone gutters of lengths sometimes exceeding one meter. Such gutters, covered with stone plates, generally occur at either end of a conduit.

Beginning at the small courtyard between 56 and 60, an unusually large-dimensioned conduit leads westward, cf. plan. We followed it for a space of 45 m, past room 116, whence it, however, continued in a westerly direction. As will be seen, it collects the water from the courtyard, the forecourts of 118, 108 and 117, but also from the alley situated east of the first-mentioned room. At its mouth it has a width of 20 cm, which gradually increases to close on 40. It is built of stone, plastered, and covered with flat stone slabs. South of room 60 it runs near the floor, but as it passes through the north wall of room 49, it at the same time turns in a downward direction. Prior to the closing up of the doorway between 81 and 49, the water from the north-to-south running alley that is here found, also ran this way. After the doorway had been closed up, water was collected here as this alley rises towards the south.

During earlier building periods, when the establishment was partly laid out on a different plan, the drainage arrangements were of similar construction. Here and there beneath the floors we came upon conduits that had drained forecourts which, although built over, are still in existence. A very complicated drainage system from Stage I is given an account of in a preceding chapter. Occasionally these had crumbled into debris, and then it was not possible to ascertain what function the conduits had fulfilled, i. e. where they had started from and where debouched.

Architectural details.

Of the two categories of buildings in Teotihuacan that in the form of ruins have survived into our time, the monumental edifices and the dwelling-houses, the former have naturally come in for the lion's share of our interest. Very few plans of dwelling-houses have been published. Nevertheless Charnay in his day reproduces the plan of a "palais toltèque".[10] Nine years later Starr published a very plain sketch of the ruin of Teopancaxco, Barrio San Sebastian Teotihuacan,[11] in 1906 Batres reproduced a plan of "Casa de los Sacerdotes" close to the Pyramid of the Sun.[12] In 1913—14 Tozzer carried out an investigation of a ruin from the Teotihuacan culture in Santiago Ahuitzotla and drew an exact plan of the excavated building.[13] But not until the great work that under the editorial direction of Gamio deals with ancient and modern Teotihuacan do we obtain any tolerably comprehensive picture of houses that may have served as dwellings in the archaeological zone.[14] These houses, which we may suppose to have been designed with the object

[10] Charnay 1885: 123.   [11] Starr 1894: fig. 1.   [12] Batres 1906: fig. 4.   [13] Tozzer 1921.
[14] Gamio 1922, tomo 1, vol. 1.

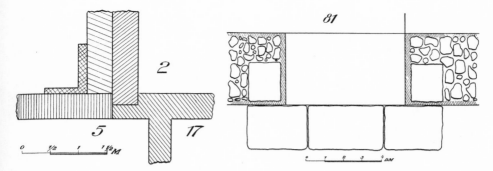

Fig. 192. Schematic sketch of corner between rooms 2 and 5. The walls are not bonded together.
Fig. 193. Entrance of room 81, schematic section seen from above. In the corners dressed stones coated with plaster and in front of the doorway three dressed stones are lying close together.

of making everyday life of priests and chiefs healthy and comfortable, are never of a personal character although variously planned. As regards their constructional elements, even these are standardized. In the description of the ruin at Xolalpan are presented a number of architectural details as well as general aspects of its architecture, direct counterparts of which are found at Tlamimilolpa.[15] Here it is only proposed to discuss certain arrangements specific of the latter locality — partly variations of the same theme — and some constructional details that have only been cursorily referred to in the preceding account.

In the official reports on conditions in Teotihuacan and certain neighbouring places that, by request, in 1580 were transmitted to Spain, the following is stated regarding dwelling-houses: "All the inhabitants of this town (Teotihuacan) and its dependencies live in houses built of stone and adobe, with flat roofs. The houses of the principal personages are curiously and elaborately constructed."[16] Mrs. Nuttall, who discovered the importance of the manuscript and translated it, adds in a note that "in a document dated 1563 mention is made of the great palaces then occupied by Alonso Bazan, a descendant of the Kings of Texcoco, who was the native lord and encomendero of Teotihuacan". The place referred to in the report is situated on the exact spot now occupied by the present town San Juan Teotihuacan, some 3 km distant from the ancient city, and centuries had then passed since the termination of its period of greatness. All its most important houses date from later times down to our days, but the huts of the Indians, on the other hand, probably differ but little as to type, though immensely as to quality, from those of Teotihuacan's era of greatness. Stone is nowadays used to a greater extent, and it has very largely been obtained from the ruins — the ancestral abodes. The presence of stone suitable for building purposes has no doubt constituted a decisive factor in the architectural development of the ancient city. Cerro Gordo,

[15] Linné 1934: 40 seq., 211—212; figs. 11—15, 339.   [16] Nuttall 1926: 80.

119

situated to the north of it, was formerly known as Tenan; this "ancient Nahuatl name of the mountain signified 'Stone Mother', or 'Mother of Stone'".[17] This mountain is an extinct volcano, and produced enormous quantities of loose stones and volcanic bombs, which were spread over the neighbouring countryside. This gave the ancient master builders a good supply of stone for the erection of houses as well as stone slabs for street-paving and the roofing-over of covered drains, etc.

Present-day houses are for the most part exceedingly poor. In ancient times they were incomparably better built, although plainly furnished. Eyewitnesses' accounts of Moctezuma's palace testify to a Spartan simplicity in one of the most magnificent palaces then existing in the New World. Woven mats served as beds, sofas or chairs; low stools, baskets, and vessels of clay, stone or wood probably constituted its principal furniture at the time when the Tlamimilolpa ruin was inhabited. In our perambulation mention was made of stone rings by which draperies were kept in place. Of doors or windows there were none. The plainness of the furnishings, soft sandals — or no footwear of any description — explain that no signs of wear could be observed in the floors. Defects were, it is true, easy of repair, but it is not likely that old floors were smartened up before being overlaid with new ones.

The material of floors and walls has been dealt with in the description of the Xolalpan ruin. Here, at Tlamimilolpa, the walls in greater part are built up of adobe, while the carefully levelled floors also here consist of 5 to 10 cm thick concrete and are coated with white finishing plaster. Thin stone flags occasionally serve as floor-paving, but even these are usually coated with plaster. An exception to this is the alley west of rooms 2 and 27, which in its southern section is paved with slabs measuring 37 by 53 cm. The construction of corners, or the effective bonding of two abutting walls, did not form part of the knowledge possessed by the builders, and occasionally the walls in the corners are literally standing apart from one another. Fig. 192 shows a complex corner which has been strengthened by an extra wall and a buttress placed in the angle itself. In places, the doorways have "door-posts" consisting of stones set on edge, elaborately dressed and of equal size which nevertheless are always plastered. The thresholds are as a rule constructed of stones, plane-cut and placed in a row, and these, too, are coated with plaster. In one case these threshold stones are lying entirely uncovered in front of the doorway, fig. 193.

Speaking generally, the walls are painted white, and in places where they have been protected, as below the floors, they are gleaming white. Occasionally they are painted red — with red iron ochre — but only seldom decorated in more than one colour. The walls of room 8 below the uppermost floor are red with bluish-grey sections, and the corresponding wall of room 1 is white, with red, horizontal lines. In some rooms, foremost in room 7, the walls had been decorated with paintings, slight traces of which remained, as related above.

[17] Nuttall 1926: 53.

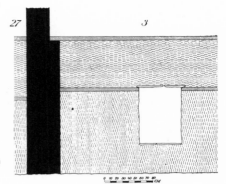

Fig. 194. Cylindrical chamber below the middle floor in room 3.

The plan of the building is strikingly plane. On levelling, it was found that from room 21 to the threshold between 23 and 33 the alley descends 19 cm. The floor farthest east in the same direction, room 55, lies 44 cm lower than the threshold in question, i. e. the difference of level only amounts to 63 cm in as many meters. Many of the rooms are on the same level, e. g. 107—113. The thresholds marked with lines on the plan are as a rule 10—15 cm high. When in a suite, a room is at a higher level than the preceding one, the next is often lower, as is also apparent from the sections.

When new floors were to be laid, the space between the old floor and the new was filled up in various ways. The sections show that this interspace usually varied from 0.5 m to 1 m. The filling in some cases consists of adobe, and the average size of these sun-dried bricks is 50 × 20 × 15 cm. Ordinarily, the filling consists of stone, sand, earth and artifacts. Below the lowermost floors, artifacts occurred less numerously, in the upper floor-fillings fairly abundantly. The floor in room 38 was laid on a bed of clay, in which was embedded a layer of wooden poles with a diameter of 5—8 cm, packed close together. These had completely disintegrated, but empty tubes now marked their positions. In the clay bed stood a small clay vessel, a so-called "candelero", fig. 195. Also in the floor itself in room 2 was discovered a clay vessel of the same type as fig. 215. In spite of its thin ware and fragile shape, it was entirely undamaged.

How the roofs were constructed, we do not know. From Juan Bautista Pomar, a mestizo born in Texcoco, who on his mother's side descended from the royal family of that city-state, we have, however, obtained information as to the ancient architecture in this nearby locality. He composed his work on his country and its history in the latter half of the 16th century. The roofs of the houses were flat and constructed of wooden beams, between which strips of wood were carefully fitted. These were so exactly fitted together that the covering earth did not dribble through. His further description applies very well to the dwelling-houses of

Fig. 195. Incense burner(?) or "candelero", found in the clay bed of the floor, room 38. (²/₃) 35. 8. 800.
Fig. 196. Stylized serpent's head. Architectural detail of stone discovered at Hacienda Metepec, 3.5 km south-east of the Pyramid of the Sun. It is of the same type as the heads on the façade of the earlier central pyramid of Ciudadela. (¹/₃) 35. 8. 2396.

Teotihuacan, and he mentions interesting details such as wooden door-posts and roof-supporting columns of the same material.[18] In the foregoing have been mentioned round holes in the floors, in which wooden columns supporting the roofs were planted, and that wall-piers in room 18 were built round a wooden post. In rooms with forecourts, the part of the roof next to the light-admitting aperture were occasionally supported by masonry columns or piers. In room 2 these rise from the floor, while in room 1, on the other hand, they rest on the floor next below, with which they are not chronologically connected. For some reason, the roof of this room must have been heavier than was usually the case, for the western wall had been similarly strengthened, cf. figs. 188 and 192.

In room 3 there are two arrangements that have no counterparts in any of the other rooms. Thus, in its north-western corner there is a miniature chamber, see fig. 183. Its roof is the floor next above, its floor is the lowest floor of the room, and its walls are built up of small stones. The chamber measures 80 cm in height and 95 cm in length and width. It contained nothing whatever, and there was hardly any dust on its shining white floor, so its purpose is inexplicable. Nearer the centre of the room, in the topmost floor but one a hole had been made, almost exactly circular, with a diameter of 72 cm. It was covered with two thin stone slabs. Through the floor-filling a cylindrical shaft had been dug, 96 cm deep, with a bottom consisting of two stone plates, figs. 183 and 194. On its bottom stood a dismantled incense burner, clay vessels, etc., account of which will be given in connection with the finds. In all probability this shaft had been constructed simultaneously with the room being provided with the topmost floor.

Beside metates and other stone implements, gutters for drains, etc., large, elaborately shaped stones were found, which no doubt had been decorative architectural details. Where or how they had been employed is uncertain, neither did the positions in which they were found provide any clue to this. Certain thin

[18] Pomar 1891: 68—69. Cf. also Vaillant 1939: 45.

122

plates with stepped sides had evidently been attached to the edge of the roof in the manner seen in the houses of the codices. These plates retained some traces of paint. On one of them, the back side and the edges are red, the front side yellow, green and red in different fields. Other slabs are profiled corners, and these, too, carry traces of paint that in every case had been applied over white ground.

The Tlamimilolpa ruin is throughout of a utilitarian character. Ornaments often exist in order to hide constructional faults, are uneconomical and useless. Functionalism and utility are, however, all too obvious. On our tour of the establishment, and in the discussion of the different building periods, emphasis was laid on the sparse occurrence of platforms with façades of the type that was found surrounding the courtyard of the Xolalpan ruin and, its modest dimensions notwithstanding, lent it a certain degree of monumentality. This building element so characteristic of the monumental erections of Teotihuacan, appears to have been used less and less in proportion to the growing of the Tlamimilolpa establishment. This absence of luxury and striving for pure utility is otherwise foreign to Teotihuacan, where labour and artistic creativeness were abundantly lavished on its monumental buildings.

OBJECTS EXCAVATED AT TLAMIMILOLPA

A considerable quantity of artifacts were recovered both in the earth above the floors of the ruin and in the fillings below them, as well as in graves and caches. The majority originate from the days of the Teotihuacan culture. An insignificant number represents the epoch next following, the Mazapan culture, while artifacts from the Aztec era are remarkably numerous, above all fragments of an amazingly large number of vessels of varying types. To the above may be added ceramics from more or less remote regions, and a number of objects dating from epochs earlier than the Teotihuacan culture, or at all events before the latter had developed its characteristic style. These objects had probably been embedded in the sun-dried brick that had been used as building material and, when the latter disintegrated and reverted to earth, become mixed with objects of later periods.

Space does not allow of a detailed account and illustration of the finds to such an extent as would have been desirable. The material from the Aztec era has been entirely left out. In ETHNOS, the journal of our museum, account has already been given of the most important finds from the Mazapan culture (vol. 3, pp. 167—178, 1938). As the ruin itself constituted the principal object of our exploration, only such objects as were contemporary with it will here be mentioned. Following a chronological account of the graves and of the finds recovered in the caches, the material will be dealt with comparatively, and part of the detached finds and fragments of imported ceramics will be included. The excluded material is largely similar to that of the Xolalpan ruin excavated by the 1932 museum expedition (Linné 1934).

Fig. 197. Effigy vessel, Burial 3, Tlamimilolpa. (¹/₄) 35. 8. 2045.

BURIALS

In the course of the excavations, 13 graves were discovered below the floors of different rooms. Sub-floor interment in huts is not an uncommon practice in America, but it is a somewhat different case when the dead are laid in the filling between the floors in a building complex of the kind represented by Tlamimilolpa. Some of the graves were abundantly, others exceedingly poorly, supplied with grave furniture. Even for children space had been allotted. These graves were throughout meagrely equipped. None of the graves appear to have been of a sacrificial and consequently ritual character, and even the more wealthy of them were found below rooms of no monumentality whatsoever. Why after death certain individuals have here been given a resting-place is a question which cannot be answered with certainty. The number of graves is exceedingly small in relation to the multitude of people that may be supposed to have inhabited the building. As the latter was now and again subjected to radical alterations, including additions in height and width, it is possible that persons deceased on those occasions were interred within the building.

The majority of the dead had — in cases where the position was determinable — been orientated north-to-south, and "Hockerstellung", i. e. the pose of sitting back on the heels, was also common. One of the graves differed in every respect from all the rest in that the deceased had been placed in a specially constructed grave,

124

Figs. 198—203. Pottery vessels found in Burial 1.
($^1/_4$) 198: 35. 8. 2456; 199: 2473; ($^1/_6$) 200: 2369.
($^1/_4$) 201: 35. 8. 2451; ($^1/_5$) 202: 2372; ($^1/_4$) 203: 2185.

had been cremated, and provided with grave furniture of immense quantity and of partly alien character. This grave was contemporary with, if not older than, the earliest parts of the building complex. Possibly the deceased had been a man of note, famed for sanctity or great power, and the building for that reason erected above his grave.

In the south-western corner of room 39 a skeleton was discovered. The floor had been demolished in order to make room for the body, proving this had been done after the building complex had been abandoned. There were no funerary offerings. No other graves of later date were discovered. But there can be no doubt that a certain number, from the Mazapan period and of the same character as those of Xolalpan, had existed although they had been made too near the surface and subsequently deleted by agricultural operations.

Burial 1.

The earliest of the graves, already referred to in the foregoing, was situated in room 16, in the north-eastern corner and below the third floor, figs. 185—186. It formed a partly enclosed chamber constructed in conformation to the surrounding part of the building, but was in the south and west not partitioned off from the hard-packed filling on top of which the floor had been moulded. Its length was about 1.5 m, height and width 1 m. To the north and east it had walls which did *not* form part of the house, but had been constructed at some earlier date. The eastern one consisted of adobe, like the adjoining house wall. In fig. 186 these two walls are not distinctively marked out, but as the house wall is of even thickness right down to the bed rock, "tepetate", the width of the wall of the grave will nevertheless be apparent. The northern wall had also been built up of adobe, but unlike the eastern, its surface was not smooth and polished, and between each course of bricks it had a row of small, red stones. The roof of the grave consisted of a layer of small pebbles, about 15 cm thick, cemented together with mortar. On this roof the north wall of room 16 had been built, fig. 185. The interior of the grave was filled up with whole or broken clay vessels and other artifacts, considerable quantities of charcoal, shells, and some few skeletal fragments. This was covered by a layer of closely packed charcoal. Between this and the roof there was layer of a yellowish substance, some 2 cm in thickness. Examination has proved this to be either ferric sulphate or much weathered pyrite.[1]

The body had been cremated in the grave itself. Round it quite a number of funerary offerings had been placed. The clay vessels had been put together on top of, or inside, each other. But many more had been broken up at the edge of the grave and then thrown into it. Of some vessels only smaller fragments had landed in the grave. The objects themselves bear witness of this having been the case, because fragments of one and the same vessel — often recovered in different parts of the grave — are of entirely different colours owing to whether they have been in direct contact with the fire or been protected by other potsherds or vessels. The custom of destroying the property of the dead is founded on a similar conception as that of depositing his belongings in the grave. To the Indian way of thinking, the objects in question possess a soul which must be released in order to enable their owner to make use of them. The fire having burned down, the whole thing was tightly packed together, involving the breaking in pieces of many of the more brittle vessels — some having besides been crocked by the heat — and finally the whole affair had been roofed over with a layer of stones. That the heat must have been considerable is evident from a number of obsidian knives having become bent. Experiments have shown that knives of this kind will bend from their own weight at 1,000° C. and that the fusing-point lies at 1,120—1,130° C. This explains why so very little skeletal remains were found. That portions of baskets, textile fragments and pieces of bark-cloth had survived in a charred state is due to their having happened to lie beyond the centre of the fire, at a point where the air-supply was very limited. The obsidian knives that had been deformed by

---

[1] Analysis has revealed a high proportion of Fe_2O_3, SO_3, H_2O; a very low percentage of MgO, SiO_2, and the absence of Al_2O_3, TiO_2, MnO, CaO, P_2O_5. This analysis and others given in the following have been carried out by Dr. Ragnar Blix of the National Museum of Natural History (Naturhistoriska Riksmuseet), Stockholm.

Figs. 204—210. Pottery vessels, Burial 1. (¹/₃)
204: 35. 8. 2377; 205: 2375; 206: 2357; 207: 2382.
(¹/₄) 208: 35. 8. 2180; 209: 2373; 210: 2359.

the heat on the other hand go to prove that special steps had been taken to obtain an exceedingly high temperature in the cremation of the corpse.

The most important types of the objects recovered are reproduced in figs. 198—255. Variations naturally occur within the groups, but only within narrow limits. As a large proportion of the clay vessels were blackened by fire, in many cases the original colour cannot be stated. The complete inventory has the following appearance:

6 *tripod vessels* of classical Teotihuacan type. Had been broken up outside the grave, into which only parts of them had landed. Two of them are exactly alike: straight sides, thin brown ware, probably wholly coated with cinnabar, fig. 201. Another, like the foregoing, but at the bottom edge provided with a torus, fig. 198. A fourth has been decorated ·with horizontal and zigzag lines, incised before the firing. The fifth has low sides, 8.5 cm, but a large diameter, ca. 20 cm. Its decoration consists of two triangels, the bases of which coincide with the bottom edge while their apices touch the top edge. The triangles, which had been incised before the firing, are filled in with impressed circles and painted red. The remaining tripod has rectangular, hollow feet, on the outside decorated with excised apertures.

5 *tripods* of Teotihuacan type. Low, slightly curving sides, and comparatively large, hollow feet. One of them unornamented but for the profiled bottom edge, fig. 216.

127

Figs. 211—218. Pottery vessels, Burial 1. (³/₈)
211: 35. 8. 2222; 212: 2243; 213: 2171; 214: 2157; 215: 2218.
216: 35. 8. 2355; (¹/₄) 217: 2356; (¹/₂) 218: 2367.

The remainder are ornamented with rows of circles, three of them with two rows, fig. 204, and the fourth with three.

6 tripods of modified Teotihuacan type. Of thick ware and with sides that are straight, but out-curving at the top so as to form a wide rim. Feet small and conical; ornamentation consisting of large patterns, incised before firing but after the drying of the vessels. In this, and in the plainness of the motive, these vessels differ from the classical tripods with symbols resembling hieroglyphs or representations of gods often scratched out after the firing. The lines are deeply incised and often filled with white paint. Four of the vessels had been partly painted red before being fired, figs. 206—207, 209—210. Fig. 205 has both red and black fields. Fig. 208 is strongly blackened from the fire in the grave.

2 tripods of alien type. One of them, fig. 199, proved capable of reconstruction, is of dark, polished ware, with soft and wide flutings slantingly disposed. The other, of yellowish-red ware, could not with certainty be reconstructed.

9 tripod lids, only two of which were complete. (In shape similar to those in figs. 21 and 38, Linné 1934.) All are unornamented except one, the edge of which is decorated with knobs resembling coffee beans, and it is coated with cinnabar.

115 (approx.) small tripods. Their number cannot be given with exactitude because in addition to 94 that were complete or practically so, there was a large number of fragments which, judging from the bottom parts, must have belonged to at least 20 vessels. As will be apparent from fig. 212, this group is classable with the above-mentioned tripods of modified Teotihuacan type, figs. 205—210. In shape, as in size, and also in decoration, they vary within narrow limits. Height and diameter fall between 4.7—5.9 and 5.3—7.1 cm, respectively. The thickness of the ware is considerable. The ornamentation consists of two pairs of incised lines, with slanting strokes between them.

Figs. 219—230. Miscellaneous pottery objects, Burial 1. ($^3/_8$)
219: 35. 8. 2250; 220: 2212; ($^1/_4$) 221: 2178; 222: 2246; 223: 2262.
224: 35. 8. 2181; 225: 2280; 226: 2188; 227: 2217.
228: 35. 8. 2150; 229: 2175; ($^1/_2$) 230: 2230.

The spaces between the lines are painted red. The rim is generally painted red on edge and inner side. The slanting strokes are as a rule eight in number, usually divided into 4 groups, i. e. 4 rows, or set together 4 and 4, i. e. in 6 rows, fig. 212. Occasional exceptions to this rule occur: 5, 6, 7 or 10 lines in groups of 2, or in some cases spread round the vessel.

2 tripods of the same type as the foregoing, but somewhat larger. These are wholly blackened by the fire. Height 7 and 7.6 cm.

2 small tripods of conical, upward widening shape. Edge of rim turned outwards; light brownish yellow ware, no ornamentation. Fig. 222.

3 small tripods, shallow, flat-bottomed, conical feet, fig. 226. Diameter 4.6—6.1 cm.

8 spherical tripods. Feet small and conical, rim cylindrical. Ornamentation consisting of soft-contoured vertical flutings, fig. 213; incised horizontal lines or impressed circles; 4 unornamented. To these vessels belong cylindrical lids, the inner diameter

of which slightly larger than the corresponding outer measurement of the vessel. The lids have handles which are either conical, or else flat with sides cut in steps and a square perforation, fig. 213. At the edge of the lid are two holes with corresponding ones in the neck of the vessel. Through these, the lid could be firmly tied on to the vessel. Height 4.1—5.9 cm.

3 lids, each with three hoop-shaped handles, or bowls with feet of that description, fig. 221. Coarse workmanship, unpolished surface. Diameter 16.8—17.2 cm.

2 almost identical bowls, each with three conical projections attached to the inside of the rim and slightly inclining inwards, fig. 218.

4 cups, with lip. Elegant shape, thin ware, no ornamentation. The lip is proportioned on a rather large scale, fig. 211. Height 11.1—11.9 cm.

14 vases with tall, cylindrical neck and rudimentary body; brim horizontal, with a diameter larger than that of the widest part of the vessel. Most of these vases

Figs. 231—239. Mortuary offerings, Burial 1.
(³/₄)
231: 35. 8. 2277; 232—233: 2277 b; 234: 2273;
235: 2450.
236: 35. 8. 2398; 237: 2219; 238—239: 2402.

are heavily blackened. One of them is
very small and of lighter coloured ware
than the rest, fig. 214. Two are larger,
heights respectively 9 and 9.9 cm, fig. 215,
the remainder not differing much in size,
height 5.9—6.1 cm. The necks of the
smaller ones are remarkably narrow.

17 flat dishes with low, raised rim. Dark-
coloured ware, in many cases polished,
figs. 225 and 229. Diameter 6—17.1 cm.

4 jars with rounded bottom and of somewhat
unusual shape. They belong to the rather
rare category of purely utilitarian vessels,
fig. 200.

1 bowl, flat-bottomed and devoid of ornamentation, fig. 202. The largest vessel of
the collection. Fragments of it were recovered in widely scattered parts of the
grave, and some of them were wholly
fire-blackened while others do not appear
to have been in contact with the fire at
all.

6 bowls with flat bottom, curving sides and
exceedingly rudimentary feet, fig. 203.
They are black, polished, and with a surface of almost metallic lustre. One of
them is ornamented with incised curved
lines, fig. 217.

27 bowls with flat or slightly rounded bottom,
rounded sides and outward-curving rim,
figs. 224, 228. Originally brown, reddish-
brown, red or black, and polished, but
now largely discoloured by fire; a proportion of them have split up from the
heat. In some of them remains of copal
were found. The smallest of the group is

of a slightly different shape, fig. 227.
Diameter 6.5—13.1 cm.

2 bowls of thin ware, with rounded bottom,
sides almost straight, rim not outcurving,
fig. 230.

1 bowl with rounded sides and bottom, of
thick, coarse ware and with unpolished
surface. The rim is ornamented with
crowded impressions. Diameter 16.5,
height 5.5 cm.

6 miniature vessels, 5 small pots of similar
shape and size, fig. 220, and one small,
asymmetrical, badly shaped saucer, diameter 3.3—3.8 cm.

2 "candeleros". One of them is cylindrical,
with exceedingly thick walls, and its
square-cut rim is ornamented with impressed dots, fig. 223. The other is two-
comparted, resembling two clumsy pots
joined together, and decorated with impressed dots and lines, fig. 219.

1 ear-plug of pottery. It is hourglass-shaped,
of good finish, and polished, fig. 235.

770 (approx.) objects of pottery. They are
quite small, figs. 238—239 show the largest
and the smallest, all of evidently careless
manufacture, and of roughly similar
shape: cylindrical, with more or less tendency to hourglass-shape but always with
a depression at one end.

118 (approx.) objects of unbaked, or only
slightly fired, clay, fig. 237. In a degree
even higher than the last preceding objects, these are of crude manufacture.
They consist of three lumps stuck one on
top of the other (in two cases four lumps).

130

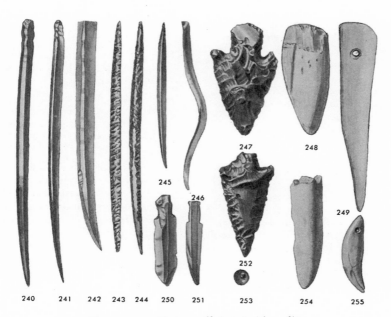

Figs. 240—255. Mortuary offerings, Burial 1. (^{3}/$_4$)
240: 35.8.2179; 241: 2152; 242: 2489; 243—244: 2396; 245: 2395; 246: 2490; 247: 2399; 248: 2492; 249: 2491;
250: 2401; 251: 2397; 252: 2400; 253: 2493; 254: 2378; 255: 2214.

Their number cannot be exactly given, because part of them have been broken up through the brittleness of the material. A ball of somewhat larger dimensions, and of similar material, was also recovered.

6 *heads,* and some fragments of figurines of slightly fired clay. Three of them are larger and of greyish material, fig. 231, two of very light-coloured, almost white, clay, fig. 234; the sixth, probably repre- senting the head of a bird, is painted yellow, figs. 232—233. Among the figu- rine fragments may be mentioned a large foot of the light-coloured ware, and parts of small arms and legs from figurines with movable limbs, of the dark-grey ware.

2 *obsidian points,* figs. 247, 252.

4 *obsidian knives* with finely flaked edges. They are originally of the ordinary type, i. e. flake knives, but notwithstanding the

fragile material not only the razor-sharp edges but also the greater part of the blade-surface have been finely flaked, figs. 243—244.

39 *obsidian knives* of the flake type, figs. 240 —242. These are of the same material as the preceding ones, viz. very light-coloured and bright, brownish-green ob- sidian. In proportion to their length they are remarkably slender, and very sharp- pointed. One specimen has by chipping been given two points, fig. 245. About half their number has been bent by the heat of the fire. Fig. 246 shows the most deformed of them all.

2 *obsidian tools,* short knives provided with tangs like arrow-heads, probably so as to enable them to be hafted and used as some kind of tool, figs. 250—251.

1 *miniature metate,* without feet, and a fusi- form muller pertaining to it. Length 9

and 6.8 cm, respectively. These well made
objects may well have been suited to preparation of medicines and the like.

1 bead of light-greenish jade; polished, fig.
253.

1 pendant of soft, green mineral; elongated,
somewhat cylindrical shape. Incomplete.

Pieces of slate. These show signs of having
been shaped, but no reconstruction is
possible. Part of them provided with red
painted lines.

10 circular sheets of mica, and some others of
irregular shape. These are very thin, and
translucent like slightly stained glass. Diameter 2.9—3 cm.

1 slab of pyrite, broken in pieces, but was
capable of being reconstructed. Diameter
ca. 6, thickness 0.4 cm. May have been
polished and used as a mirror.

1 object of pyrite, rounded and highly polished, fig. 236. Analysis reveals a high
percentage of iron and sulphur; specific
gravity 4.48.

1 piece of pyrite, of rectangular shape and
with one side slightly convex and polished;
1.1 × 0.9 × 0.1 cm. Was no doubt originally set in the eye of a mask of the type
shown in pls. 3—5.

Metal-resembling substance, small, irregular
shaped pieces. Analysis has shown them
to contain copper and iron, but no zinc,
tin or antimony.

2 bone implements, short and tapering, though
not sharp-pointed. Have possibly been
used for flaking off knives from obsidian
blocks. Figs. 248, 254.

1 thin, flat bone object with a blunt point
and a hole pierced for a suspension cord
or the like, fig. 249.

1 tooth, incisor of a rodent or some small
predatory animal; perforated through the
root portion. Probably used as a pendant, amulet, or something of that kind,
fig. 255.

8 shell ornaments. Six of them are bell-
shaped, of a type similar to that of fig.
259, pierced or notched at the pointed
end; made from *Oliva reticularis* LAMARCK
shells. Have been in contact with the fire.
Maximum length 4.4 cm. One flat pendant of oval shape, pierced near the edge,
1.5 × 1.8 cm, *Spondylus princeps* BRODERIP;
and one of unwrought shell of *Chama
coralloides* REEVE.

Marine shells. A great quantity of shells of
the following species:
Chama coralloides REEVE
Fasciolaria gigantea KIENER
Lithophaga aristata DILLWYN
Pteria margaritifera LINNÉ
Spondylus americanus GMELIN
Spondylus princeps BRODERIP
Strombus pugilis LINNÉ
Thais fasciata REEVE
Turbinella scolymus GMELIN
Turritella cumingi REEVE
Pinna maura SOWERBY.

To this considerable quantity of artifacts, over 1,200 in number, may be added
30 odd fragments of a large "incensario", a large number of small charred fragments
of textiles, baskets and of bast paper. These will be dealt with in the comparative
section under their respective headings.

Burial 2.

The topmost floor of room 22 had partly been demolished through cultivation
work, and the second floor at a 45 cm lower level had also been broken through
here and there. In its north-eastern corner we continued down to the tepetate,

Figs. 256—262. Mortuary offerings, Burial 2. (³/₅)
(¹/₃) 256: 35. 8. 197; 257: 207; 258: 208; 259: 209; 260: 210; 261: 214; 262: 211.

175 cm below this second floor, which belonged to Stage II. Directly on the rock bottom a youth, an individual past the stage of childhood, had been interred. Of the skeleton hardly anything but some teeth remained. The mortuary offerings were fairly numerous, consisting of:

2 jars of roughly similar shape and of dark-coloured ware. Necks decorated with lightly scratched vertical lines. One of the jars fairly well polished except for fields bounded by large circular lines, fig. 256.

3 bowls of the usual type: flat bottom and curving sides, and of dark, polished ware, cf. figs. 203 and 217. The smallest of them has no feet, while those of the remainder are rudimentary. Diameter 12.1, 16.2 and 23.7 cm, respectively.

2 bowls of rounded shape, unornamented. One with three ordinary feet, the other with annular foot. Diameter 9 and 14 cm, respectively.

3 bowls of the yellowish-red ware, with annular feet, decorated with incised horizontal lines, dots and S-figures, cf. fig. 299; broken.

1 dish, of coarse ware and clumsily shaped. Diameter 12.1 cm.

3 miniature bowls. One with rounded bottom, the centre portion of which is bent upwards. Diameter 7.2 cm. The other two are flat-bottomed, with low and straight sides. Diameter 5.2 and 6.9 cm, respectively.

1 miniature jar of the same type as that seen in fig. 278. Height 3.6 cm.

1 clay figurine, manufactured in a mould. Face and head-dress slightly damaged, fig. 257.

1 stone bead, of greyish-green rock, fig. 258.

1 small bowl, made of lava, fig. 260.

8 shell pendants, points of shells — Conus interruptus BRODERIP — that have been cut off and pierced on one side for suspension, fig. 259.

2 bone implements. One blunt-pointed needle, part of the eye broken off, fig. 261; the other an awl, or bodkin, with one end flattened, fig. 262.

In room 91 a trial shaft was sunk through a large hole that had been made in the central portion of the floor. Here, too, the second floor, 50 cm lower down, had been damaged, evidently through the digging of a pit for maguey planting. This operation had caused the ruin of a grave dating from Stage II. Judging by some still remaining skeletal fragments, this grave must have lain directly below the second floor. In the breaking up of the floor, the grave had been demolished, but within the margins of the hole which measured 2 m² were discovered the skeletal remains, and also the bottom portion of the vessel seen in fig. 197. The lid belonging to it was found embedded in the filling of the pit — earth, pieces of flooring, potsherds, skeletal fragments, etc. — but in spite of the most careful search and sifting of the earth, it was not possible to collect all the parts, wherefore the head could not be reconstructed.

Burial 4.

Below the middle one of the three floors of room 1 was discovered a grave which, like the next preceding ones, is referable to Stage II. It lay on a level with the doorway of room 2, and about 1 m from the west wall. The deceased lay in an extended position, head towards the north. The skeleton was so brittle that it crumbled to dust even when lightly touched with a camel-hair brush. The deceased appeared to be of the male sex, adult, though not aged. The mortuary offerings were as follows:

2 bowls of the usual type: flat-bottomed, with curving sides and without feet, cf. figs. 203 and 217. Diameter 13.9 and 16.3 cm, respectively.

1 miniature jar of the same type as in fig. 278. Height 4.5 cm.

2 ear-plugs, with plane surfaces, fairly well polished. Diameter 2.8 and 3 cm, respectively.

1 jar, of the same type as in fig. 256. On the polished surface vertical lines had been scratched round the neck, and others in four groups along the body of the vessel. Height 12.6 cm.

1 jar, of conical shape, with flat bottom and rounded lower part. Ornamented in red with three large, round patches, at the top joined together with a border en-

circling the jar. Painted before firing. Height 11.2 cm.

1 bowl with gently rounded bottom; brownish-red and polished. Height 7.2, diameter 12.5 cm.

1 bone needle, fusiform, pointed at both ends; rather thick, but with a small eye. Length 15.8 cm.

2 obsidian figurines. Stylized human figures, figs. 263—264.

3 obsidian knives. One of them large, lanceolate, with one end squarely broken off, but otherwise of the type seen in fig. 271. Length 13.5 cm. The other two quite like each other, fig. 270.

1 obsidian point, neatly made, edges slightly convex, and with a rounded haft. Length 8.3 cm.

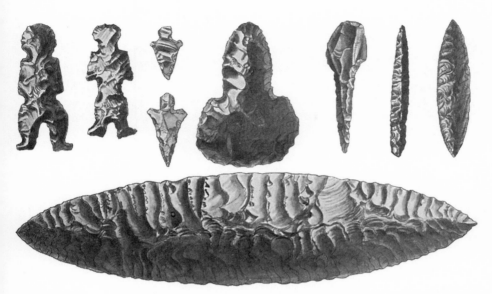

Figs. 263—271. Obsidian objects from Burial 4 (figs. 263—264, 267—270) and from Burial 5 (figs. 265—266, 271). (²/₅)
263: 35. 8. 501; 264: 502; 265—266: 1030, 1035; 267: 506; 268: 505; 269: 497; 270: 504; 271: 1023.

3 obsidian tools. Two of them are drill points, and the third a ladle-shaped scraper, possibly used in tapping maguey plants for pulque, figs. 267—269.

Shells, fresh-water shells, *Unio discus* LEA.

1 tripod vessel, incomplete. Has had three cylindrical feet, and is decorated with plain negative painting circles in a red field. Contained yellow clay (pigment?). Height 8.2 cm.

Burial 5.

Room 38 came into existence during Stage III, cf. fig. 185. Large quantities of filling had to be brought along in order to raise the floor of the newly added room to a level approximating that of room 37, with which it communicated. Before that, an individual was interred in its south-western corner. This grave had not been protected in any way, and the skeleton was badly damaged through the weight of the filling which was nearly 2 m in thickness. The deceased appeared to have been an adult male individual, and was lying on his right side in Hockerstellung. The list of mortuary offerings comprises the following objects:

1 black jar with three small feet, of a type similar to that in fig. 256. Height 8.3 cm.
2 bowls with flat bottom, curving sides and rudimentary feet, of the usual type seen in figs. 203 and 217. The larger one is black and polished. Diameter 15.6 and 10.3 cm, respectively.

1 cylindrical bowl, flat-bottomed and with rudimentary feet. Diameter 7.6 cm, height 4.5 cm.

2 *miniature dishes.* Plain, and slightly rounded. Diameter 4.3 and 4.9 cm, respectively.

2 *miniature jars,* broken into fragments,
painted red inside and out after firing;
possibly paint-pots.

12 *clay objects* of the same type as in figs.
238—239, but smaller.

1 *bone awl,* thin and very sharp-pointed.
Length 13.8 cm.

1 *bone needle* with a small eye, very thin,
point broken off.

1 *stone bead,* of triangular longitudinal section and pierced through lengthwise, 1.9 ×
1.7 × 0.9 cm.

1 *piece of slate,* thin and of irregular shape.

3 *mica slabs* of rectangular shape. The shorter
sides are left in the rough, while the longer
sides have been cut straight and clean. Ca.
11.7 × 18 cm.

6 *mica plates,* small and very thin. 5 of them
are circular, with a diameter of 3 cm, and
one elliptical, 3.1 × 3.8 cm.

4 *obsidian knives,* lanceolate. The largest one
is an uncommonly beautiful piece of work,
fig. 271. The smallest has been turned out
from an ordinary flake knife, chipped
into shape. Lengths 19, 6.3, 5.8 and 4.7
cm.

9 *obsidian points,* three larger (length 5.7—
7.1 cm) and six smaller (length 2.2—3.1
cm), thin and flat, which undoubtedly
have been arrow-heads, figs. 265—266.

2 *shell ornaments.* One is a piece of shell —
Spondylus americanus GMELIN — ground
into rounded shape, 5 × 3.9 cm, with a
small perforation in the middle; the other
a small bell-shaped ornament of the type
shown in fig. 259; *Oliva reticularis* LA-
MARCK.

Pieces of slate, crushed into bits so that the
original shape cannot be determined. They
carry traces of rich decoration in red and
yellow.

Copal. Some lumps which have only been
partly consumed by the fire.

Shells, *Thais deltoidea* LAMARCK.

Burials 6—8.

Below the floor of room 109 and quite close to the treshold separating it from
room 108 were the remains of a new-born baby, or fetus. The floor having been
damaged and water having seeped through, the greater part of the skeleton had
perished. The mortuary offerings only consisted of 4 cylindrical clay beads.

In excavating the north-western part of room 107, just below the floor and
close to the south wall, we happened upon another baby, or fetus, grave. While
following in a westerly direction the big sewer that starts from the courtyard
between rooms 56 and 60, we did some test-diggings here and there. It was then
that this grave was unexpectedly found. It contained nothing beyond a few badly
damaged skeletal fragments and a flat-bottomed bowl of a type similar to that
recovered in Burials 9 and 10, though very low. In its bottom there is incised
ornamentation consisting of three groups of arc-shaped lines. Diameter 27.8, height
5.4 cm. Inside the bowl lay a flat piece of stone with irregular edges.

In following the drain leading from the forecourt of room 100, below the floor
of room 96 we came upon another grave of the same type as the foregoing. Over
the dead child, or fetus, lay some fragments of a large cooking pot. Of mortuary
offerings there were only two obsidian knives of the flake type, 6.3 and 9 cm long,

Figs. 272—273. Painted tripod vessels, Burial 13. (¹/₃). Fig. 272 in the Museum of Teotihuacan. Fig. 273: 23. 8. 513, extended design from a cylindrical jar identical with fig. 272.

respectively, and a spindle whorl. The latter is cylindrical, with its upper half shaped like an inverted cone; its height exactly equals its diameter (1.6 cm).

All the above graves derive from Stage III.

Burials 9—10.

In room 10 were also found infant graves from Stage III, i. e. below the topmost floor. The interval between the floors had in consideration of the relative levels of the adjoining rooms, 9 and 15, been restricted to 23 cm. This not allowing sufficient space for graves, openings had been made through the lower floor, and thus the graves were partly situated below its level. The holes that had in this way been cut measured ca. 25 × 45 cm, and were orientated east to west. Grave 9 lay close to the south wall, near the steps leading to room 11, and grave 10 immediately east of the drain coming from room 9. In grave 9 had been placed an earthenware bowl with another bowl set upturned over it in the way of a lid. These were found farthest east, having been pushed in a little below the floor, and close to the infant's head. On the floor, west of the opening, were two bowls, one in the same way covered by another. The first-mentioned bowls were empty, but the latter contained a piece of slate and an obsidian knife of the flake type. Thus the child appears to have been supplied with food and a "cutlery set". In grave 10 there was only one bowl, but in it had likewise been placed a piece of slate and two obsidian knives. Strangely enough, parts of the skeleton were found within the bowl and the remainder outside it. All these bowls are of the ordinary flat-bottomed type, with curving sides and three diminutive feet and of brown or brown-black ware, cf. figs. 203 and 217. Diameters 23.8—26 cm. The pieces of slate are unwrought.

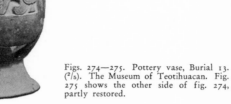

Figs. 274—275. Pottery vase, Burial 13.
(^{2}/$_5$). The Museum of Teotihuacan. Fig.
275 shows the other side of fig. 274,
partly restored.

Burial 11.

The floor of room 50 had in parts been torn up. In one of the holes were discovered 5 smashed bowls of the ordinary, flat-bottomed type, a few bone fragments, and, along one of its sides, below the floor, 3 undamaged bowls. The colour of these, which were all of one kind, ranged from light-brown to brown-black, the surface of the latter being lustrous, and the diameter from 20 to 29.5 cm, cf. figs. 203 and 217. The smallest but one had in its bottom a flowery pattern composed of incised lines. The above probably constituted the remains of a ruined child grave of the same kind as the preceding ones, and like them dating from Stage III.

Burial 12.

The uppermost floor in room 49 was for the most part found entirely destroyed. Close by the north wall, at a depth of ca. 1 m below the floor, some bones of an infant were discovered. In this grave, also dating from Stage III, the following mortuary offerings were found:

7 *miniature dishes,* roughly shaped, of light-grey and soft ware. Diameter from 4 to 4.6 cm.

2 *miniature bowls,* clumsily made and of ware resembling the foregoing. Diameter 1.7 and 2.3 cm, respectively.

1 *obsidian knife* of the flake type, length 7.1 cm.

Mica plates, very thin and some of them cut into shape.

1 *unwrought stone,* painted white. It has the appearance of a pile of ground maize. The

Figs. 276—285. Mortuary offerings, Burial 13. ($^3/_4$)
276: 35. 8. 523; ($^1/_3$) 277: 515; 278: 522.
279: 35. 8. 523; 280: 527; 281: 524; 282: 526.
283: 35. 8. 525; 284: 530; 285: 525 a.

remainder of the objects mostly resembling children's toys, possibly manufactured by a child, it does not seem impossible that this stone too played the part of a toy and actually was meant to represent the leading commodity of life.

Burial 13.

Of the graves dating from Stage III, the beyond comparison most important one was situated in room 6. Very shortly before our visit in October, 1934, the owner of Tlamimilolpa, while engaged in agricultural pursuits, happened upon a floor of gleaming whiteness — the floor of the room numbered 6 in our plan. He had cut a hole through it, and from curiosity widened it, and looked for "treasure". What he got for his trouble was, however, a grave. Acting on the advice of a relative of his, Joaquín Oliva who has been referred to in the foregoing, he carefully saved up the grave equipment. Joaquín knew that tourists would buy antiquities both old and new, but also that private collectors set much store by such finds as the complete furniture of a grave. That this amateur grave-robber had been conscientious in his work was evident from the fact that nearly all minor fragments of such clay vessels as had been recovered in a damaged state were duly found in situ. Although this grave after its discovery had been subjected to fairly rough treatment, it must be regarded as important. The mortuary offerings were rich and variegated, and of high value to comparative studies. This particularly applies to the typical tripod vessels being found in association with the imported vase. The skeleton had not aroused any particular interest in its finders, and the sparse remains of it were only capable through its much-worn teeth of bearing evidence of the deceased having been of considerable age. He had been equipped with the following objects:

Fig. 286. Clay figure with movable limbs, Burial 13. (¹/₃) 35. 8. 531.

2 tripods. These are of the same size, and of almost identical ornamentation. This has been applied after firing, and on a ground especially laid on for the purpose, figs. 272—273.

1 vase, carved decoration, orange ware. Of a type not indigenous to Teotihuacan, figs. 274—275.

2 jars. One of spherical shape with a narrow mouth, three short and thick, out-spreading legs, fig. 277. The other is of the same type as that in fig. 256, but badly shaped and proportioned. Height 9.3 cm.

1 bowl, of the yellowish-red ware, with an annular foot, decorated with incised

horizontal lines, dots and S-figures. An excellent example of this type of vessel, fig. 299. Diameter 20.3 cm.

1 bowl of the flat-bottomed type, with curving sides and rudimentary feet; of unusual depth in relation to height. Diameter 23.3, height 9.6 cm.

2 dishes, with rounded bottom and of plain workmanship. Diameter 6.3 and 10.1 cm, respectively.

17 miniature dishes, slightly rounded. Twelve larger, diameter 6.2—7.5 cm, and five smaller, diameter 4.1—4.7 cm.

18 miniature jars, rather coarsely shaped and roughly of the same size, fig. 278.

1 clay stamp, plane, with checker pattern, figs. 276 and 279.

1 clay ornament, shaped like a small mussel. Originally no doubt one of a series of similar ornaments attached as a border along the lower edge of some tripod vessel, fig. 281.

2 large figurines with movable limbs. Both limbs and bodies are hollow; the heads are made from the same mould. One of the figures has lost its right arm, and the other one had after its discovery been played to bits by children so that only the head and legs remained. They are painted in red and yellow, fig. 286.

1 stone bowl, manufactured of translucent and streaked tecali, "Puebla marble"; close to the brim a groove has been cut, fig. 284.

1 stone ornament, made of a somewhat spotted, light-green kind of rock, polished, fig. 280.

2 stone beads. One smaller, cylindrical, well polished, and of light-green jade. Dia-

meter 0.8, height 0.6 cm. The other larger, of irregular shape, and rather flat. Also made of some greenish mineral, but unpolished. Diameter 2.2—2.3, height 0.8 cm.

2 *rings of mussel shell, Cardium isocardia* LINNÉ. The convex side only partly ground smooth; closely around the excised hole runs a red painted circle, figs. 283 and 285.

1 *mother-of-pearl ornament, Pinna maura* SOWERBY. Shaped like a spade, thin, and of violet iridescence, fig. 282.

CACHES

Below the floors of the ruin were discovered vessels and other objects that were unconnected with graves but, for reasons unknown, had been purposely deposited in the floor-filling. The custom of depositing offerings below or within a building while it was being erected still prevails here and there among the Indians. In ancient Mexico this custom was very popular, as we know from the caches that have been discovered in the temple buildings of Teotihuacan, in many other archaeological sites of Central Mexico, and in the Maya area.

In Tlamimilolpa no definite system in the relation of the votive offerings to the architecture is discernible. Upon this, the architecturally stereotyped character of the building, devoid of any outstanding feature, may possibly have a bearing. In one case a cylindrical chamber had been provided for the housing of offerings, but otherwise little had been done for their protection. One category of objects, large and richly decorated "incensarios", had even been deliberately destroyed when deposited.

In two cases vessels had been placed in the floors themselves, moulded into them, as already mentioned in connection with "Architectural details", p. 121. In three cases we found black, flat-bottomed bowls of the kind typical of Teotihuacan (cf. figs. 203 and 217) standing on floors that had been built over. In room 18 a bowl of that type had been set on the lowermost floor close to the north wall, and in the south-east corner of room 7 another such bowl was found, likewise placed on the earliest floor. The same was the case in room 37, but that bowl contained 2 obsidian knives of the flake type and pieces of slate or irregular shape but painted with red strokes. The jar of yellowish-red ware, fig. 300, cannot either by mere accident have found a place exactly underneath the treshold between rooms 157 and 174, resting on a small stone slab. That a large bone of a whale should have been carelessly left behind under the second floor of room 46 also seems somewhat improbable. While incensarios were recovered from various periods — in Burial 1 and beneath the earliest floor in rooms 1, 3, 7 and 16, i. e. Stage I — the caches dealt with below date from the latest period, Stage III.

Figs. 287—291. Part of content of Cache 1. (¹/₂)
287: 35. 8. 2126; 288: 2127; 289: 2138; 290: 2137; 291: 2013.

Cache 1.

In connection with the "Architectural details", a small cylindrical well-like space below the topmost floor but one in room 3 was mentioned and illustrated, figs. 183 and 194. A circular hole had been made in the floor, a shaft had been sunk through the filling and its bottom was paved with two stone slabs. On these a number of objects had been placed, whereupon this small chamber had been closed up by means of two thin stone flags. A fresh filling had been laid on the floor and another floor, the top one, had been moulded over it. Hence there can be no doubt that the cylindrical chamber originates from Stage III.

The whole floor of this small chamber was covered with objects. In the centre had been placed a large and crudely made conical bowl with a reinforced brim, and laid on top of it was an up-turned bowl of the same kind but somewhat smaller and with a hole in the bottom. These two bowls constituted the lower part of an "incensario" of a type of which a detailed description will be given below. The remaining parts of the incensario were contained in the bowls. It had been intentionally taken to pieces — not broken up. The large face-mask that enters into the composition of objects of this kind was painted red and of the same type as those which are reproduced in plates 3—5. This incense burner forms part of the collection that was reserved for the Teotihuacan museum.

Arranged in a circle round the bowls were two cylindrical tripods and four bowls. One of the tripods and two of the bowls were also retained at Teotihuacan. The bowls and the tripods are exactly alike. The former are simple, unornamented and brown or blackish-brown, and carry traces of faintly glossy black paint, fig.

288. The tripods are also brown and of fine, hard and thin ware, fig. 287 and pl. 2. As will be apparent from the plate, the feet, bottom edge and head are coated with red paint, proved to be cinnabar. The head, as well as the thin, solid feet, have in both cases been manufactured in the same mould. They were loosely attached to the vessel while they still were damp. The head represents the characteristic features of the Fat God.

The other artifacts include a flat ring of obsidian, fig. 289, which reposed in the bowl here illustrated, a bone needle, and a tube of bone. They lay on the floor between the tripods. The needle is very well made, circular in section, but flattened towards the eye, fig. 291. Its length, 20 cm, is remarkable. Of great interest is the bone tube, fig. 290. It may have been used for storing needles but may equally well have been a sucking-tube, in which case it had a magical use. Lastly, in another bowl there were four shells of four different species: *Chama coralloides* REEVE, *Pecten ventricosus* SOWERBY, *Fasciolaria gigantea* KIENER, *Oliva reticularis* LAMARCK. Of skeletal remains there were no traces whatever, and the roofing slabs had so well answered their purpose that hardly any dust at all had filtered down into this small chamber which presumably had been arranged as a place for offerings.

Cache 2.

A small collection of clay vessels, small in size and of no very great practical usefulness, was discovered in room 27. They had been placed in a row on the middlemost floor, along the south wall, and protected by two stone slabs leaned against the latter. The following list of these objects starts from the east:

1 jar with round body and wide mouth, decorated with shallow, vertical grooves. Height 5.1, diameter 5.5 cm.

3 jars, round-bodied with flat bottom, short neck and wide mouth. All of them ornamented with shallow, vertical grooves or lines. Height 5.1, 7.1 and 7.6 cm; diameter 5.5, 7.5 and 8.2 cm, respectively.

2 tripods. One undecorated, cylindrical, and with hollow feet rounded at the lower end. Height 6.7, diameter 7.1 cm. The other, of light yellowish-red ware, slightly conical shape widening upwards; feet conical and solid. Ornamented with two bands in relief. Height 7.1, diameter 8.6 cm.

2 vases with tall, cylindrical neck, dwarfed and compressed body and brim which is spread out almost flat and disproportionately large (cf. fig. 215). Height 11.2 and 13 cm, respectively.

Cache 3.

Below the floor of the alley connecting rooms 94 and 99, at a depth of 20 cm, while doing some trial digging we came upon a large and wholly undamaged vessel, an unornamented jar with ovoid body and low, rounded brim. Height 58, diameter

50 cm. No doubt it had been used for storing fluids. It stood on a bed of clay, and beside it was a bowl of the ordinary flat-bottomed type with curving sides and three small, conical feet. Fragments of similar large vessels were recovered both at this place and, in 1932, at Xolalpan, although by no means in any great numbers, while they were common at Las Colinas and Zoquiapan, in the neighbourhood of Calpulalpan. In 1932 we found at Las Palmas two similar jars which possibly derived from the Mazapan culture (cf. 1934: fig. 96). It is possible that large vessels of this type were used for storing water during the dry season. Even 60 years after the arrival of the Spaniards it is stated that "the natives drink stored rain water".[2]

COMPARATIVE NOTES AND STUDIES

The artifacts recovered at Tlamimilolpa are partly of the same character as those of Xolalpan (Linné 1934). In the following will only be discussed the finds collected from graves and caches, and objects of major interest discovered under the floors of the ruin. At the same time as fresh material is adduced attempts will be made to connect it with cultural impulses that have issued from, or reached, Teotihuacan. The pottery has been placed last, in spite of its being incomparably most important both in quality and quantity. By that means this group of objects, which give occasion to the greater part of the comparative studies, will be in closer contact with the concluding section. Of the extensive pottery material, only a minor portion can for reasons of space be dealt with. Some of the material has already been published in the Museum's journal, ETHNOS (cf. p. 14). We hope later on to have occasion to recur to certain groups of objects, particularly incensarios and trade pottery, as well as to the large ethnographical collections that will yield valuable information to archaeology.

TOOLS AND ORNAMENTS OF OBSIDIAN, STONE AND MICA

It is only among objects made of obsidian that we find any of higher class. These are good examples of highly developed technical skill, and correspond in every respect to the Xolalpan finds. As material for fashioning delicate tools, obsidian was the equivalent of our steel. Projectile points and flake knives dominate as regard numbers in possessing 112 and 133 representatives, respectively. Of ex-

---

[2] Nuttall 1926: 54.

Fig. 292. Stone built into the wall at the entrance of room 8, below the first floor. Draperies or hangings were kept in place by means of such stones, cf. p. 104. (2/5) 35. 8. 749.

quisite quality are the knives from Burial 1: delicately shaped, thin-bladed, and exceedingly sharp, figs. 240—242, while those finished by fine-flaking bear evidence of a marvellously advanced technique, figs. 243—244. Scrapers of various types also occur in large numbers. Some of them may possibly have been used in tapping pulque, fig. 267, seeing that they in point of shape much resemble the iron scrapers nowadays in use. Among the obsidian objects are also small human figures, "eccentric" objects, in appearance exactly similar to those from Xolalpan, figs. 263—264. Counterparts of them are known from the Maya region, and these are among the elements that supply unequivocal evidence of communications in that direction.[1] It is worthy of note that "eccentric" flints have recently been found in Oklahoma. They are strikingly reminiscent of the Maya objects of that kind and, if they are really genuine — which seems to be the case — their presence is hard to explain.[2] As novelties can only be described two small knives from Burial 1, figs. 250—251, which evidently have been hafted, drill points from Burial 4, figs. 268—269, and a ring from Cache 1, fig. 289.

Most numerously represented among objects of stone or lava are plasterer's floatstones. Of these are 59, and they are on the whole of the same type as those from Xolalpan (Linné 1934: figs. 268, 270). One of the recovered metates had originally three legs. Especially remarkable is a very small one which was found in Burial 1, and which, as regards size, has a toy-like appearance. Its careful workmanship and its presence in this grave is more likely to suggest having been used for grinding medicines, or the like. Other implements include a number of stone balls, whet-stones, smoothing stones and axes. The last-mentioned are only two in number, but they are very well ground, although of rather plain types (Linné 1934: figs. 251, 255). Of weapons, there were only two points of quartz, and a stone ring which may possibly have served as the head of a club. Of interest are three rectangular stone knives in view of the fact that implements of exactly the same type are still in use among the Otomí Indians, hafted as scrapers and used in the preparation of maguey fibre.[3] The "square knife" type is extremely archaic, and occurs sporadically in both North and South America. In the Peruvian coast and

[1] Linné 1934: 152—153. [2] Clements and Reed 1939: 27—30. [3] Montell 1937: 312; fig. 6.

10   145

in the border regions between Peru and Bolivia, and in Chile, it has also been found in copper. In El Gran Chaco it also appears in hard wood as well as copied in iron.[4]

While on the subject of architectural details I mentioned divers building elements made of stone, and depicted a sculptural detail, fig. 196. Several fragments of large, seated figures representing the god known to the Aztecs as Ueueteotl, the Old God, and the bowl he carries on his head, were recovered.[5] He is the earliest Mexican deity to be sculpturally represented; his image occurs in finds made below the lava deposits of Copilco, and this god occupied an honoured position in the pantheon of the peoples of the Valley of Mexico down to the time of the arrival of the Spaniards.[6]

A small bowl made of lava was found in Burial 2, fig. 260, and in Grave 13 another of tecali, Mexican onyx, fig. 284. The latter material formerly was — and still is — popular for ornamental purposes. The principal deposits are located at Tecali in Puebla. On an earlier occasion I have mentioned certain objects of this material which had been archaeologically recovered in localities that are widely separated, such as Ulua Valley, Chichen Itza, Oaxaca, Isla de Sacrificios, Tepic, and Guasave in Sinaloa.[7]

The personal ornaments consist of beads and small pendants, in some cases of jadeite. They are remarkably few in number. The earthenware figurines are profusely provided with ornaments, which makes the paucity of finds of this kind all the more striking. Notwithstanding the abundance of objects in Burial 1, there was only one small jadeite bead, fig. 253. In this connection it may be mentioned that nothing but a fragment of an earthenware ear-plug was found below the floors, one in Burial 1, fig. 235, and two plain ones in Burial 4. The supply of obsidian from mines near Teotihuacan and Pachuca must have been ample. Jadeite, on the other hand, was an article of import. Deposits has not so far been located, but everything points to Oaxaca and Guerrero being the home of Mexican jadeite.[8]

Thin plates of slate, fashioned into shape, were unfortunately only recovered as fragments. The majority of these had been painted red and in some cases also white. Frequently the patterns appear to have been well executed and of complex design. They were probably of the leaflike type depicted by Seler and Gamio, and by the former called "Votiv-Opfermesser oder Votiv-Lanzenspitzen".[9] Still more likely it seems that they served decorative purposes in the service of religion.

Mica that had been worked up was of fairly common occurrence, usually in the form of small round plates. Rather large and thick rectangular plates were recovered, out of which the circular discs had been cut. One of the uses of these objects could be ascertained, namely that of having ornamented certain parts of incensarios.

[4] Nordenskiöld 1921: 146—147; fig. 57.   [5] Cf. Peñafiel 1890, vol. 1: pls. 86—87, 1900: pl. 61; Seler 1915: figs. 28—30; Gamio 1922, tomo 1, vol. 1: pls. 22, 122; Dieseldorff 1926, vol. 1: pl. 29.   [6] Linné 1938: 106.   [7] Linné 1934: 139.   [8] Ball 1941: 36.   [9] Seler 1915: 432; fig. 22; Gamio 1922, tomo 1, vol. 1: 217—218.

Of peculiar character are a rounded object, fig. 236, and fragments of a circular plate, both from Burial 1. The latter, which has the appearance of rusty iron, may have been a mirror. Analysis has shown both of them to contain a large proportion of sulphur and iron, and they are undoubtedly iron pyrite (FeS₂). There can be no doubt that certain pre-Spanish objects described as being of iron are nothing but pyrite. Weathering has made them look rusty. The diameter of the flat disc is 6 cm, which roughly corresponds to the average size of the Mexican pyrite mirrors included in Nordenskiöld's study of convex and concave mirrors in America.[10] Unfortunately the surface is so badly weathered that it is impossible to determine the way in which it is ground. Nordenskiöld has, however, found that the majority of pre-Spanish mirrors — all of them from Mexico, Ecuador, and the Peruvian coast — are convex and consist of pyrite. In Musée de l'Homme, Paris, there is one which forms part of Charnay's collection and is stated to have come from Teotihuacan. Nordenskiöld further adduces a Mexican picture-writing in which among other things is seen a man using a mirror. The picture-writing in question is said to originate from Cholula. Mirrors were naturally in great demand as an article of trade, and even formed part of the barter goods with which the great raft that Bartolomé Ruiz in 1526 encountered off the coast of Ecuador was loaded.

OBJECTS OF BONE

Objects of bone recovered from burials, caches and floor-fillings were but few and, with one exception, of little interest. They consist — apart from the pierced tooth, fig. 255, which represents an exceedingly ancient form of hanging ornament — of short, pointed, though not sharp bone instruments, awls or bodkins, and needles. The first-mentioned may have been used splitting off knives from obsidian blocks. The bodkins might, provided penitential rites were here practised similar to those of the Aztecs, have been used for piercing the tongue and other parts of the body so as to obtain blood for sacrifices. Nuttall, quoting Jacinto de la Serna, an author from the middle of the 17th century, supposes that in the so-called candeleros (cf. figs. 195, 219, 223) slips of paper soaked in the sacrificial blood, were burnt together with copal.[1] Sometimes copal or beeswax is said to have been found in candeleros.[2] In "Historia de los mexicanos por sus pinturas" mention is in fact made of objects that may have been candeleros.[3] The needles are long and thick, cf. fig. 291. What purpose such needles served is hard to tell. Of practical use they could hardly have been for anything else than "upholstery" work. In sewing

[10] Nordenskiöld 1926: 105—106.   [1] Nuttall 1904: 13.   [2] Leon 1905: 188; Seler 1915: 496; Thompson 1930: 105.   [3] Phillips 1883: 627; Radin 1920: 58.

147

together woven mats for low stools that are seen used by persons of high degree in the codices, they ought to have been of good service.

Among the finds made in the earth covering the floors may be noted fragments of four rasping bones. Of these, two are to a certainty human thigh-bones, one of them even retaining its condyle intact. The fourth is made of horn. This musical instrument and its geographical distribution I have dealt with in an earlier work.[4]

Below the floor of room 48 was found a portion of the crown of a human skull. Two sides of this four-sided piece of bone had been cut to a straight edge, one of them having been smoothed down to exceeding fineness. It conveys an impression of being an unfinished piece of work. Objects manufactured from parts of the human skull are unknown to me from the Teotihuacan culture.

·The bone tube, fig. 290, is a rare and interesting object. Judging from its position in Cache 1 it can scarcely have formed part of an ornament, in the way it was, and still is, the case with similar objects in Darien.[5] If it did not serve for a needle case, which is not very probable, it was most likely a sucking or drinking tube of ritual character.

Birket-Smith,[6] Lindblom[7] and Berg[8] have studied the occurrence and uses of this class of object, the first-mentioned particularly in North America, Lindblom in Africa and Berg in Europe, especially among the Lapps. The writers just referred to show that the drinking tube, in its practical use, is a very ancient culture element which, at all events in America, derives from a common origin. The Eskimo from East Greenland to Bering Strait and the Aleut use drinking tubes for practical purposes, while south of that region the object has passed into an instrument of exclusively shamanistic or ritual employment. These sucking tubes, which are found among a considerable number of tribes, are of bone, wood or stone. In South America they only occur in the farthest south, viz. among the Yaghan of Tierra del Fuego. The sole intervening instance is that of the Chocó Indians of Panama, among whom in 1927 I saw a medicine-man blowing on his patients through a tube.[9] The same procedure occurs among certain North American tribes. Highly interesting is Birket-Smith's well-founded opinion regarding "the oldest tubular pipe simply as the sucking tube of the medicine-men".[10] The southernmost range of the connected North American distribution area of this culture element includes Mexico. While the medicine-men of the Tarahumara[11] and the Tepehua[12] use tubes for sucking out illness from their patients' bodies, the Aztecs of past ages applied these instruments to ritual purposes. This is depicted in the Codices[13] and is related by Sahagun. In his accounts of the annually recurring feasts he mentions that sucking tubes of reeds, "caña hueca", were used in drinking pulque and for sucking

[4] Linné 1934: pp. 128, 155, 204—207.   [5] Lothrop 1937: 201.   [6] Birket-Smith 1929, vol. 2: 143—145, 243, 312—313, 1929 a: 29—39.   [7] Lindblom 1941: 48—74.   [8] Berg 1941: 98—108.   [9] Nordenskiöld 1928: fig. 47.   [10] Birket-Smith 1929 a: 37—39.   [11] Bennet and Zingg 1935: 258—260.   [12] Lumholtz 1904, vol. 1: 352.   [13] Nuttall 1903: 73.

up the blood out of the body of the person sacrificed during the second annual feast [14]:

> . . . .
> "Und den Wein hebt man viermal weihend
> empor vor dem Gefangenen,
> darnach trinkt er mittels eines Saugrohrs.
>
> . . . .
> Und ein anderer Priester
> bringt das Adler-Saugrohr.
> Sie stellen es in die Brust des Gefangenen,
> an die Stelle, wo sein Herz gewesen war;
> sie saugen es voll Blut, tauchen es ganz in das Blut,
> dann heben sie es ebenfalls weihend zur Sonne empor.
>
> . . . .
> Auf die Lippen der Steinbilder, der Idole
> bringt er das Blut der Gefangenen,
> mittels des Saugrohres lässt er sie davon kosten."

Though unworked, the following bone object is worthy of being mentioned. Both the topmost floor — which lay just below the ground surface — of the southern part of room 46, and the second 40 cm lower down, had been damaged and partly removed. Through the resulting opening a shaft was sunk down to the bedrock. At a depth of not quite 2 m below the top floor a bone of considerable size was found among the filling. Eager searching for further bones of that description met with no success. The bone proved to be from a whale, viz. the right humerus of a *Balaenoptera* (probably *davidsoni*). Of this genus, the species in question is found from Bering Strait to the Mexican coast. Whether bones of the present kind, or large fossil animal bones such as are to be seen in the Museum of Natural History in Mexico City and in the museums at Puebla and Oaxaca, gave rise to myths of giants, is a question that must be left unanswered. Díaz Lozano, in his account of the discovery of fossil elephant skeletons in the northern part of the Valley of Mexico, also mentions that numerous remains of extinct animals, such as mammoth, mastodon and glyptodon, had been discovered in the valley.[15] The natives of Tlaxcala told to Cortés and his followers, when in 1519 they marched against Tenochtitlán-Mexico, according to Bernal Díaz del Castillo,[16] "that their ancestors had told them, that in times past there had lived among them men and women of giant size with huge bones ... So that we could see how huge and tall these people had been they brought us a leg bone of one of them which was very thick and the height of a man of ordinary stature, and that was the bone from hip to the knee ... They brought other pieces of bones like the first ..." Together with costly things of many kinds, similar bones were also sent to the emperor: "several large bones

[14] Seler 1927: 69, 71—72; cf. Sahagun 1938, vol. 1: 125—127. [15] Díaz Lozano 1922—1923: 37—51.
[16] Díaz del Castillo 1908, vol. 1: 286.

were also sent, uncovered at Coyuhuacan, which in accordance with the common native tradition and the declaration of the doctors were pronounced to be the remains of giants".[17]

Probably the fossil bones gave rise to the giant myth, and the whale bones may have lent support to it. Massive bones of mystical, gigantic marine animals must have had an imposing effect, been endowed with enormous power, etc. In 1927, among the Cuna Indians of Panama, I met a medicine-man who, among a multitude of other things, also included fossil shark's teeth in his pharmacy.

SHELLS AND SHELL WORK

Of the shells recovered in graves and caches, some are natives of the Pacific Ocean, others of the Atlantic, and only one freshwater species was represented, viz. *Unio discus* LEA. The remaining part of the mollusc material, which was fairly large, has been disregarded because here, as in the case of the artifacts, we are mainly interested in objects directly connected with the excavated ruin. The species of shells included in the inventories of finds given in the foregoing are geographically distributed as follows[1]:

Natives of the Pacific Ocean	*Natives of the Atlantic*
Conus interruptus BRODERIP	*Cardium isocardia* LINNÉ
Chama coralloides REEVE	*Fasciolaria gigantea* KIENER
Lithophaga aristata DILLWYN	*Oliva reticularis* LAMARCK
Pecten ventricosus SOWERBY	*Spondylus americanus* GMELIN
Pinna maura SOWERBY	*Strombus pugilis* LINNÉ
Pteria margaritifera LINNÉ	*Thais deltoidea* LAMARCK
Spondylus princeps BRODERIP	*Thais fasciata* REEVE
Turritella cumingi REEVE	*Turbinella scolymus* GMELIN

Commercial intercourse must evidently have been brisk in both directions, as half of the marine species comes from the west coast and an equal proportion from the Gulf of Mexico. The presence of different species of marine shell in finds from the Early Cultures down to Aztec times in the Valley of Mexico may prove a valuable guide in solving the question of the trade routes of remote antiquity. In contradistinction to what is the case with artifacts, with shells there is never any uncertainty as to their "place of manufacture". Of great help as regards the ancient disposition of the trade routes are those to this day trafficked by the Indians when they set out on trading expeditions, apparently more from tradition than practical

[17] Bancroft 1883, vol. 5: 81—82.   [1] All mollusc determinations have been made by Nils Odhner, Ph. D., of the National Museum of Natural History (Naturhistoriska Riksmuseet), Stockholm.

reasons. The Indians are, and formerly were, exceedingly keen on trading and fixation of the ancient trade routes would be of great importance when it comes to determining cultural influences as to time and place. By that means it would be possible to ascertain whether agreements between certain artifacts are accidental, resulting from superficial or causal, indirect contact. Shells are easy of transportation, and there are numerous instances of species that from some reason or other had become popular having, probably through many middlemen, travelled considerable distances.

Spondylus princeps was much favoured by the Maya and the Aztecs, by the earlier Pueblos and by the ancient Peruvians.[2] From the Maya region there are instances from Labna, Ulua Valley, Pusilhá[3] and San José[4] in British Honduras, and its shells were possibly known in Huastecan territory. The shortest distance as the crow flies from Labna to the Pacific Ocean is upward of 700 km, and consists partly of exceedingly rough-travelled country. A yearly tribute of 1600 shells was paid by Colima to Moctezuma. From Peru, where *Spondylus princeps* does not occur, trading expeditions were dispatched northwards in order to obtain these much-sought-for shells. In the first advance to be made from Darien on Peru, Bartolomé Ruiz's vessel encountered a large trading raft. It was loaded with textiles, pottery, etc., and these wares were intended to be bartered for "conchas coloradas", i. e. shells of *Spondylus princeps*.[5]

Fasciolaria gigantea, which is most numerously represented, is the largest of all American shells and also attained a wide popularity in olden times. Shells of this species are depicted in relief on the façade of the earlier of the central pyramids of Ciudadela and on the wall-paintings in Templo de la Agricultura.[6] Positive evidence of shells of this species having been used as trumpets we do not possess, but from one or two incomplete specimens it appears probable. Shell trumpets were fairly common in Mexico, besides occurring in Central America as well as sporadically in the West Indies and South America, though not to any great extent in North America. Shell trumpets were also manufactured from *Strombus, Turbinella, Triton*, etc.[7] *Fasciolaria gigantea* was the symbol of Tecciztecatl, an Aztec moon god[8] — the shell itself was known as *tecciztli* — and among the Maya this shell is depicted in combination with certain gods.[9] Shells were generally represented in connection with water. Stylized *Oliva* shells were in Maya hieroglyphic writing given a special function, the sign for zero, as shown by Förstemann as early as 1880.[10]

South-west of Teotihuacan, on the shore of Lake Texcoco, stood a village named Tequizistlán, in earlier times called Tecciztlan, which, according to Nuttall, had

[2] Richards and Boekelman 1937: 167.   [3] Boekelman 1935: 259, 262—266.   [4] Thompson 1939: 181.
[5] Oviedo 1855, vol. 4: 122.   [6] Gamio 1922, tomo 1, vol. 1: fig. 40; pl. 27; Lehmann 1933.
[7] Izikowitz 1935: 227—231, 248—250.   [8] Seler 1923: 752.   [9] Tozzer and Allen 1910: 296; pl. 1.
[10] Förstemann 1886: 4—5.

been named after *tecciztli*.[11] As already mentioned, this was the Aztec name for *Fasciolaria gigantea*. On the earliest map of the Valley of Mexico, which is in the possession of the Uppsala University library — and erroneously ascribed to Alonso de Santa Cruz — the place is adjoined by a hieroglyph unmistakably representing a shell.

Objects manufactured from shell are in comparison with unworked shells exceedingly few in number and not particularly remarkable for good workmanship. On the contrary they are strikingly primtive, which is rather strange in view of the exquisite work produced by the Maya, and the exceedingly beautiful and with marvellous skill manufactured shell ornaments from the Huasteca. It would appear as if importation was only of secondary importance as regards raw materials for the manufacture of ornaments. Shells played an important role in religion. The mere fact of their being aquatic must have provided an incentive to people whose material life — and therefore also religion — was dependent on the life-giving water.

Most numerous among the shell objects were the bell-like pendants of the type illustrated in fig. 259. The base of the shells was cut off, and the top either pierced with a hole or carved through with a slit. The shells from Burials 1 and 5 were of *Oliva reticularis*, and those from Grave 2 of *Conus interruptus*. At Ticoman, Vaillant found objects of shapes identically similar to those of the same shells from the first mentioned of the above graves.[12] These had been brought from the Atlantic, while the shells forming the material of those from Burial 2 are native of the Pacific. Simple ornaments manufactured in this way, which may perhaps also occasionally served as dancing rattles, we have from tribes on various cultural levels. Boekelman makes some interesting statements as to the occurrence of *Oliva porphyria* LINNÉ shells. His proofs that certain objects are in fact manufactured from this shell, and not from *Oliva reticularis*, scarcely strike one as conclusive. *Oliva porphyria* belongs to the Pacific, "yet its generally-accepted habitat being Lower California".[13] It is of course not impossible that shells of this species may have been carried all the way from there and via Teotihuacan or Tenochtitlán even as far as Honduras, but it comes more natural to suppose that the shell actually in question is the species of *Oliva* that lives in the Atlantic. From Roatan Island, Honduras, there are similar danglers. They are anyhow stated to have been manufactured from *Oliva porphyria* shell.[14]

In Burial 13 where found two rings made from shells of *Cardium isocardia*. On the outer side they are only partly ground smooth, and they are decorated with a red ring painted round the aperture, figs. 283, 285. In the same grave there was also a small, spatulate, mother-of-pearl ornament, fig. 282, and among unworked shells in this grave was found its raw material, *Pinna maura*. The simplest orna-

[11] Nuttall 1926: 58.   [12] Vaillant 1931: 312; pls. 84, 93.   [13] Boekelman 1935: 266.
[14] Strong 1935: 71; pl. 15.

ments of all consists of rounded portions of shell, ground into shape and provided with a hole drilled near the edge. One of them was pierced in two places and was made from *Spondylus princeps*.

Particularly interesting is the small earthenware shell that formed part of the inventory of Burial 13, fig. 281. It is probable that, together with a number of its kind, it originally decorated the bottom edge frieze of a tripod. It is so naturalistically executed that the shell upon which it was modelled has been capable of being determined as *Pecten ventricosus*. Its naturalism has been exaggerated, so that the effect arrived at has, from an artistic point of view, even surpassed nature. It is a remarkable thing that even Indian artists have perceived the decorative value of this shell, which has also been appreciated by their colleagues of different periods and in different parts of the Old World.

BASKETRY, BARK PAPER AND TEXTILES

Among the objects that had been deposited in Burial 1, over 1.200 in number, there were also weavings, baskets and articles made from bark paper. As already mentioned, the deceased person had been burnt in the grave itself, and the mortuary offerings had been put into the grave without any apparent system. Part of the textiles etc, had by the pottery been protected from direct contact with the fire, in consequence of which they had merely been charred and thus preserved. In spite of their not being much to look at, these fragments nevertheless must be counted as archaeological rarities, both in these parts of Mexico and among ancient relics from the cultures with which Teotihuacan was more or less in contact.

Baskets and mats.

One large and two smaller baskets had originally been deposited in the cremation grave. As to their shape, the fragments do not provide much of a clue. They must have been more or less flat-bottomed, and the two smaller baskets had an outcurving and down-turned rim, fig. 295. They are, as will be apparent from figs. 293—295, made in coiled basketry technique: a continuous coil which begins at the centre of the bottom and rises to the rim. The coil is the warp, and the successive circles are wrapped and fastened together by sewing with a flexible weft. The warp or foundation in all cases consists of a bunch of fine elements, probably stems of some grass. The weft, the binding stitches, which have the twofold object of holding the filler together and of attaching it to the completed course of coiling below, are noninterlocking. Two different techniques were used, as can be seen from the schematic figures appended to the figs. 293—294.

153

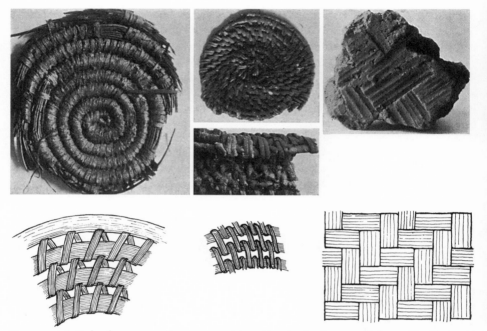

Figs. 293—296. Basket fragments, 35. 8. 2224 a—c, and impressions in clay from a twilled mat, The Museum of Teotihuacan. In the bottom row is schematically shown the technique of the baskets and the mat, while the lower photograph in the centre, fig. 295, shows the rim of one of the baskets.

Coiled basketry is still being largely manufactured in Mexico, and in the market place of San Juan Teotihuacan it is possible to buy baskets made in the same way as those from Burial 1. Particularly in North America, the technique of coiling played an important part.[1] In South America, on the other hand, coiled basketry has an area of distribution mainly limited to south and west, but is here undoubtedly among the earliest of culture elements.[2] The only fairly detailed report from Mexico, known to me, of archaeological basket material has been published by Zingg. It deals with remains probably of the ancestors of the modern Tarahumara.[3] From regions in the neighbourhood of Teotihuacan, Vaillant mentions a bit of coiled basketry in a case at Copilco.[4]

In addition to the charred remains of baskets and weavings, we found impressions in clay of coarse, probably knitted, textiles. These had probably been of the same kind as those still in use. But impressions of twilled mats were also in evidence. In the filling under the topmost floor of room 8 was found a piece of

[1] Weltfish 1930: the map, fig. 2.　　　[2] Nordenskiöld 1931: 92—93; map. 30.　　　[3] Zingg 1940.
[4] Vaillant 1935 a: 250.

clay bearing imprints from a twilled mat, in all probability from a bed-mat, petate (Mexican *petatl*), fig. 296. In Ticoman and El Arbolillo, Vaillant discovered impressions from the same type of mats.[5] Such are still in common use among the Indian population and, like the baskets, are kept for sale in San Juan Teotihuacan. The technique is that of "over-two under-two" twill plaiting.

Bark paper.

In Burial 1 were also found fragments of bark paper. As bark-beaters of stone had been found under circumstances indicating that they had been used by the Teotihuacan people, these finds are, per se, not surprising. That the implements in question had been used in the manufacture of paper is beyond all doubt.[6] Unfortunately the fragments are far too scanty to convey any idea as to their original character. Even today paper is being manufactured entirely by the ancient method in regions remote from the main highways. It is exclusively used in the manufacture of spirit figures which are employed for magical purposes.[7] It may not be entirely impossible that the charred paper fragments originate from a codex. Smith found crumbled codex leaves in a grave at Uaxactun,[8] and Stirling came upon remains of a codex in a mound at Cerro de las Mesas, Vera Cruz. The paper had perished altogether, "but the white sizing with which they had been covered, and the painted designs, remained bright and fresh".[9] The above examples, recovered during latter years' field-work, give hope that the small number of codices we possess from pre-Spanish times will be added to through archaeological discoveries.

Textiles.

Few examples of the textile art of pre-Spanish Mexico and Central America are known. The elaborate robes worn by the personages depicted in Mayan sculptures and in the mural paintings of Teotihuacan and Monte Alban, those seen on clay figures and vessels, the garments that are enumerated in the inventories of tributes drawn up by the Aztecs, and those mentioned by the Conquistadores, nevertheless reveal that anciently textile art occupied a high standard. The accomplished skill attained by the peoples of the Peruvian coast was with certainty not equalled, because the possession of wool lent to the Peruvian weavers an advantage that those of ancient Mexico were never able to make up for. They were restricted to working with nothing but henequen or agave fibre and cotton,

[5] Vaillant 1931: 315, 1935 a: 250.   [6] Linné 1934: 136—137, 197—204.   [7] Montell 1936: 190—191, 1936 a: fig. 2.   [8] Smith 1937: 216—217.   [9] Stirling 1941: 291.

of which the latter had, contrary to conditions in Peru, in many parts of Mexico to be imported from the low-lying countries.

It is only in Museo Nacional in Mexico that I have seen archaeologically recovered textiles, stated to have come from Nochixtlán in Oaxaca. They are rather trifling, but so also is the case with those referred to in the literature. Blom mentions "a few charred scraps" from the sacred Cenote at Chichen Itza and in a cave near Comitán, in Chiapas.[10] A year or two prior to his visit the cave had been discovered by the local natives. Such earthenware vessels as had been found had been destroyed and the same fate befell a large piece of cloth. Blom, however, recovered fragments of white cotton cloth. "Among these fragments we found two different kinds of weaving ... the one having three wefts together, and the other two, the weft being finer and thinner than the warp. On some of the fragments the original edge is preserved and two pieces are sewn together with long stitches ... I am certain that they must date from the later part of the Old Empire Period." Thompson found a fragment of cotton textile at San José, in British Honduras. It was of small proportions, and he is not even sure but that the fragment may be recent.[11] At Zacatenco, Vaillant recovered in a burial of the Early Period a small cloth fragment "preserved miraculously in the brain of a skeleton whose bones had rotted completely. It seems not to be cotton, but some fibre more like henequen".[12] In a grave at Ticoman he found "a gray powdery substance ... that looked like the remnants of a feather robe".[13] A remarkable find was made during excavations in the great pyramid of Cholula.[14] Here an earthenware vessel in a grave contained some charred cloth. In a report issued by Instituto de Biología in Mexico City the material is declared to be wool. The grave is not with certainty stated to be pre-Spanish, and that the Indians shortly after the Conquest should have come into possession of woollen cloth does not appear very probable. It is true that it did not take long ere sheepbreeding was under way, not least from the personal interest taken in it by the first viceroy, Antonio de Mendoza, but that a "pagan" burial should have taken place in Cholula is not very likely.

Textiles have also been found in caves in Sonora[15] and Coahuila.[16] At least the material from Coahuila seems to indicate a certain relationship to the Basket-maker culture.

Miss Elisabeth Strömberg of the Northern Museum (Nordiska Museet), Stockholm, has subjected the charred textile remains from Burial 1 to a searching technical examination. This work gave some interesting results, as will be apparent from her report which here follows.

---

[10] Blom 1930: 165—167.   [11] Thompson 1939: 183.   [12] Vaillant 1930: 38.   [13] Vaillant 1931: 315.
[14] Romero 1935: 19—20; fig. 13.   [15] Ekholm 1939: 8.   [16] Krickeberg 1937: 200.

TECHNICAL ANALYSIS OF TEXTILES RECOVERED IN BURIAL I

By Elisabeth Strömberg.

Seeing that so few textiles from ancient Mexico have hitherto been recovered and preserved, a detailed presentation of the finds made at Teotihuacan may not be uncalled for. In consequence of the ravages of time to which they have been subjected they do not tell us anything about the character of the garments used, or of domestic textiles on the whole, but they nevertheless afford some information as to what materials were in vogue and provide us with examples of the fabrics that were produced.

In the grave were found large numbers of scraps and fragments both of textiles in a proper sense, and of bark-cloth. Thin sheets of unspun fibre resembling wadding and strings of unspun fibre, are also present. All of this is quite charred and apt to crumble to dust at the slightest touch unless handled with exceeding care, and consequently a satisfactory examination can hardly be accomplished. It is, however, possible to establish that the fragments originate from nine different kinds of cloth. Microscopical examination performed at the Central Testing Station at Stockholm (Statens provningsanstalt) revealed that four of them are manufactured of bast fibre, and five of cotton. Experiments made with modern fabrics show that vegetable textile materials on the whole retain their volume in charring. Hence the thickness, structure and general appearance of the fabrics may be inferred from the fragments, but on the other hand nothing can be ascertained regarding their degree of flexibility, elasticity, original colour, etc.

The greatest number of the fragments come from rather heavy, very loosely-woven cloth of bast fibres. Three distinctly different thicknesses are here distinguishable. The frequency of the threads varies — on an average — between 7 and 12 threads per cm. The yarn is S-spun,[1] and the material is probably agave fibre, which still is used for textile purpose in Mexico, pl. 6, fig. c. All these specimens of loose-woven cloths produce the same appearance of having been manufactured without any particular care or skill. The weave-closeness varies a great deal even in the same fragment, and the yarn is of uneven thickness and spun with varying hardness. Many selvages are preserved, the longest one being 13 mm. In the case of primitive weaving methods it is frequently the selvages that indicate

S   Z

---

[1] The terms S-spun and Z-spun, S-twined and Z-twined, have been adopted by the International Cotton Committee at Paris 1937. Cf. H. C. Broholm and M. Hald, Costumes of the Bronze Age in Denmark. Copenhagen 1940, p. 13. The figure to the right shows the directions of twisting in yarn, strings and cords when held in vertical position. Cf. Vivi Sylwan, Woollen textiles of the Lou-lan people (Reports from ... the Sino-Swedish expedition, Publication 15, Stockholm 1941) fig. 2.

the manner of manufacture, but here the building up of the cloth is regular right out to the edge, and no extra arrangement of the threads is present to reveal anything of the implements used.

Two small fragments, one of which is seen in pl. 6, fig. f, are also made of bast fibre. They probably form part of the same piece of cloth. Francisco de Castañeda, in a report which in 1580 he sent to Philip II, mentions that in pre-Columbian times the Indians of Teotihuacan paid a tribute to their rulers consisting, inter alia, of "blankets made of coarse agave fibre", and of the inhabitants of the nearby Tequizistlán he says that "they used coarse mantles of agave fibre".[2] One is tempted to suppose that these "coarse blankets" were manufactured of something very similar to these little fragments. In one direction the yarn is properly S-spun, while in the other direction it is very coarse and very loosely S-spun. This gives the cloth a repp-like appearance, and makes it porous but yet stout. The closeness of the texture amounts to 6 and 3 threads, respectively, to 1 cm.

The occurrence of cotton cloth of so many different kinds is of especial interest because it has probably been imported. Castañeda expressly states that "the cotton they use for clothing is brought from the region of Panuco".[3] All the specimens of cotton fabrics convey — in contradistinction to the bast cloths — the impression of a highly developed art of spinning and weaving. As for example the specimen seen in pl. 6, fig. h, which shows a piece of repp cloth of irreproachable evenness, woven of exceedingly fine and evenly S-spun yarn. The closeness of the fabric amounts to 14 and 52 threads per cm, respectively. The fineness of the threads which lie the closest, and almost cover the surface of the cloth, is closely comparable to modern cotton number 40 (international numbering). This means that one gramme of cotton has been spun out to a thread 64 m in length. In another fabric of gossamer thinness — not here depicted — the yarn is finer still. Here the closeness of the threads comes to 24 and 42 per cm, respectively. Whether these fabrics were imported in the finished state, or were locally manufactured, is of course impossible to tell, but the smallest spindle-whorls found in the ruin at Tlamimilolpa weigh no more than 2 g, and cannot very well have been used but for spinning an exceedingly fine thread. The heaviest of the spindle-whorls, which undoubtedly had been used on a spindle for spinning agave fibres, weighed 86 g.

Pl. 6, fig. a, shows a piece of bast cloth, with 8 threads per cm in both directions. In the warp direction can here be discerned a straight line where corresponding weft threads coming from opposite directions, are laid round each other between two warps and then return in the following shed, see fig. 297. The cloth may possibly have been patterned in tapestry-weaving, and this may be a colour partition. It may even be due to other causes. It had no decorative effect in case the cloth was one-coloured. It is in fact only just discernible to the naked eye.

Only four small fragments present a more elaborate technique of weaving or

[2] Nuttall 1926: 63, 68.   [3] Nuttall 1926: 79.

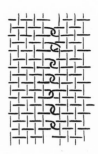

Fig. 297. The joining of the wefts in the fragment pl. 6, fig. a.

plaiting. Two of these are depicted in pl. 6, figs. b and d. In one direction Z-spun cotton threads run together by twos and in the other there are twos of carded, though not spun, cotton strands. For the sake of simplicity the former are here referred to as warp, and the latter as weft, and the side of the cloth that is seen in the pictures is in the following referred to as the right side. On the face of it, the fabric in question appears to be simple twill, in which the weft passes over two and under two of the threads of the warp, and the weave reverses so that the diagonal lines that are characteristic of twill turn on themselves and form diagonal lozenges. In reality the fabric is made up of a single warp-system while the weft-system is doubled. At the back of each pair of unspun cotton yarns visible on the right side there runs another pair only visible on the wrong side of the fabric. These two pairs partly run together over and under two pairs of warp threads, see fig. 298, but at regular intervals they separate, and while the weft of the wrong side is regularly woven in, the weft of the right side is left lying free over not less than 6 pairs of warp threads. The result is seen to the right in fig. 298 in which the pattern has been reconstructed as far as with certainty can be done. In order to achieve this in a loom with stretched warp, a fairly elaborate shedding harness would be required. From the above scanty fragments it is of course impossible to form any definite conclusions as to the method of their manufacture. They may just as well have been hand-plaited as woven in the strict sense of the word. The warp runs to ca. 7 pairs of thread per cm, and the weft to ca. 6 threads. With its loose-lying, unspun cotton fibres, in particular the right side must have been very little durable. Hence it is hard to believe that any large objects were manufactured in this technique. It was probably used for decorative purposes or for small objects that were not exposed to much wear.

Unfortunately this archaeological find contains nothing but detached fragments, disturbed from their original sites. In one case only it is possible to speak of a fairly preserved, connected whole, pl. 6, fig. g. This consists of a lump of furled and folded cotton cloth, tightly twisted together at one side. Opposite this compressed side there is no definite termination, however. Probably there was some sort of continuation.

159

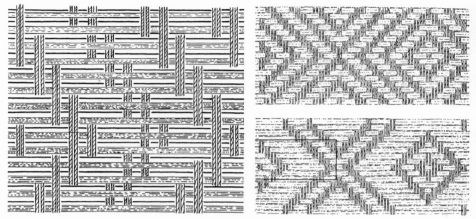

Fig. 298. Diagram showing the interlacing of the threads in the cloth pl. 6, figs. b and d. Narrow all-black lines represent wefts, that in reality are visible only on the wrong side. To the right the pattern of the same cloth reconstructed; above the wrong side and below the right side.

Another shapeless mass resembling the foregoing but of finer cotton fabric has been broken up in such a way as to present itself in transverse section. In the folds and between the layers there are numbers of small, round seeds that with remarkable frequency occur detached among the charred dust, or sticking to the smaller fragments, as seen in pl. 6, fig. a, near the right-hand bottom edge. Typical even of the smaller fragments is that several thicknesses of the same or different kinds of cloth occur directly superposed one another in a number of tiers. In other instances there are thicknesses of bark cloth, or of unspun waddinglike fibre, between the tiers. Among the undisturbed contents of the earthenware dish, pl. 6, fig. e, can be seen a number of small "parcels" consisting of a bundle of grass straws, or some other kind of vegetable stems, wrapped in bark cloth. One of these "parcels" is seen right in the surface in the upper part of the dish, somewhat to the left of its median line. Among the detached finds there are similar bunches, tightly wound round with strings of unspun fibre. As the cloth fragments are far too insignificant in themselves to allow of any conclusions as to their use — nothing about them gives any definite indication that they were part of the deceased's clothing — the above observations have been recorded because they tempt one conjecturally to advance the suggestion that at any rate some of these cloth fragments may be the remains of some sort of enclosure, bags or bundles, for containing seeds, grass, or other parts of plants deposited in the grave for magical purposes, or maybe as food for the deceased.

Figs. 299—300. Yellowish-red pottery. Fig. 299 from Burial 13, fig. 300 found underneath the treshold between rooms 157 and 174.
(³/₁₀) 35. 8. 517 and 910.

POTTERY

The pottery of Teotihuacan expresses itself in but a small number of forms. The decorative techniques vary, but the decoration itself is seldom remarkable for artistic inspiration, and no interest was taken in naturalistic representation. The art of the potter appears to have been bound by tradition but we are not, at any rate for the present, able to trace its line of development. It looks as if a range of types created by leading artists had unchanged been handed down as an inheritance. No appreciable connection with the people that inhabited the region prior to the pyramid-builders can be discerned at least in that part of their pottery, which is embedded in the adobe of which the Sun Pyramid was constructed. Certain types, such as the flat-bottomed bowl with out-curving rim, the cylindrical tripod vessel and the "candelero", are "zonal fossils". In the following will be discussed some ornamental methods and vessel types in the Tlamimilolpa collection as well as comparative notes with a view to ascertaining a possible exchange of culture elements.

Painted pottery is not typical, while in the Pyramid of the Sun painted potsherds outnumber those otherwise decorated.[1] All-red bowls occur in Burial 1, polished red ware in which the paint is derived from iron oxide. Tripods found in the same grave are decorated with incised lines and painted red fields and in one case with black ones, figs. 205—210, 212. Thereby as well as in shape and ware they differ from the "classic" tripods.

Negative painting is exceedingly common in the material obtained from the Sun Pyramid, but rare in "classic" Teotihuacan pottery.[2] Its infrequent use is connected with a lack of interest in painting of any kind. A tripod vessel from Burial 4 and a few fragments, including one of trade ware, fig. 320, represent this technique in our collections. While on the subject of the Xolalpan material I collated data

[1] Noguera 1935: 56; Pérez 1935: 93.   [2] Noguera 1935: pp. 7—10, 57—60; pl. 1.

concerning negative painting, i. e. the method as such, its distribution and origin.[3] Since then there have been adduced fresh material, fresh instances and points of view.[4] The locality where the method originated is unknown but Lothrop, who is well acquainted with both Middle and South America, writes: "the weight of evidence seems strongly in favor of north-western South America as the point of origin".

"Al secco" painted pottery is a Mexican speciality. Painting after firing on a prepared ground is known by various, not particularly happy names. On earlier occasions I have myself used the inappropriate term "in fresco", but as the paint may more correctly be described as having been laid on a dried ground than on a moist one, "al secco" more aptly describes the process.[5] From Tlamimilolpa we have fragments of more than twenty vessels decorated by the al secco method. The colours are red, pink, yellow, and turquoise-green and the ground is generally white. Black lines separate the colour-fields which are never toned down so as to merge one into the other. Our finds vary as to age. The earliest fragments were picked up close to Burial 1, the latest ones above the floors. The al secco technique appears mainly restricted to Mexico and the Maya region. Beside clay vessels also calabashes,[6] stone vessels,[7] house walls[8] and leaves in codices,[9] were in this way decorated. In north-western Mexico portions of the coating were cut out and replaced with paint of another colour[10] and the same method is to this day practised in the case of a kind of lacquer work in Michoacán.[11] In archaeological excavations at Sinaloa, Ekholm found gourd vessels decorated in an identically similar technique.[12] The excision method is closely related to the method referred to below of scraping away portions of the surface of clay vessels and filling them up with paint. Lumholtz specially notes that the male calabash decorators of Uruapan cut out the patterns while all the rest of the work falls on the women. It may be possible that lay workers shaped the vessels, which were subsequently decorated by the "learned" priests of Teotihuacan. They are usually decorated with signs of a hieroglyphic character, which in identical form occur on vessels carved after firing. Some of these ornaments are undoubtedly symbols of definite significance.[13]

Two almost exactly similar tripod vessels from Burial 13 are the best preserved examples of this decorative technique, figs. 272—273. The groups of white figures, two on each vessel and similar to each other, are painted on light brick-red ground. Apparently unessential details have been painted in the same manner, which may be an indication of a copy having been made from some other painting. The photograph, fig. 272, shows the specimen we left behind in Mexico and the drawing, fig. 273, half of the decoration on the one we brought home. The decorative groups

[3] Linné 1934: 162—167; map. 1.   [4] Butler 1936: 452—457; Lothrop 1936: 9—13, 29—30.
[5] Linné 1934: 168—171.   [6] Linné 1938: 67.   [7] Saville 1899: 354.   [8] Toscano 1940: 38.
[9] Seler 1915: 520.   [10] Spinden 1928: 183—184.
[11] Lumholtz 1904, vol. 2: 380; Molina Enriques 1925: 115—124; Francisco León 1939.
[12] Ekholm 1940: 10—15.   [13] Linné 1941: 174—186.

consist of a central figure flanked by flower stems with flowers and leaves. The figure represents the upper part of a human form provided with an oval shield, a large head ornament with the head of a bird, or with the mask of a bird framing the face, and a complicated garment. The latter shows a certain resemblance to the carapace of a tortoise. This, and the T-shaped nose ornament, might possibly connect the figure with the Aztec goddess of the agave, Mayauel, "she of the maguey-plant". She was also known as "One Eagle", her symbol was the agave plant and she was related to the *octli*, or pulque, gods.[14] In Codex Laud (p. 9) she is represented seated on a tortoise. The *octli* gods and their relations possessed fairly definite spheres of action, but their insignia varied, from which it may be inferred that at some earlier time their functions had been different. Their characteristic paraphernalia consist of a T-shaped nose ornament and a head-dress composed of white heron feathers, a bandage of unspun cotton, or a crown of paper. The diffuse fields of the head-dress, rather garishly reproduced in fig. 273, might correspond to a bandage of unspun cotton. From this, liquid drops are seen to fall, and drops also occupy the spaces between the flower stems. Seler depicts two potsherds painted in the same technique, with rain drops falling from stylized clouds.[15] The decoration of the tripod vessels was surely not intended merely for esthetic effect but had a definite significance, a sort of picture-writing that probably expressed a prayer for material prosperity, perhaps life-giving rain for the vegetation or stimulating pulque for mankind.

Not much interest was taken in the vegetable world and the plants here represented can hardly be called realistic. They are, however, uncommonly life-like, contrary to those on the famous "butterfly urn" decorated in the same technique and found in the neighbourhood of the Pyramid of the Moon.[16] What plant is intended is uncertain; agave it is not. Certain points of correspondence with the hieroglyph for Tlacopan, Tacuba of our time, no doubt exist. According to Peñafiel the first part of the word, *tlaco*, is derivable from *tlacotl*, Spanish jarilla.[17] In Mexico, jarilla would seem to mean plants belonging to the order *Compositae*.[18] But certain signs suggest that the plant in question may be a lobelia and thus belonging to the order *Campanulaceae*. Certain species of lobelia are medical plants.

Pottery carved after firing is a distinctive feature of Teotihuacan. The designs were carved or scratched out of the surface of the fired vessel and usually filled in with cinnabar. Even when no paint was used, colour contrast was obtained between the basal clay of the vessel and the polished slip. Among funeral offerings in the graves of Xolalpan this pottery is well represented.[19] At Tlamimilolpa there was not a single vessel of this type but only some few fragments which, however, entirely agree with the Xolalpan material. This technique was also practised among

[14] Spence 1923: 294 seq.   [15] Seler 1915: fig. 179.   [16] Peñafiel 1890, vol. 1: pls. 74—75, 1900: pl. 22; Seler 1915: fig. 178; Lehmann 1933: 65.   [17] Peñafiel 1885: 205, 1897, vol. 2: 280   [18] Gamio 1922, tomo 1, vol. 1: 25 seq.   [19] Linné 1934: frontispiece; figs. 17—18, 21—22, 24—29, 38, 41.

the Maya. Lothrop cites instances from Old Empire sites, Uaxactun and Copan. He also depicts a tripod vessel of Teotihuacan type carved after firing from Escuintla in southern Guatemala. The decoration presents in style a mixture of Teotihuacan and Maya.[20] A fragment from Tlamimilolpa constitutes a connecting link with the next following method of decoration. In this case the top part of a cylindrical bowl has been decorated before, the lower part after, firing. The respective styles are different.

Pottery incised before firing dominated at Tlamimilolpa. Of the clay vessels, close upon 250 in number, that were recovered from Burial 13, one half were decorated in this way. As already mentioned, they had partly been painted before firing, and as in style, material and shape they differ from the "classic" tripods and in their general character convey a foreign impression, they have an appearance of having been manufactured outside of Teotihuacan. Some few fragments of this pottery were found in the filling below the floors. In a class by itself is a vessel found below the floor in room 73, fig. 301. Its decoration resembles that seen on vessels carved after firing, but has been executed before the firing of the vessel, and inter alia consists of a symbol which I have dealt with in a minor paper.[21] It is of exceedingly poor workmanship. Possibly its maker was a beginner or a bungler who dabbled in scholastic art.

Carved decoration before firing deepened the effect, and became softer and less constrained than when applied after firing, figs. 177 and 308. The stiffness that characterizes symbols and hieroglyphs is less pronounced in the numerous fragments of vessels decorated by this method. While during the process the clay still was soft, the tools left fine marks but on a harder surface the edges became scratchy. We have it from Lothrop that "pottery vessels decorated with carved designs appear to have first been manufactured in Middle America by the Maya, who had developed this technique well before the end of the Old Empire period".[22] Fragments recovered at Xolalpan indicate connections with the Maya[23] and so do a few small fragments from Tlamimilolpa. Lothrop's opinion that the Maya have been the pioneers also in this special branch of pottery technics may not be indisputable seeing that it presupposes the peak period of Teotihuacan as having coincided with the decline of the Maya Old Empire. That still remains to be proved. In southern Guatemala and western Salvador pottery vessels carved in Maya style have been found. According to Lothrop there are, however, also comparable vessels which may be attributed to the Pipil.[24] Under that appellation are included tribes which have migrated southwards and, tradition says, were descendants of "Toltecs" that had Teotihuacan for their centre. It is generally supposed that their emigration took place in the 11th century, but Lehmann maintains that they migrated in several waves, the first of which occurred as early as

[20] Lothrop 1936 a: 147—149; fig. 6.   [21] Linné 1941: 174—186.   [22] Lothrop 1936 a: 140.
[23] Linné 1934: 96—101.   [24] Lothrop 1936 a: 148—149.

Fig. 301. Tripod vessel decorated before firing. Its feet, which had been knocked off, were cylindrical. The vessel was recovered below the floor in· room 73. (²/₅) 35. 8. 2618.

the 4th century. Unless the Pipil had learnt the art in Guatemala, the method, provided Lehmann's dating is correct, must have been anciently established at Teotihuacan.

It must, however, be considered an open question whether a stubbornly orthodox profession of the — to many — only saving doctrine that culture elements, with their appurtenant distribution apparatus, can only arise once, be necessary in this case. Vaillant is of opinion that carved pottery of the Maya was derived from painted decoration.[25] A similar development may also have taken place at Teotihuacan. Mural painting is of ancient origin, and fragments of al secco painted pottery have been found in the adobe of the Sun Pyramid.[26] Between mural painting and al secco painting there is undoubtedly some connection, as also with clay vessels with carved decoration. The motives on the richly decorated bowl from Calpulalpan are intimately connected with, and small-scale copies of, the mural paintings of Teopancaxco as well as with those in grave chambers at Monte Alban (cf. pp. 86—87).

Mouldmade decoration frequently occurs, but only fragments of three moulds were recovered. The question arises as to whether in a community as highly advanced as Teotihuacan, the manufacture of pottery was "home industry" or, perhaps more probably, was carried on by certain craftsmen and ceramic artists.

[25] Vaillant 1935: 135.   [26] Noguera 1935: 17.

It is strange that nowhere in Teotihuacan have there been discovered any remains of a potter's workshop. An abundance of vessels spoilt in the firing usually betrays the site of such places. Moulds have been in extensive use for making decorative details, heads of figures, feet for tripod vessels, spindle-whorls etc. A good example of this is seen in fig. 287 and pl. 2. The feet and the face of the Fat God are in both these vases, which were recovered in two exactly similar specimens, made in the same moulds. Particularly in the manufacture of the small heads that decorate the walls of tripod vessels immediately above the feet, moulds have been used. Thin ornaments were also mouldmade and stuck on to vessels that were still moist, figs. 305, 307. In the former case the potter happened to fix the left edge ornament too near the opening leading into the handle. He saved the situation by cutting away half of the ornament. Decorative details of "incensarios" were often made in moulds, industrialized mass-production. Of great interest are flower-like ornaments appearing on fragments of three vessels, two of which were found above the floors in quite different parts of the ruin, and the third below a floor. A crack in the mould, which has left a distinct impression, proves that these ornaments beyond any doubt have been manufactured in the same mould. Many of the 91 spindle-whorls that were recovered are mouldmade. Two of them are seen in figs. 311—312. The former is decorated with a stylized bird motive, the latter with a simple motive, but, in return, has its other side ornamented with an impressed design. Both of them have been given a finishing touch by hand. The spindle-whorl seen in fig. 311 was recovered under the second floor in room 21 together with fragments of pottery imported from the Maya region, fig. 331 and pl. 2.

Pottery with impressed ornaments is of fairly frequent occurrence, and of the recovered stamps, 18 in number, some are capable of being used for decorating clay vessels. These stamps carry a "negative" pattern, fig. 310. The others are in the way of printing blocks with relieved pattern and were used for imprinting paint, figs. 276, 279, 309. One is a fragment from a cylindrical stamp, a later type, judging from its distribution.[27] Identically impressed ornaments do not necessarily prove that the objects originate from the same locality, as even stamps can be reproduced by means of moulds.[28] Figs. 302—304 show examples of pottery with impressed ornaments. Touching up was not infrequently practised, as used to be the case with mouldmade objects. It does not appear possible to draw any definite line between "negative" stamps and moulds. On comparatively solid objects the impression was made before the clay had dried, but in the case of thinner ware the part to be decorated of the outer walls as well as the stamp were moistened.

Figurines were encountered in large numbers, both above and below the floors, and in Burials 1, 2 and 13. The majority were fragmentary, but complete and undamaged specimens were also recovered. How such a vast quantity of figurines

[27] Linné 1929: maps 3—4. [28] Museo Nacional, Mexico City.

Figs. 302—314. Pottery objects found at Tlamimilolpa. (¹/₂)
302: 35. 8. 786; 303: 184; 304: 360.
(¹/₄) 305: 35. 8. 1831; (¹/₄) 306: 1489; 307: 289; 308: 787.
309: 35. 8. 1960; 310: 483; 311: 181; 312: 228; 313: 1323; 314: 2727.

and parts of figurines, came to be present at Teotihuacan is a question not ever likely to be definitely answered. If the people like the Aztecs destroyed and replaced their household and temple equipment at the close of each calendar-round of 52 years, then each household must have possessed an exceedingly numerous collection of penates. But if they, like the Huichol, considered their household gods passé after five years, their presence would be easier to understand. They were of varied kinds and of different eras, from the Early Periods to Aztec times. The material is too vast for anything but a cursory glance in the present work. Among the conventional Teotihuacan types, numerical predominance is held by those which inappropriately are known as the portrait type. An exquisitely beautiful head of this type had been adapted to a pendant. From either side a perforation had been made for the suspension cord. Mouldmade heads are very numerous. Occasionally the entire figurine has been made in this way, though usually only the head which in some cases has not been joined on to a body. Many of the figurines that are not mouldmade bear witness of having been produced by real artists, figs. 313—314. Here human beings make their appearance from among the swarm of gods, demons and magical or symbolic representations.

Only a few of the gods in which Teotihuacan in all certainty abounded can be identified: Ueueteotl, Tlaloc, possibly Xipe and the Fat God. In appearance they resemble their namesakes among the Aztec gods. But whether they exercised the same functions as in the Aztec era is by no means certain. The ideas that underlie the symbols are capable of being twisted, changed and finally altogether transmuted. But this is a risk which has to be run in order to give some life to the past. Rather likeable in all his humanity is the Fat God, he must have been a powerful deity, if we may judge from the profusion of his images. He did not, however, survive the Teotihuacan culture. A study of the geographical distribution, in what connections he appears on pottery vessels, or in combination with other figurine types, the emblems on his headdress, etc., would provide an interesting field. Possibly his cradle stood in the Totonac region. Anyhow he constitutes a connecting link with the peoples of the Atlantic coast and the Maya.

Figurines with movable limbs were recovered in two twin specimens in Burial 13, and fragments of smaller ones in Burial 1, cf. pp. 131 and 140. They resemble present-day dolls and are characteristic of the Teotihuacan culture. Seler-Sachs depicts one from Tuxtla, but thinks it possible that it had been imported from the highlands.[29] Bodies and limbs are frequently found but complete figures are rare. Finds from the Peruvian coast show that dolls were popular toys also in ancient times, and from other localities in South America similar observations have been made both archaeologically and among more or less secluded tribes of the present day. Seeing that the deceased found in the graves were adult people, there can hardly be any doubt of the figurines having been idols and not dolls. In Xolalpan we found two figurines, made in the same mould, in a child's grave, but it does not necessarily follow that they had been dolls.[30] To this day figurines are being used by secret societies in the south-eastern districts of the Valley of Mexico in religious ceremonies of magic character, and it is similarly related from other parts of America.[31]

Nuttall and Wardle have given some attention to these figures.[32] They cite Diego Duran when he records that on the first day of the third month, Tozoztontli, a day intimately connected with the planting of the crops (the 24th of March), cords were stretched above the maize fields. To these cords were tied small idols, or rags resembling scarecrows, or children's playthings:

"Iten este dia se hacía una abusion y supesticion que en algunas partes y en casi todas el día de hoy lo he visto hacer y era que de árbol á árbol por encima de las milpas ataban unos cordeles, colgaban de estas cuerdas algunos idolillos ó trapos en fin alguna cosa de trecho á trecho que los que no lo saben y entienden creran que son espantajos para pájaros ó juguetes de muchachos y en realidad no es sino supersticion y abusion."[33]

Wardle is of opinion that these objects were "probably representatives of the goddess Cinteotl", the maize goddess, and that they acted as patrons of the crops.

[29] Seler-Sachs 1922: 552; pl. 10. [30] Linné 1934: 83; fig. 112. [31] Disselhoff 1939: 303.
[32] Nuttall 1886: 328 seq.; Wardle 1905: 213—216. [33] Duran 1880: 274.

To suppose without further evidence that figurines with movable limbs represented Cinteotl, and that they were used in the way described by Duran, would be rather rash. According to Sahagun, the third annual feast, "the little awakening", took place on the 18th of March.[34] The Julian calendar was ten days behind our era in 1559, when Sahagun had practically finished his work. In addition, the Aztec year had lagged behind by 10 days, counting from the fall of Tenochtitlán, on account of no leap years having been intercalated.[35] As, therefore, planting was done in good time before the rainy season, which begins in the middle of May, the seed was greatly in need of protection both against animals and malevolent powers. There is nothing to prove that the figures represent Cinteotl. They vary, however, between such narrow limits that they may quite well represent one particular deity. Seler and Spence point out that Cinteotl is not a female deity and as a rule the figures carry no female traits.[36] The childish form of the limbs contrast with bodies and heads of no childish character whatever. The hands, which are closed but not clenched, are noteworthy. Cinteotl of the Aztecs carries in one hand the rainstaff and in the other the throwing stick. What his supposed predecessor in Teotihuacan carried in his hands, we do not know. The large figures from Burial 13 have yellow bodies but red-painted faces. Yellow is in Mexican pictures the colour of the dead body, but in Codex Borgia[37] Cinteotl is yellow, while in Codex Aubin he wears a red garment.[38] If the functions of the figurines consisted in the guarding and awakening of the crops, the red colour would undoubtedly have been right and proper, but hardly so the colour of death.

The shapes in which the pottery occurs are in relation to the number of vessels comparatively few. Domestic pottery is rather rare and of cooking vessels only some few fragments were recovered. Most of the vessels from Burial 1, as well as the miniature vessels from other graves and Cache 2, seem principally suited to medicine men with magical or real practice. Among mortuary offerings some types are comparatively rare. A form as specific as that seen in fig. 211 occurs in Utatlan and Zacualpa, Guatemala, and in Copan.[39] Vessels with a spout are, in contradistinction to the rest of America, comparatively common in Mexico. The tall-necked vases of Burial 1, figs. 214—215, have their counterparts among the Mixtecs[40] and at Monte Alban.[41]

The cylindrical tripod vases mounted on rectangular or cylindrical legs and sometimes provided with slightly conical lids are most characteristic of all Teotihuacan pottery types. The walls are frequently decorated with a frieze of mould-made heads or round buttons immediately above the feet. Otherwise the ornamentation varies, as already mentioned. The type is of sparse occurrence in the Mixtec and Zapotec regions but is more common, in a more or less varied form,

[34] Seler 1927: 77. [35] Seler 1902: 181. [36] Spence 1923: 178. [37] Seler 1904—1909, vol. 1: 224, 241, vol. 2: p. 52. [38] Seler 1902: 147. [39] Lothrop 1936: 80; fig. 75. [40] Museo Nacional, Mexico City. [41] Caso 1932: fig. 52 c, 1935: figs. 48, 52, 1938: fig. 29.

among the Maya. It would undoubtedly be interesting to study this vessel type among the latter, its appearance in time and space, and the variations of its ornamentation in style and technique. Thompson has encountered tripod cylindrical vases at San José, British Honduras. He draws attention to their resemblance to their Teotihuacan counterparts. He also mentions us that similar finds have been made "in Uaxactun II and also on an apparently contemporaneous horizon at Kaminaljuyu, Guatemala ... San Jose sherds are certainly not of Teotihuacan origin, but the presence of cryptocrystalline calcite and dolomite tempering indicates importation. Whether the Maya area influenced Teotihuacan or vice versa, or whether a third area was the source of inspiration for both cannot at present be determined." When cylindrical vases appear during San José II and Uaxactun II, important chronological data concerning Teotihuacan are obtained. According to Thompson's two tables "Peten ceramic sequence", San José II covers the period 435—633, or 577—853, A. D., dependent upon which of two correlations he has used for this outline of Maya history.[42] Vaillant is of opinion that Uaxactun II ended even before 600 A. D.[43] and Caso agrees with Thompson's first table.[44]

In Burial 3 was discovered an effigy vessel consisting of two parts, fig. 197. The lower section is provided with human legs, the upper with arms in relief. The head, which is hollow and has its mouth open, is stuck on over a perforation made in the upper section of the urn. The ware is of the same kind as in the typical Teotihuacan ceramics. Peñafiel depicts a similar vessel from Teotihuacan, but the inferior quality of the reproduction forbids any detailed comparison.[45] A certain family likeness may be noted between effigy vessels from Calipan in Puebla[46] and those from Teotitlán del Camino in Oaxaca.[47] The peculiar pose of the hands is identical and constitutes a connecting link. There also exists a very distant relation from San José.[48] Archaeological finds from the district of Santa Cruz Quiché and Kaminaljuyú in the highland of Guatemala are, however, much more closely allied to fig. 197. In the latter case the resemblance is striking. But this effigy urn is of exquisite workmanship and richly ornamented, evidently the work of an eminent artist, and alongside of it our specimen looks like a rather poor country cousin. Pictures of this figurine in the Illustrated London News are accompanied by the following interesting remarks: "The specimen in question is archaeologically important as it almost duplicates pots from the tombs at Uaxactun" ... "It is with the objects representing the Early Old Empire stage at Uaxactun (perhaps about 200 A. D.) that the Kaminaljuyu artefacts have the closest correspondence."[51]

Both from the instances cited above and from others that will be brought forward

[42] Thompson 1939: 93—94, 224—225; figs. 40, 43, 93; tables 17—18.   [43] Vaillant 1935: table 3.
[44] Sociedad Mexicana de Antropología, Boletín No. 1. Primera sesión de la Mesa Redonda sobre problemas antropológicos Mexicanos y Centroamericanos (del 11 al 14 de julio de 1941). Table, p. 9.
[45] Peñafiel 1900: pl. 20.   [46] Noguera 1940: pls. 5—6.   [47] Seler 1895: pl. 13; Danzel 1923: pls. 61—62.
[48] Thompson 1939: pl. 17.   [49] Lothrop 1936: fig. 88.   [50] Kidder 1936: fig. 2.
[51] Sept. 11, 1937, p. 437 and Aug. 29, 1936, p. 359.

Fig. 315. Mask belonging to incensario recovered from Burial 1.
(¹/₃) 35. 8. 2383.

in the following, it will be seen that communication with the Maya existed. Whether Teotihuacan was the donor or the recipient is uncertain. In the case just referred to, it appears as if an attenuate culture wave had reached it from the south, but when it comes to the tripods, the reverse seems more likely to have taken place. As to methods of ornamentation, it may not be impossible that in both regions development has independently produced similar results. In addition, some third region — as yet unknown to us — a contributor to them both, may perhaps have to be taken into account. The comparative material is still all too scanty, but when the extremely important researches at Kaminaljuyú have been published, one may hope that momentous questions regarding the relations of the Teotihuacan culture to the Maya will come nearer their solution, and·a great step be taken towards the dating of Teotihuacan.

Incensarios.

In Cache 1 was discovered a complete incensario, though it had been taken to pieces, and in Burial 1 many parts of another one were found (pp. 142 and 132). In many places below the floors these objects were met with in a more or less damaged condition and always incomplete. Fragments of them were to be seen almost everywhere, both below and above the floors.

Judging by the finds in Cache 1 and Burial 1, these objects consisted of a bottom part composed of two rough bowls and an earthenware tube. One of the bowls was placed upside down on top of the other, and the tube was projecting upwards from a hole in the bottom of the former. On the upper bowl and in front of the

171

tube an altar-like arrangement was built up around a large face-mask. Figs. 316—317 show the incensario found in Burial 1, reconstructed as far as we have believed ourselves capable of doing without unduly drawing upon our imagination. For practical reasons the bottom bowl has been left out. The various parts were lying all mixed up together and largely broken to pieces. The bowls, the tube and the mask are of comparatively good material, but plaques and ornamental details are exceedingly brittle. The parts had once been loosely fitted together by means of a yellowish kind of clay. It is probable that some perishable material also was used because — among other things — two large plaques have defied all attempts at restoring them to their proper position. To guide us in the reassembling work we had the marks from the cementing substance. The entire object had further been coated with thinly fluid white paint, and as that had been applied in its fully assembled state, unpainted surfaces indicated the original position of certain details. Unfortunately this incensario is, technically as well as artistically, the poorest of all that we found. It was only on the mask that any particularly elaborate painting had been bestowed. Over the white ground had been laid a yellowish-grey tint and a face-painting consisting of a row of yellow circles reaching from the mouth to the cheek-bones, and from there across the face and nose, cf. fig. 315 and pl. 3. The face, as will be seen, is adorned with a large panache fitted to the forehead, large ear-plugs and a large nose-ornament.

More or less complete incensarios were found below the second floor in rooms 6, 42, 47, and beneath the earliest floor in 3, 7 and 16. Below the undermost floor of room 1 four incensarios were discovered in hollows in the filling. Bowls and tubes were absent, and all other parts — not including the masks — were badly damaged. They had evidently been deposited immediately before the moulding of the floor. They were embedded in ashes and surrounded by considerable quantities of yellowish clay. In some cases were found bits of charcoal and remains of charred textiles. Three of them had been placed together in east-to-west orientation. The predominant colours of the decoration of the masks were, counted from the east, red, green, white. North of them lay the fourth one, which was decorated in white and green. It is possible that the colours bore symbolic significance, but speculations coordinating them with the face-painting of the Aztec gods would no doubt be unsafe. Lehmann, who has given much attention to directional symbolism considers that colours played an important part in this respect, and Sahagun relates that Quetzalcoatl is reported to have had devotional chambers in the four points of the compass, north, east, south and west, and that they were coloured red, yellow, white, and green, respectively.[52] Shellhas points out that the Maya connected the four cardinal points with each of four colours, and that yellow denoted air, red signified fire, white stood for water, and black for earth.[53] Blue or green symbolized water or rain, and was also the colour of

[52] Cf. Sahagun 1927: 269, 1938, vol. 3: 110; Lehmann 1933: 82, 1939: 50.   [53] Schellhas 1904: 17.

Figs. 316—317. Incensario from Burial 1, partly reconstructed. Height 60 cm. 35. 8. 2383.

the mountain gods of the Aztecs, while red was the colour of the maize goddess and the young maize sprouts. To the conceptional world of the Teotihuacan culture we possess few guides. Codices and chroniclers do not help us much, and thoughts and ideas roused by the material objects generally evade being laid by the heels.

The different specimens differ from each other as regards details, but all of them appear to have been constructed like the one of Burial 1. The decorative details have largely been manufactured in moulds. To a large extent they undoubtedly possessed symbolic significance, and some, such as birds and flowers, have proved capable of identification, while others were of abstract purport.[54] Some were star-shaped, and then frequently with a circular depression in the centre, in which had been fastened round plates of mica of the same kind and size as those recovered from the graves. Some of the incensarios must have been rather fantastic creations, and their makers must have been virtuosos, for whom no manual difficulties existed. It would seem as if in this realm the pottery artists have given free rein to their imagination which they had to curb in the case of the ritual clay vessels, with their standardized shapes and sparing decoration. Both the decorative details and the masks had been painted in different colours, often astonishingly well preserved. To these interesting objects we hope to have an opportunity to recur in a special monograph, but as certain of the colours are not permanent, some details have already been reproduced in colour. Some masks, probably mouldmade, are here

[54] Cf. Linné 1941: fig. 6.

173

seen in pls. 3—5. On them greater care has been expended in manufacture, finish and painting, and the material is often of better quality. As will be seen, they are very much alike, and, though they can hardly be called realistic, give a fairly good representation of the racial character, and bear the cast of callousness and serene composure. The eyes are either depressions with painted iris, or openings in which small finely polished plates of pyrites have been fixed by means of the yellowish clay (pl. 3). The majority of the masks have a large nose-ornament, which is either unattached, fig. 315, or attached to the mouth, pls. 4 and 5.

That the objects here being dealt with served as incense burners is possible, though far from certain. The two bowls and the tube speak in favour of the supposition, and so do the ashes and the charcoal that we found associated with them. Gamio found charcoal even in the objects recovered by him that are referred to below. There is ample scope for conjectures, for beyond conjectures we cannot get for the present. By some sort of name they must be known and we have here used for the generally accepted appellation. For their supposed employment they must have been exceedingly unpractical. Lifting off the upper bowl, along with the flimsily constructed and very fragile "altar", must at all events have been a thicklish process. The absence of vent-holes also argues against the incense burner theory.

Only some few incensarios have been depicted, and to my knowledge none whose construction one can be quite sure of. Gamio, however, has by word and illustration related how, in 1911, he found two "braseros rituales" in situ in pre-Spanish building remains in Santa Lucía, at Azcapotzalco.[55] The upper part resembles figs. 316—317, but in one specimen the tube is replaced by an elongated, conical projection of the upper bowl. The bottom section is of hour-glass shape, the lower bowl in our figure being replaced by two bowls set bottom to bottom. Arrangements of this kind were apparently unknown in Tlamimilolpa. It is astonishing how it was possible to deposit objects of such fragility in the filling of the floors that had been moulded on top of them without getting them broken to pieces. This interesting find has also been published by Mena, accompanied by remarkable, and highly subjective, determinations as to what deities are represented by the masks and appurtenant equipment.[56] Beyer has ventured to doubt that all the parts have been correctly placed in the reconstruction done at the museum, and in addition that in one case the "altar" has been built up from parts of at least two incensarios.[57] But as there have been recovered incensarios lacking both bowls and tubes, it appears possible that such parts were collected and that new combinations were constructed with what material there was at hand. The fragile material, and the anything but stable setting up of these objects, seem to indicate that they used to be put together for more or less temporary use.

These incensarios are typical of the Teotihuacan culture. With the sparse

[55] Gamio 1922, tomo 1, vol. 1: 196—200; pls. 114—117. [56] Mena 1914: 329—333. [57] Beyer 1922: 283—289.

Figs. 318—319. Pottery vessels, trade ware. Purchased from local inhabitants. (²/₃) 35.8.2510 and 2511.

material that is in existence it is not yet possible to point to any progressive development from simpler forms. Like its characteristic pottery, incensarios appear to be exponents of the peculiar, by leaps and bounds progressing, explosive development of this culture. Searching for their origin elsewhere does not offer much encouragement. A certain affinity to the Zapotecan funerary urns is traceable, and among both peoples the artists worked with a very high degree of technical skill. A more remote resemblance is met with in the incense burners of the Maya that have a figure posing in front of the vessel itself, and more or less combined with it. Closer kinship is, however, presented by the incense burners of the Guatemalan highland that consist of an hour-glass-shaped bottom section and a lid with a seated figure on top of it.[58] The bottom sections are strikingly similar to those of Gamio's find. The hollow figure on one found at Kaminaljuyú has details closely allied to corresponding parts of our incensarios and it serves the same purpose as the tube. Here one is no doubt justified in pointing to a link with Teotihuacan. Threads connecting Teotihuacan with the highland of Guatemala have already been emphasized in the foregoing. If so be that the notion was imported into Teotihuacan, the naturalistic figure was broken up and reduced to a mere coulisse. The fact is that the Teotihuacan artists appear to have had a definite aversion against any realistic representation of the human body.

Trade pottery.

During its golden age Teotihuacan maintained widely extended trading connections, and of this also the Tlamimilolpa pottery bears witness. A large proportion of clay vessels and potsherds differ entirely from the products of the native industrial artists, which are in a class by themselves both in form and material and in the style and technique of their decoration. Whether the fairly primitive vessels, ornamented with simple linear engravings, that were for the most part recovered

[58] Dieseldorff 1933, vol. 3: figs. 130—131; Kidder 1936: fig. 6; Lothrop 1936: fig. 101.

from Burial 1, figs. 205—210 and 212, are to be regarded as being entitled to right of domicile, I cannot say for certain. Only reasonably authentic examples of trade pottery will here be presented, as in many cases nothing short of comparative studies in well-stocked foreign museums will yield definite information as to origin. The pottery from the Mazapan culture and from the Aztec era has as before-mentioned been left out.

Already in connection with the archaeological finds from Chalchicomula and Calpulalpan I stated my conviction that the yellowish-red pottery was not native of the Teotihuacan culture area, but imported goods. In Chalchicomula it was fairly numerously represented though unaccompanied by the typical Teotihuacan pottery, while in the Calpulalpan district it was present everywhere, cf. pp. 37 and 78 —79. The yellowish-red ware — Vaillant's "thin orange", called "eggshell orange" by Longyear — occurs in extremely varied forms, but preponderant in numbers are bowls of the type seen in fig. 299. In these, both shape and ornamentation varies within an extremely narrow margin. The main part of the finds from the localities referred to above consisted of bowls of this type. In Burial 1 were found fragments of a vessel which unfortunately was not capable of reconstruction, and in Burials 2 and 13 there were, respectively, three bowls and a single one. Beside this standardized type there are vessel forms presenting most amazing contrasts with the Teotihuacan potters' products, with their strict adherence to tradition and scantiness of variety. The ornamentation is generally of a distinct character. The ware is of a very superior quality, and it has therefore been possible to make the vessels very thin. Fragments of two small vessels of undeterminable shape are no thicker than up to 1.5 mm. In the manufacture of decorative details, stamps and moulds have often been employed. Painting on coated ground occurs in fragments found in the bottom stratum of room 60, although it may quite possibly have been laid on long after the manufacture. It is also worthy of note that an incomparably greater proportion of perforations from mendings by the "crack-lacing" method occur in this class of pottery. This suggests a certain difficulty when it came to replenishing supplies.

Vaillant demurs to my theory, stated in 1934, that the yellowish-red ware was an imported article. "It would be far more probable that the clay was extracted from some non-volcanic formation in or near the Valley and the vessels manu- factured in various Teotihuacan sites, so that the ware would thus be in style and occurrence a purely Teotihuacan trait."[59] Nevertheless, I adhere to my supposition.

The petrographic analysis that in 1934 was carried out by Dr. Gunnar Beskow, and showed that the material of the yellowish-red pottery fundamentally differed from that of typical Teotihuacan tripod vessels, has been continued.[60] This work has unfortunately not yet been concluded, but on some future occasion I hope to publish the definite results. Preliminary examination reveals that the material of

[59] American Anthropologist, n. s. vol. 37, 1935, p. 505.   [60] Linné 1934: 213—214.

176

fragments from Chalchicomula and Calpulalpan corresponds to that previously analyzed from Teotihuacan. Fresh samples from there are producing similar results. Among the Kaminaljuyú finds there are bowls which in colour as well as appearance are similar to those of Teotihuacan. Miss Anna O. Shephard has examined them, and in a letter of February 20th 1941 states that the material differs from Beskow's analysis of 1934. As the latter has been checked up and been found to agree with the later ones, it is evident that there must have existed different manufacturing centres for export to Kaminaljuyú, and to Chalchicomula, Calpulalpan and Teotihuacan. That this specific pottery should have been manufactured within a large, hitherto unknown region by the same methods, and influenced by the same esthetic conception, but with varying material, is of course possible. But perhaps the potters changed their locality, or were moved from one place to another. Thus it may be that perambulation within certain limits should also be taken into account. From the Peruvian coast it is related that in 1889 potters wandered long distances, and in places where the clay was good, and profitable business expected, they would stay for a time. Their methods were very archaic.[61]

At Xolalpan were recovered fragments of a tripod vessel with carved ornamentation of Totonac character. Beskow found that the clay greatly differed from that of the material handed him for comparison, a typical Teotihuacan tripod vase which was all that could be desired as regards being of local manufacture.[62] But, although not from the Valley of Mexico, the first-mentioned vessel had not either come from any locality near the one from which the material of the yellowish-red ware had been taken. The same probably applies to a good many Tlamimilolpan finds, as well as to a vessel acquired by purchase, fig. 177. This is heavy and massive, and lacking the swing and elegance of the typical tripods, lent to them by their gently curving sides, as compare the simple and technically rather poor vessel, fig. 189. The ornamentation is of a typically Totonac style.

Of the same hard, yellow ware is a vase from Burial 13, figs. 274—275. It is damaged, but of the ornamented portion there was only missing a small fragment in the top right corner in fig. 275. The edge carries traces of green paint, but the rest of the decoration has been carved out of, or engraved in, the freshly made vessel while still soft. A number of fine lines have, however, been applied after it had dried. In places the instrument used has scored the surface, and the lines are nowhere flanked by slightly raised ridges. Certain excised portions being more than 3 mm deep, a good shading effect has been attained. The motive consisting of serpent's teeth, tongues and feathers, is suggestive of a Quetzalcoatl representation, but hardly presenting any links with the art of Teotihuacan. Its form is foreign to the Central Mexican highland, but typical of the Central American Pacific coast. Vessels of a similar shape occur, however, on the Atlantic coast of Mexico, from which locality I am most inclined to believe that the vessel in'

[61] Brüning 1898: 259.   [62] Linné 1934: figs. 117, resp. 21; 213—214.

question originates, and in the Maya region. In Ticul, Charnay acquired a vase which both in shape and decoration exhibits a strong family-likeness.[63] It is possible that both of them originate from the same exporting centre. From El Carmen, in Campeche, an intermediate locality, comes a specimen of similar shape.[64]

It ought to be mentioned that this vase quite possibly was not recovered from Burial 13 but may have been added to the collection by the owner of Tlamimilolpa. If so, his object was to provide us with a stronger inducement to decide upon the excavations we subsequently carried out at this spot. Unlike all other broken artifacts recovered from Grave 13, its missing parts proved impossible to find in spite of our energetic search of the place where it was alleged to have been found, cf. p. 139.

Among the numerous fragments of imported pottery may be noted that of Coyotlatelco. Some are almost identical with examples depicted by Tozzer,[65] while others differ from those published by him and by Noguera, fig. 327. All of them were recovered above the floors, and Noguera emphasizes that pottery of this type survived into Aztec times.[66] Two small vessels, figs. 318—319, were purchased from local inhabitants. They were stated to have been discovered in the ruins of a house beneath a field in the adjoining section of the village of San Martín. Material and ornamentation seem to indicate Cholula as their place of origin. As in the case of fig. 332 this is, however, by no means certain. A large number of pottery fragments are nevertheless more justly ascribable to that important centre of export, or to Tlaxcala. One of these is here depicted, fig. 330.

Many fragments speak a plainer language. The majority of them come from the Totonac district, figs. 322—324, 326, and the ceramic art of the Huaxtecs is also well represented, fig. 325. With the possible exception of the first-mentioned, all are above-floor finds. From Oaxaca we have strangely enough no sure representative, but parts of an incense burner, with gleaming black surface and polychrome decoration, bear witness of connections with the Mixtec area. These, too, were recovered above the floors. The most northern importations came from Michoacán, and those from farthest away were from the Maya. Fragments were recovered of four Maya vessels: one below the bottom floor of room 16, next to Burial 1, and another below the bottom floor of room 21, figs. 328—329 and 331, respectively, cf. pl. 2. The rest were from parts of the ruin that had been demolished. These fragments are of outstanding interest. Of this find Vaillant, who himself had the opportunity of studying it, gives the following classification: ... "trade sherds of Peten Maya type corresponding to the Uaxactun II—Holmul II-IV tradition".[67]

It should be added that only two fragments of plumbate ware were recovered, both above the floors. Their presence is not very surprising, as this peculiar pottery

[63] Charnay 1885: 319, 1887: 375; Hamy 1897, vol. 1: pl. 27.

[64] Reseña de la segunda sesión del 17 Congreso Internacional de Americanistas, México 1912; Maler's plates, III: 5.   [65] Tozzer 1921: pls. 18—19.   [66] Noguera 1935 a: 160.   [67] Vaillant 1938: 543.

Figs. 320—332. Fragments of trade pottery. (Ca. 1/2)
320: 35. 8. 1305; 321: 742; 322—323: 759 (outer and inner surfaces).
324: 35. 8. 618; 325: 605; 326: 484; 327: 685.
328—329: 35. 8. 2501 (outer and inner surfaces); 330: 709.
331: 35. 8. 185; 332: 708 (outer surfaces).

"is the most widely dispersed pottery now known in Mexico and Central America, while the period during which it was manufactured must extend back of the Spanish Conquest by at least 700 years".[68]

It is strikingly evident that imported pottery has only to a very small extent influenced the native art. But this appears generally to have been the case in ancient America. It may, however, be that future research will modify this view. Tradition must have been very strong in Teotihuacan, as might have been expected in view of the powerfully theocratic government of the state. And it is even possible that an important part was played — if not by national self-sufficiency — at any rate by a lingering aversion to, and distrust of, anything that was "foreign".

[68] Lothrop 1933: 97.

179

RECAPITULATION OF RESULTS

An extensive building from the classic period of Teotihuacan was partly excavated at Tlamimilolpa, east of the church of San Francisco Mazapan. The uncovered portion of the ruin occupied an area of more than 3,500 m² and comprised 176 rooms, 21 forecourts, 5 courtyards and numerous alleys. On two occasions the part of the complex that was subjected to a thorough examination had been radically rebuilt. For this, no practical reason could be discovered. The remains of the three sets of buildings that had been erected one above the other gave no evidence of any development as regards planning or technical methods. The rooms were grouped together in fairly small "tenements". Many tenements in the centre were not interconnected, and could only have been reached by means of entrances situated in different directions. A well-built system of drains, technical building details, mural paintings, etc., bore witness of a highly developed habitation culture. The layout does not convey the impression of having been the residence of a single person of rank, but more likely the quarters of the functionaries of the temple city, lodgings for pilgrims, or something in that line.

A large number of artifacts were collected. The earth stratum above the ruin contained great quantities of Aztec potsherds, but, on the other hand, the Mazapan culture was but poorly represented. Below the floors were discovered 13 burials and 3 caches. The earliest burial differed from the rest in that the deceased had been burnt in the grave itself. More than 1,200 objects, including charred remains of textiles, baskets and bark-cloth, were found in this grave. The mortuary offerings in the rest of the burials are much of the same character. This indicates short time-spans for the different building periods.

The stone objects consist of tools, fragments of sculptures, specimens of stone-cutter's work for technical use in building, a vessel of tecali, etc. Ornaments are few and those of jadeite are rare. Objects made of obsidian include numerous knives and points for arrows and spears, and eccentric objects with direct counterparts among the Maya. A slab of iron pyrite may have been a mirror. It is exceedingly weathered and has the appearance of rusty iron.

A small quantity of needles, bodkins, and other bone implements were recovered. Of these, the most interesting is a sucking or drinking tube. Worthy of remark is the presence of a whale bone. The mollusc material is abundant. One-half of the species originate from the Pacific Ocean and the rest from the Atlantic. Only one freshwater species was represented.

The textile fragments reveal that fibre of agave and cotton had been in use and supply valuable information about the thickness, structure and general appearance of the original cloths. Those made of cotton give an impression of a highly developed art of spinning and weaving. Most of the fragments come from loosely-woven cloth of bast fibres of varying thickness, but even more complicated techniques had been in use. The basket fragments show two variations of the coiled basketry technique. The bark paper fragments are too small to convey any information as to the character of the original objects.

Except for the "al secco" technique, painting played a minor part in the ornamentation of clay vessels. Between this kind of painting and pottery carved after firing there exists a connection. The decoration is frequently of a similar hieroglyph-resembling character, and may possibly have been executed by learned priests on pottery vessels manufactured by laymen. Pottery objects incised before firing were numerically predominant. Carving after firing, a decorative technique typical of Teotihuacan, is but poorly represented.

Moulds and stamps were in frequent use. Figurines display a pantheon of great variety. Here are included deities that bear an outer resemblance to Ueueteotl, Tlaloc and possible also Xipe, of the Aztecs. From the Totonacs had perhaps been imported, or to them exported, the oft-represented Fat God, who did not survive the Teotihuacan culture.

One complete, and one almost complete, "incensario", as well as a considerable number of fragments of these objects were recovered. The former was left behind in Mexico, but the latter has partly been capable of restoration. The masks appertaining to the incensarios are beautiful of shape and richly painted and occasionally provided with eyes made from pieces of iron pyrite.

A considerable number of potsherds tell a tale of far-flung commercial relations. For example, pottery was imported from the Totonacs, Huaxtecs and Mixtecs, from Cholula and Michoacán, and from Peten Maya. Lack of comparative material has so far rendered impossible any determination of the origin of other trade objects. The yellowish-red ware seems in all possible probability to have been imported. Vessels of apparently similar material and of corresponding shape have been recovered at Kaminaljuyú close to Guatemala City. They would not, however, seem to have been manufactured within the same region as this type of ceramics from Teotihuacan, Calpulalpan and Chalchicomula.

Certain pottery vessels recovered in the graves belong to types of less frequent occurrence. These are also found in Oaxaca, in the Guatemalan highland and in Copan. An effigy urn has a near counterpart in Kaminaljuyú. The tripod vessel that is so wholly characteristic of Teotihuacan also occurs in the highland of Guatemala and on the slopes towards the Pacific coast, in Copan, in Uaxactun and other ancient cities in the Peten district and in British Honduras. Archaeological finds in San José reveal the existence of an evident connection with classical Teotihuacan. Similar finds are made in Uaxactun II and in the contemporaneous horizon at Kaminaljuyú. San José II and Uaxactun II are by Thompson dated to 435—633 A. D. To interconnection with Teotihuacan, I shall recur in the following. The latest literature dealing with these problems only reached me after the preceding chapter had been sent to be printed.

PART IV

GENERAL SUMMARY AND CONCLUSIONS

The Ethnographical Museum of Sweden's expedition in 1932 confined its activities to Teotihuacan. For various reasons we thought the best purpose would be served by a continued exploration of the Teotihuacan culture during this second expedition. In this respect our reconnaissance of the Chalchicomula district proved disappointing, as it yielded a negative result. At our short visit in the surroundings of Calpulalpan, on the other hand, we encountered material of great interest for the principal object of our work. In Teotihuacan we were again favoured by fortune. Our labours at that place have resulted in no inconsiderable contribution to our knowledge of the life of its inhabitants during that ancient city's period of greatness. The most important results of the researches made in the Chalchicomula district, at Calpulalpan, and in Teotihuacan have been epitomized in the foregoing, pp. 55, 89—90, and 180—181. The material has also been comparatively dealt with, pp. 48—54, 77—88, and 144—179.

Origin of the Teotihuacan culture.

One feature is possessed in common by the American high cultures, viz. that of successive development never yet having been capable of being followed from a modest beginning. It would appear as if in this case there existed no laws for the rise, high tide and decline in the development of the Indian cultures, or for the history of their development. For want of some better explanation, the reason for this is usually said to be that, generally speaking, archaeological research in America only began some way into the present century. That much is, however, evident that there is no question of radiation from any single centre, but radiation from a number of directions by variously developed elements, and that certain peoples absorbed more than others. Certain peoples appear to have been gifted not only with the power of creating culture but also, in a higher degree than others, of its assimilation.

It seems as if the roots and the initial development of the Teotihuacan culture are not to be found in Teotihuacan. This is shown by Noguera in an exceedingly important work which deals with the material that was obtained when, in 1933, a tunnel was excavated through the Sun Pyramid.[1] In the adobe, of which the pyramid was constructed, artifacts from the earlier inhabitants of Teotihuacan were found. These artifacts do not represent a stage preceding the later classical Teotihuacan culture, but there are certain other points of contact in existence. This earlier culture, Teotihuacan I, possesses elements in common with the last of the Early Cultures that Vaillant calls Cuicuilco-Ticoman, and also no doubt was contemporaneous with it. Apart from elements of which the origin has not yet been capable of identification, it is closely akin to the cultures that flourished in Michoacán, Jalisco and Guanajuato.[2] Teotihuacan I occupied almost the same level of development as the Cuicuilco-Ticoman culture, of which there were offshoots in the Chalchicomula district. A similar or identical culture is found in the most ancient strata below the pyramid of Cholula. If Teotihuacan I built "pyramids" like the teteles of Chalchicomula, these must have been entirely absorbed by the gigantic architectural achievements of the following epoch.

A wide gap exists between Teotihuacan I and the epoch next following it, Teotihuacan II, at any rate if we may judge from the pottery. Apparently another people had taken possession of the place. This people, whose culture had evidently already been fully developed, has been named Toltecs, a term which has brought about a great deal of confusion. A clear course of development can in certain respects be made out during the following periods, Teotihuacan III and IV, with possibly yet another added, but the culture had immediately come out in full blossom. Its largest city and religious centre probably was Teotihuacan, but it spread over certain parts of Central Mexico[3] and maintained connection with cultured peoples of the surrounding regions. The closest correspondence, at any rate as regards pottery, is strangely enough found in the highlands of Guatemala. There are good reasons for hoping that the explorations of the great archaeological site of Kaminaljuyú in the outskirts of Guatemala City may also throw light on the history of Teotihuacan. A part of that site, Miraflores, has given the name to a culture, Archaic-Miraflores, "from which, it now appears, must have come the basic elements common to both Teotihuacan and Old Empire Maya".[4] To the Toltec question and the foreign connections of Teotihuacan, I shall recur in the following.

People, language and culture.

Of the people that erected the temple pyramids of Teotihuacan we know but little. The chroniclers' records of the "Toltecs'" knowledge and conceptions, social

[1] Noguera 1935.
[2] Vaillant 1932: 488, 1938: 541—542, 1940: 299; Vaillant and Vaillant 1934: 120, 124—125; Cf. Lehmann 1921: 13, 14, 17. [3] Noguera 1932: the map. [4] Kidder 1940: 122.

organization and political conditions, are of slight value. They have, for one thing, hardly any connection with the peoples of the Teotihuacan culture and, for another, those peoples lived so long before the days of the Aztec informants that no actual facts are likely to have been preserved by tradition — even if the latter actually referred to the people in question.

Although, at all events in certain cases, a fairly complete picture might be composed — like a piece of mosaic — it would never amount to a monograph like Krickeberg's great work on the Totonacs. An imposing but not easily surveyable material has, however, been brought together in the monograph on the nature and culture of the Teotihuacan valley that has been published under the editorship of Gamio.[5]

Physical anthropology has shown that the inhabitants were brachycephalic and that they practised cranial deformation.[6] Unfortunately the skeletal material brought back by us has not yet been subjected to detailed scientific examination. The majority, though not all, of the skulls are artificially deformed of the fronto-occipital variety, cf. one skull from Chalchicomula, fig. 96. These people had good teeth, though often strongly worn down, probably by the stone powder rubbed off the metate in the grinding of the daily maize. Caries of the teeth is of rare occurrence. The fact of these people having been brachycephalic is remarkable, seeing that both the Basket-makers of Coahuila, the pyramid-builders of Cuicuilco in the Valley of Mexico, the Otomí and the Aztecs were dolicocephalic and did not deform their skulls. The peoples of the Atlantic coast, on the other hand, possessed precisely these distinctive anthropological features.[7] This may indicate that the new possessors of Teotihuacan came from the east, while the earlier ethnical stratum, Teotihuacan I, was of a westerly orientation. But it may on the other hand be possible that both the Totonacs of the coast and the people of the Teotihuacan culture had a common origin.

As regards their language, Lehmann asserts that they spoke an archaic form of the Nahuatlan languages, Nahuat, belonging to the Utaztecan, or Uto-Aztecan, stock.[8] While the languages belonging to the Aztec group had the phoneme *tl*, in Nahuat, *t* was used in its place.[9] If Lehmann is correct as to this, which Mason appears rather inclined to believe, linguistic evidence runs in direct opposition to anthropological evidence regarding the home of this people.

Certain aspects of the culture is capable of reconstruction. The spiritual side of it has almost entirely vanished away, but images of gods, ritual objects, hieroglyph-resembling ornaments, etc., afford indirect information. A cautious use of the earliest chroniclers' descriptions of the Aztecs' religious conceptions and ceremonies may perhaps yield some measure of material. The material culture is more easily reconstructed. In this, ethnographical studies are our best and surest help.[10] The

[5] Gamio 1922.   [6] Hrdlička 1912: 5—6.   [7] Seler 1915: 441—442; Krickeberg 1925: 53, 1937: 217.
[8] Lehmann 1920, vol. 2: 978 seq.   [9] Mason 1940: 69.   [10] Cf. Montell 1936, 1936 a: 60—66, 1937: 301—318.

maize is planted and harvested by means of the same rude implements as to this day among Otomí Indians west of the Valley of Mexico. The metate still remains indispensable in the Mexican cuisine. Now, as anciently, pulque is still being prepared. The manufacture of pottery is in outlying districts carried on exactly in the ancient way, though the products are crude and today only serving practical purposes. Certain specific types, such as the so-called "shoe vessels", are still being used, at all events in certain parts of Oaxaca. Paper is manufactured among the Otomí by methods of extreme antiquity, and used for religious purposes. The bark-beaters of stone that are still in use, are exact counterparts of the archaeological finds. The women weavers of Teotihuacan undoubtedly worked with implements of roughly the same nature as to this day are used by Otomí women in the neighbourhood of the Valley, among whom are still in use garments represented on the clay figurines of Teotihuacan. In these parts even today the natives use agave fibre in textile manufacture, a material also formerly used in Teotihuacan, and stone implements employed in the preparation are here archaeologically recovered. Spindle-whorls picked up in the fields are occasionally still doing service in villages in the Valley of Mexico. The sandals that are worn today are also of archaic type, although the soles may have been cut out of discarded motor tyres. Baskets, satchels and mats of the same kinds as were used by inhabitants of Teotihuacan, are to this day being marketed in the modern equivalent of the ancient city. Yaqui Indians from Sonora are drawn together in regiments, one of which was at the time of our Mexican sojourn quartered at Tlaxcala. They have retained a great deal of their ancient customs and practices. Their masked dances are capable of contributing to a certain degree of reanimation, as it were, of the masked figurines of Teotihuacan, and among their primitive musical instruments, the rasping bone is found in the archaeological collections.[11] Of weapons, the spear-thrower still survives, and is used in duck-hunting on Lake Texcoco.[12] In ancient days, the life of the common people was probably much the same as that of the modern peon. More than today it does, however, appear to have marked the contrast between the working-day and the feast-day, the latter having a strongly religious character.

Many of the Teotihuacan huts have been built of stones collected from ancient buildings, the floor often being that of a ruin below the hut. The block of ruins at Tlamimilolpa, 3,500 m² of which were excavated, shows how people of the better classes were housed. These dwellings must be regarded as very good. They were for a certainty never higher than one storey and had no windows. Points of general resemblance with certain old pueblos in south-western U. S. A. undoubtedly exist. Many of the 176 excavated rooms had been provided with a large, rectangular opening in the ceiling for admitting light and air. In the floor there was a corresponding depression for the collection of rainwater. This was carried off

[11] Montell 1938: 145—166. [12] Linné 1937 a: 63—64.

185

by well-built drains, which in some cases could be stopped up so that the water remained in the small basin. The building material for the most part consisted of adobe covered by a thick layer of plaster. The latter, like the floors, was ground smooth and usually painted white. A considerable number of stone implements, i. e. plasterer's floats, that had been used for spreading plaster on floors and walls, were collected. Occasionally the walls were red, yellow, or decorated with simple patterns in red and white, and in some cases embellished with paintings. Various shades of red and blue, as well as plain white, were the only colours used, so far as can be judged from the fragments preserved. Considering that the remains of the walls were but low in height and frequently badly damaged, it may safely be supposed that the decoration of the rooms had originally been much richer than we were able to ascertain.

As regards furniture and fittings, neither the building nor the finds could tell us much. Stone rings built into the wall next to the doors indicated that certain rooms, grouped into "apartment suites" of varying size, could be partitioned off by means of hangings, or the like. Impressions in a lump of clay of a woven mat showed that the petate (Mexican: *petlatl*), to this day in use as a bed-mat, formed part of the furniture. There are metates (*metlatl*) to prove that maize was ground within the building complex, but no kitchen premises could be located anywhere. Only a small number of fragments of cooking vessels were found. The grinding-pan or small mortar, the molcajete (*molcaxitl*) and the griddle, comal (*comalli*), must apparently have been inventions of a later era, although they became, and still remain, indispensable kitchen utensils. The tortilla (*tlaxcalli*), the inevitable griddle-bread, was evidently unknown. Obsidian implements of a certain type indicate, on the other hand, that pulque was a familiar beverage. The objects in question bear close resemblance to the type of iron scraper nowadays in use. There even exists a tradition, more moralizing than founded on fact, laying the blame for the downfall of the "Toltecs" upon over-indulgence in pulque-drinking.

The Tlamimilolpa ruin is probably of a somewhat later date than that of Xolalpan, seeing that in the former the platforms typical of the latter had been built over with constructions of a later period. In addition, the pottery was partly different. For example, carving after firing was very rare, while pottery incised before firing dominated. Of painted decoration, only "al secco" played any appreciable part. Moulds and stamps had been in frequent use in the manufacture of details on clay vessels, spindle-whorls, figurines, etc. Rather interesting among the archaeological finds are a number of large incensarios. They are built up of numerous parts, often manufactured in moulds. Their nearest counterparts are found in the highland of Guatemala.

Interesting, too, is the imported pottery, bearing evidence of lively and far-flung trading connections. But unfortunately it is only in certain cases, as, e. g., importation from the Peten Maya, that these can with certainty have taken place during the time when the building was being occupied. At subsequent periods both the people of the Mazapan culture and the Aztecs had inhabited the area. In association with pottery of the native type, a distinctly different one, the yellowish-red ware, occurs. This may in all certainty be supposed to have been imported. It was also encountered in the Chalchicomula district and in Calpulalpan, as well as having been found in Kaminaljuyú, Guatemala. From petrographic analyses it appears that vessels of yellowish-red ware recovered at Teotihuacan, Calpulalpan, and Chalchicomula originate from the same place, but that those of Kaminaljuyú — in spite of their identity of form — have come from elsewhere.

Obsidian evidently played a part in ancient Mexico similar to steel in our mechanized era. In the working up of this brittle, natural glass, these ancients had attained perfect mastery. Only the knives with triangular point and finely flaked edges that we found in the excavated tetele at Aljojuca reveal great manual skill. Compared with certain knives from Burial 1 in Tlamimilolpa they, however, look almost clumsy. The implements and ornaments of stone are of considerably inferior quality. The scarcity of axes is altogether out of proportion to the extensive work of hewing into shape, e. g., roof-beams, that must have been carried out at Tlamimilolpa. Of interest is the "square knife" of which a few specimens were recovered. Stone knives of an identical type are still in use among Otomí Indians in the preparation of maguey fibre. A circular, much weathered pyrite disk may have been a mirror. It is, however, in such a bad state of preservation that no definite proof of this is possible. Among the bone implements, which comprise bodkins, needles, tools for preparing obsidian, etc., a sucking-tube attracts one's interest. From having been an instrument of practical use among more primitive peoples, it had changed into a magical one, for use by medicine-men or employed in religious ceremonies.

Points of obsidian and of stone, the latter occurring rather sparsely, appear, judging by the varying sizes, to indicate that both spears and bows and arrows had been in use. The clay pellets most probably constituted blow-gun ammunition. This because they have been found to be of a diameter fairly constant in comparison with blow-gun pellets preserved in various ethnographical collections. In Calpulalpan they occurred in numbers that were remarkably large in relation to other artifacts. Their mean diameter is slightly larger than that of clay pellet projectiles that are found among such Central American tribes as are still using blow-guns with this type of ammunition. Studies of blow-guns from South America and the Indo-Malayan archipelago seem to prove that the volume of the tubes varies within very narrow limits. This is no doubt due to the restricted power of human lungs to effect a sudden and violent expulsion of air. On the basis of these studies the length of Teotihuacan and Calpulalpan blow-guns may be estimated at 150—170 cm.

The mode of burial often reveals interesting details relating to the people's attitude towards the eternal problem: life after death. Those interred in the tetele at Aljojuca had been given an unusually meagre equipment in the way of mortuary offerings, at any rate of the kind that withstands corruption. In many cases no offerings at all were to be seen. The dead had been buried in various poses, frequently in a doubled-up position, and as a rule with the face turned towards the centre of the mound. The two graves at Las Colinas, Calpulalpan, had been richly provided with funerary offerings. The deceased who, judging by the locality and their equipment, may have been priests, had been placed at full length. Such, too, was the case at Tlamimilolpa, alternating with the doubled-up position. It is worthy of note that infants of very tender age had been provided with food, and "cutlery sets" for their journey to the kingdom of death. The mere fact of their having been given a proper burial points to a highly developed culture. Early writers relate that the Aztecs practised varying modes of burial, with different ceremonies. Burial 1 at Tlamimilolpa shows that cremation occurred, and that rites were performed at the graveside, at which among other things large quantities of clay vessels were sacrificed, i. e. were broken. In addition, and before the fire was kindled, the deceased had been richly provided with various objects. Judging by their character, he would seem to have been a person versed in magic arts. Totalled up, the mortuary offerings came to upwards of 1,200 objects. Charred remains of baskets, bark-cloth and textiles give us for the first time an idea of the general character of these objects in Teotihuacan, at any rate as regards the last mentioned of the above categories.

As to social and political organization, we are restricted to surmises, some of which are nevertheless founded on rather safe ground. Society appears to have been strongly theocratic and public life highly tinged with religion. The epoch we are concerned with appears to have been peaceful, seeing that both Teotihuacan, Azcapotzalco, Cholula and the cities of the Calpulalpan district must have been planned without any thought having been given to defence against enemies. What weapons, worthy of the name, that have been recovered are few in number. But with man's inborn craving for plaguing his fellows and himself, those in authority seem to have ruled the community with a heavy hand. That those overlords were priests — and later on, possibly, like Quetzalcoatl, priest-kings — is placed beyond any doubt whatever. The building-works of Teotihuacan bear witness of an organization not only strict but also of first-class efficiency. The erection in adobe, without mechanical appliances of any kind, of an edifice like the Sun Pyramid, of a volume approaching one million m³, presupposes peremptory gods and adamantine will in the temporal powers. The numerous temples of Teotihuacan must have required a host of temple servants and priests. Possibly the ruins that we excavated at Tlamimilolpa and previously at Xolalpan had been allotted as dwellings to this staff. The firm hold religion had on the people is reflected in the architecture, art and handicrafts. Whether there had actually existed a kingdom in the strict sense of the word, with Teotihuacan for its capital, may perhaps be doubted. It is more likely to have been a federation of minor urban states mainly united by bonds of religion, language and culture. Indians are as a rule no state-builders, and the empire of the Aztecs was held together by the fear inspired by the formidable armies of that warlike nation.

If the innumerable clay figurines represent gods, Teotihuacan must have possessed an exceedingly populous pantheon. Some of them bear superficial resemblance to the Aztec gods Ueueteotl and Tlaloc. It seems also possible that already at this time Xipe Totec, "Our Lord the Flayed", had entered the Valley of Mexico, from his probable home in Oaxaca. Whether these gods of the old time exercised the same functions as their equivalents had among the Aztecs is uncertain. Both Tlaloc and Ueueteotl are deities of great antiquity. Particularly the former is met with in large parts of Mexico and Middle America and his worship dates back to the Early Cultures. Unique in character, and in his outer aspect genially human, is the Fat God. He also occurs on the Atlantic coast and among the Maya, and Beyer has shown that he is especially frequently represented among the Totonacs and in Teotihuacan. Possibly, however, his home lies in a quite different direction, whence he had been introduced into both those cultures just referred to.

It is possible that a detailed study of the hieroglyph-resembling symbols on clay vessels and other objects would reveal that the priests of Teotihuacan busied themselves with astronomical pursuits.[13] This presupposes some form of writing as well as a knowledge of numerical symbols. Caso takes an optimistic view of this question. It is, however, remarkable that as regards writing they appear to have remained uninfluenced by their contemporary Maya colleagues. It has, it is true, been maintained that they employed the same method for expressing numerals, but this does not, to be at least, seem to have been conclusively proved. The bowl from Calpulalpan that is reproduced in figs. 128, 170—174 appears to bear evidence of the existence of some regular form of writing. Caso has shown that the ceremonial year of 260 days, *tonalpohualli* — erroneously called *tonalamatl* — was in use. That this 260 day period arose among the Maya has been proved by Larsen and Apenes.[14] In selecting sites, the cities appear to have been orientated in relation to mountain peaks. Such is the case in Teotihuacan and in Las Colinas, Calpulalpan. No systems of buildings or "town plans" were orientated to the astronomical north, but the north-south axis always has a deviation of about 17° East. This applies both the temple pyramids, the ruin at Tlamimilolpa and the small, altar-like building at Las Colinas. This orientation, which is characteristic of the Teotihuacan culture, is to be accounted for by the axes being parallel, or at right angles, to a line drawn from the building to the point of the setting of the sun the two days of its annual zenith-passage. The first day, the 18th of May (in leap-years, the 17th), was New Year's Day in the Aztec era, and in all probability had a similar significance in Teotihuacan.

<hr>

[13] Linné 1941: 174—186.   [14] Apenes 1936: 5—8; Larsen 1936: 9—12.

Connections and age of the Teotihuacan culture.

It has been maintained that the Teotihuacan culture owed its development to influences from abroad. But in view of its exceedingly specific character, as evinced by the tangible evidence of its material remains, this appears to be a rather weak explanation. When pottery of types characteristic of Teotihuacan have been encountered in remote localities it has also been suggested that the types in question have proceeded from a third, still unknown, centre. About this, there is a smack of a suspected thief's explanation of having received the goods from a third, unknown, party. Many sensational discoveries of the last decade show, however, that an excessively negative attitude may not be entirely safe, as fresh archaeological finds are capable of overthrowing cautious theories or establishing bold surmises.

During its era of greatness the Teotihuacan culture maintained lively connections in different directions. These were no doubt partly of a commercial character. What there was that could be exported is hard to see as the plateau is rather unproductive, the only natural asset of any consequence being obsidian, which, among other places, was quarried at Cerro del Tepayo, some 20 km east of Teotihuacan. If the city was a resort of pilgrims — as Guadalupe, the northern suburb of Mexico City, became during the colonial era and still remains — it would perhaps explain the presence of objects from remote parts. Among the collections from Tlamimilolpa are found fragments of pottery from the Michoacán, Huaxtec and Totonac districts, from Cholula and the Mixtec region. The importation coming from the most distant point hails from Peten Maya. Judging by the circumstances in which these imported objects were found they appear — excepting those from the Maya — to date from comparatively recent periods. Shells bear witness of connections with both coasts, and from the Pacific even the bone of a whale had been brought. Alien styles were on the whole not adopted. The city and the culture remained true to themselves — were perhaps self-sufficing. If ideas of certain requisites for the cult, such as incensarios, had been imported, they were modified, Teotihuacanized. The only alien stylistic features that are discernible as regards art, originate from the Totonacs.

But just as objects deriving from alien peoples were brought to Teotihuacan, local ones were carried from here to distant parts. At Acapulco, for example, in a shell refuse heap were recovered ceramics of Teotihuacan type.[15] In Colima, Kelly found a restorable vessel of thin orange ware (Teotihuacan III), associated with series of local Colima wares.[16] The same explorer has in excavations at Chametla in Sinaloa, recovered "a trade spindle whorl from Teotihuacán".[17] The cultures in north-western Mexico in later times came into contact with the regions south of the specific area of Teotihuacan culture, the Mixteca-Puebla territory.

[15] Mason 1941: 287.   [16] Mason 1940: 255.   [17] Kelly 1938: 42, 53.

At the time of the Conquest cotton was introduced into the Valley of Mexico from the Pánuco region. The textile fragments from Tlamimilolpa show that even at that time cotton was being used, and it is probable that it was imported from the district just referred to. While excavating at Zacatenco, Vaillant discovered some fragments of textile ware. These, which derive from the earliest archaeological period yet isolated in Mexico, have since been found to consist partly of cotton.[18] Staub's investigations show that objects from the Huaxtec area have marked similarity with Teotihuacan,[19] and Seler, in his day, points out connections in that direction.[20] Tlamimilolpa pottery — apart from direct importations — presents features of Totonacan style, figs. 177 and 274—275. Mural painting in "Los Subterráneos" and "Templo de la Agricultura", near the Pyramid of the Sun, also includes ornaments of Totonacan style. Unfortunately none of the sherds of clay vessels imported from the Huaxtecs or Totonacs were recovered below floors of indubitable intactness in our ruin. The Fat God may have been a Totonacan deity; his sporadic occurrence among the Maya seems to argue in favour of, his great popularity in Teotihuacan against, such a supposition. Beyer, who was the first to point out the Fat God as a link of connection, has moreover drawn attention to a Totonac ritual object possessing decorative details corresponding with a mythological figure known in Teotihuacan.[21] The custom of filing the front teeth was prevalent in the coastland; and the few instances established in area of the Teotihuacan culture provide clear evidence as to its origin.[22] Various kinds of correspondences between Teotihuacan and the Totonacs have been pointed out both by Seler, Krickeberg and other students.[23] Exceedingly remarkable, although palpably incorrect, is Torquemada's statement that in Teotihuacan the Totonacs built two pyramids which, as he says, were dedicated to the sun and the moon.[24] It is, however, obvious that the cultural influence mainly flowed from the coast to the highlands.

At Tehuacan graves have been discovered of Zapotec style. In them were found clay vessels of pure Zapotec type in association with others equally obviously of Teotihuacan origin. Excavations showed, however, that contemporaneous occupation by people of neither one nor the other culture had existed.[25] In Tlamimilolpa were discovered potsherds that were trade ware from the Mixtec area, and clay vessels of a type as specific as the vases seen in figs. 214—215 are also known from that territory. At Yucuñudahui, in the district of Nochixtlán, a grave has been examined from which it is seen that the culture of the ancient Mixtecs had analogies with both Teotihuacan and the Zapotecs.[26]

Prior to the great excavations at Monte Albán there was little material evidence

[18] Vaillant 1939 a: 170.   [19] Staub 1921: 55 seq.., 1921 a: 225, 1926: 12, 21, 1926 a: 290—291, 294, 1935: 35.
[20] Seler 1915: 520—524.   [21] Beyer 1927 a: 269 seq.   [22] Linné 1940: 20—21.
[23] Lehmann 1910: 737; Seler 1915: 438—439, 461, 474, 495, 519, 585; Krickeberg 1918—1922, 1925, 1936: 502, 1937: 216—218; Gamio 1922, tomo 1, vol. 1: 293—295; E. S. Spinden 1933: 225—270.
[24] Torquemada 1723, vol. 1: 278.   [25] Noguera 1940 a: 306—319.   [26] Caso 1938: 47—50; figs. 65—73.

of connections between the Zapotecs and Teotihuacan.[27] On the basis of the material from Calpulalpan one could point to connection between Teotihuacan III and Monte Albán III. Communication with Teotihuacan is best seen from the wall-paintings in grave-chambers Nos. 104—105. Figures known from Teotihuacan, Ahuitzotla and Calpulalpan there appear in association with Zapotecan figures and hieroglyphs, cf. pp. 86—87. It would have been possible for a native artist to execute these paintings only provided he had access to figures painted by a colleague from the Teotihuacan culture area. On the other hand it is hardly possible that any Teotihuacan artist could have been their creator seeing that the hieroglyphs are purely Zapotecan. It may be that more hands than one were in operation. Caso sees in these figures representatives of the Teotihuacan pantheon. As everything points to the deceased having been local personages of power and position, the presence of the alien gods is hard to explain. That the dead in Teotihuacan had been converted to an alien religion does not seem a particularly satisfactory explanation. Perhaps these strange gods constitute evidence of "missionizing" on the part of priests called in from abroad. Medicine-men, the priests of peoples, generally do a great deal of travelling about both within and without the territory occupied by the tribe. During Erland Nordenskiöld's expedition to Panama and Colombia in 1927, a medicine-man of the Chocó tribe accompanied us for a considerable length of time. He had travelled far and wide, and studied under noted specialists. The medicine-men of the Cuna Indians on the Atlantic coast of the Isthmus of Panama thought it a great pity that he had not accompanied the expedition also to their country. This, they considered, might have resulted in a profitable exchange of useful knowledge. Among the Cayapa Indians in the extreme north of Ecuador six medicine-men from the Chocó were living when in 1908—1909 Barrett studied that tribe. They were greatly in request although the Cayapa spoke another language and had a more highly developed culture.[28]

On personal contact, jadeite-inlayed teeth is good evidence. Such teeth had been discovered close to Xolalpan, and were acquired by us by purchase in 1935. They have already been discussed in a special treatise.[29] The practice of decorating the front teeth with inlays of varying substances may be supposed to have originated among the Maya. As dental jewellers they attained mastery. Except for Monte Albán and its surroundings, authenticated instances are few outside the Maya region. Just as we do not train dentists by correspondence, neither did the Indians learn by hearsay the art of inlaying teeth with jadeite. Either the person interred at Teotihuacan was a native who had got his teeth decorated among the Maya, or a Maya who had died at Teotihuacan, or else the incrustations must have been the work of a travelling Mayan dental specialist. There are, it is true, also the Zapotecs to be taken into consideration, but the weight of the evidence leans towards

[27] Linné 1938: 167—168.   [28] Barrett 1925, vol. 2: 352.   [29] Linné 1940: 2—28.

communication with the Maya. Technical analysis of, among other things, the cement with which the "filling" was secured may perhaps solve that problem.

The peoples of the Atlantic coast appear to be largely indebted to the Maya for their culture, and from them the Zapotecs had received strong cultural impulses. It would therefore be tempting to suppose that by way of the Zapotecs the peoples of the Teotihuacan culture received elements that were essentially Mayan. This does not, however, appear to have been the case. Judging by the pottery, at the present stage of archaeological research it looks as if contact had been more intimate between Teotihuacan and the Maya than between Teotihuacan and the Totonacs and Zapotecs.

In the account given of the results achieved in the work at Teotihuacan in 1932, I also endeavoured to show that certain finds indicate contact with the Maya.[30] Material from elsewhere proving contact, even though frequently only sporadic, has also been adduced with a similar intention.[31] The Teotihuacan culture, however, had chiefly attained its development without any Mayan influence, and Spinden's assertion does not fit the case: "The principal motives of Toltec decorative art are obviously related to the earlier more brilliant work of the Mayas".[32] It is the originality of the Teotihuacan type of pottery that makes it with such certainty distinguishable from purely Mayan ware. Saville reproduces objects from Guatemala which might have been manufactured in Teotihuacan, but were made of "native clay". The rather uncommon type of clay vessel seen in fig. 211 also occurs in Utatlan, Zacualpa and in Copan. The richest comparative material yet found derives from Kaminaljuyú, in the outskirts of Guatemala City. The vessel in the form of a human figure, fig. 197, has here a counterpart, only of far superior class. Certain definite points of resemblance between incensarios of Tlamimilolpa and others from the Quiché district and in Kaminaljuyú undoubtedly exist. The tripod vase typical of the Teotihuacan culture also occurs in the Guatemalan highlands, on the slopes towards the Pacific coast, in Uaxactun and other cities in the Peten district, in British Honduras, and in Copan. Occasionally similarity also extends to the technique of decoration.

Thompson has been able to date the Teotihuacan element in San José, British Honduras, to San José II, embracing the period 435—633 A. D. in accordance with the Goodman—Martínez Hernández—Thompson correlation. He has subsequently mentioned that pottery of the Tzakol period, correlatable to Teotihuacan II (III?) and Monte Albán III, has been recovered in a building in Uaxactun. The latter can be dated through stelae to 593 A. D.[33] The Tzakol ceramic phase is abundantly represented in the Peten district.[34]

[30] Linné 1934: 58—59, 96 seq., 152—153.
[31] Seler 1915: 482—486, 1915 a: 121—123, 128; Gann 1925: 276 seq.; Saville 1930: 195—206; Termer 1931: 185; Stone and Turnbull 1941: 45. [32] Spinden 1928: 169.
[33] Sociedad Mexicana de Antropología, Boletín No. 2. Primera sesión de la Mesa Redonda sobre problemas antropológicos Mexicanos y Centroamericanos (del 11 al 14 de julio de 1941). P. 14. [34] Smith 1940: 247.

In the foregoing it has been mentioned that a peculiar type of spouted cup, fig. 211, which was recovered in Burial 1, Tlamimilolpa, extended as far as Copan. Longyear also states that tripod vases with covers, "al fresco" decoration, Tlaloc vases, and yellowish-red bowls, also occurred at that place. He emphasizes that the tripods had been found in fairly early Copan horizons, and that there exists no appreciable difference between those of Copan and their Teotihuacan counterparts.[35]

The material obtained from Kaminaljuyú, which is of exceeding importance for the clearing up of the connections maintained by Teotihuacan and possibly also for establishing its own origin, has so far only been published in summary reports. As early as 1936, Kidder, who had led the researches, declared that "some of the pottery appears to bear close resemblance to that of Uaxactun, some to that of Teotihuacan".[36] In the following year he wrote that "the pottery evidences trade relations with northern Peten during the Tzakol period (middle to late Old Empire) and with Teotihuacan".[37] Pottery of Teotihuacan type is described as "slab-legged, cylindrical-bodied tripods with lids, several of them stucco-coated and painted with elaborate designs in color».[38] There are further present, as already mentioned, yellowish-red bowls and anthropomorphic vessels of the same type as fig. 197. On the basis of his explorations in Kaminaljuyú, Kidder finds that the early Maya Old Empire was contemporaneous with a well-developed stage of the Teotihuacan culture.[39] Whether by this he alludes to Teotihuacan II or III is uncertain. Personally, I have a leaning towards the latter alternative. The dividing line between these two periods has not yet been clearly established. A remarkable thing is that "in fact, Mexican rather than Maya influence seems to have been preponderant in the region, at least during the period of the tombs that were excavated".[40] Thompson points out that "any Maya historical reconstruction must now satisfy conditions in the Valley of Mexico before it can be accepted as a correct interpretation of facts in the Maya area".[41] Now the tables are turned. Formerly Teotihuacan was believed to be of considerably more recent date than the Maya. Only Seler and Lehmann went to extremes in the opposite direction. It is remarkable that as early as 1913 Maudslay was able to form the conclusion "that the ruins between Mixco and the City of Guatemala might belong to the same culture as that of Teotihuacan".[42] It must be mentioned that the first intensive investigation at Miraflores, Kaminaljuyú, was carried out by Gamio. He also pointed out the Mexican influence in that area.[43]

Communication has thus existed between Teotihuacan and the Guatemalan highland, Peten, British Honduras and Copan. Its exact nature has not yet been ascertained. Thompson has suggested that some intermediate centre of radiation,

[35] Longyear 1940: 269—270.   [36] Kidder 1936 a: 131.   [37] Kidder 1937: 144.
[38] Kidder and Thompson 1938: 507.   [39] Kidder 1940: 122.   [40] Kidder and Thompson 1938: 508.
[41] Thompson 1940: 138.   [42] Maudslay 1913: 14.   [43] Gamio 1926—1927.

hitherto unknown, may have exercised an inspiring influence in both directions. Exportation from Teotihuacan to San José he rules out as entirely improbable, and there is nothing suggesting the possibility of the Mayan area having influenced Teotihuacan. As regards Guatemala, he also takes account of a Mexican invasion. Most students seem to incline towards trade contact. Whether this took place more or less directly with Teotihuacan or with some region not yet known, is a matter which should be capable of being revealed by comparative analyses of material. The yellowish-red ware, mostly annular-footed bowls, fig. 299, occurs in similar material in finds from Teotihuacan, Calpulalpan and Chalchicomula. On the other hand it differs altogether from that of typical Teotihuacan tripod vases. Miss Shephard, who is the leading authority on technical pottery analyses, has written to me that it does not either agree with the yellowish-red ware of Kaminaljuyú. In spite of its being identical in form, this type of pottery must have been manufactured in different regions. Of these, one must have purveyed its wares to Mexico, the other to Kaminaljuyú. Conclusions, it thus seems, must therefore be worked up with caution. Fragments of vessels from Peten, recovered in Tlamimilolpa, prove direct trading interchange. For the existence of trading relations also speaks Smith's pointing out that "the grave material from Kaminaljuyú had a large percentage of Tzakol types but not so the pottery found in the building fill and general digging".[44] But the Mexican influence has also been attributed to the Pipil. By these are meant emigrants from Central Mexico who are supposed to be descendants of the Toltecs. A few words about the Pipil and the Toltec question may therefore not be out of place.

Pipil.

In certain parts of the Guatemalan highland and the slopes towards and the lowlands on the Pacific coast, in western Salvador and scattered places in Honduras there live, or were living, peoples who had immigrated from Central Mexico. They are known by the collective name of Pipil. Other emigrants penetrated as far as Nicaragua, and possible even as far as Costa Rica. These aliens were referred to as early as by the chroniclers, such as Fuentes y Guzmán, Mendieta, Motolinía, Oviedo, Palacio, Alonso Ponce and Torquemada. Their language belongs to the Nahuatlan stock and is closely related to Aztec, but part of them speak an archaic dialect, Nahuat, which Lehmann holds was also spoken in Teotihuacan. He has devoted attentive study to the Pipil question from a linguistic point of view, made his own speech-recordings, worked up earlier material and compiled an exhaustive bibliographical collection.[45] He is definitely of opinion that emigration took place at different times and by different routes. To Izalco in Salvador, the immigrants

[44] Smith 1940: 248.   [45] Lehmann 1920, vol. 2: 978—1075.

arrived as early as ca. 300 A. D. Of early date are some of their settlements in Guatemala, those in the highland being, however, more recent than the occupation of the coastland. Nicaragua is by Lehmann supposed to have been reached by them not before ca. 1000 A. D. According to Historia de los Reynos de Colhuacan y de México, an emigration to the isthmus of Tehuantepec took place in the year 1064.[46] Even in Aztec times, founders of colonies were sent out. Thus Ahuitzotl (1486— 1502) despatched an expedition to Salvador. Spinden considers that in that territory there has been an "Aztec period", publishes a vase of typically Aztec character and adduces, quoting Brinton, that in 1511 Moctezuma sent a delegation to the Maya tribe Cakchiquel in Guatemala.[47] At a late date there was also an immigration into Guatemala from the Tuxtla district.[48] The dates fixed by Lehmann are no doubt open to question, but that they lay very far apart appears certain. Schultze-Jena, who has carried out exemplary linguistic researches in Mexico and Middle America, arrives at a similar result in his Pipil studies.[49] The earlier emigrants do not appear to have worshipped Quetzalcoatl, and must therefore have started out before the plumed serpent took the form of priest-king-god.

The original culture of the Pipil is little known. It is difficult to know what they brought with them and what they borrowed from the surrounding Maya. The latter were ousted by them, but even in the sixteenth century they occupied in Salvador a few small enclaves in the Pipil territory.[50] They must have been well organized and the cultural equals of their neighbours. In certain districts Termer considers them to have been the ruling class, and that would explain their having been able to retain their language.[51] Language, race and culture seldom coincide. But apart from the language, both tradition and artistic creativeness point to central Mexico as being the home of the Pipil. In their religion there are elements typical of Central Mexico, including Tlaloc, the Mexican Rain God, and tripod vases typical of Teotihuacan. In Salvador we find place-names well known from the region of Teotihuacan culture.[52] Through influence from the surrounding Maya there arose, in the realm of art, a specific Pipil style. It consisted among the earlier Pipil of a mixture of Teotihuacan and Maya elements.[53] Remarkable, too, is the existence on the Pacific coast of Guatemala of elements typical of the Huaxtec and Totonac regions, Tabasco and northern Chiapas. This also goes to prove that they must have immigrated from different directions and by different routes. When contact with their homeland was broken off, and no fresh impulses were added, Mayan influence more and more supervened.

The causes of the Pipil migrations southwards no doubt varied during different times. The Aztecs were sending out trading expeditions, probably also with a view to making preparations for future military expansion. The people in Tula are

[46] Lehmann 1938: 109.   [47] Spinden 1915: 474—479.   [48] Seler 1908: 628.   [49] Schultze-Jena 1935; cf. Sapper 1936: 85.   [50] Lothrop 1939: 44.   [51] Termer 1936: 112—113.   [52] Lothrop 1927: 216.
[53] Seler 1908: 628 seq.; Mason 1938: 215—216; Termer 1936a: 127, 1941: 18.

reported to have suffered from a severe famine since the year 1018 (1070), when a seven-year drought visited the country. Another cause for emigration was the fall of Tula in 1064 (1116). Exactly why the people of the Teotihuacan culture secreted emigrants is unknown. Overpopulation, as it acted in northern Europe during the epoch of migrations and the viking era, should perhaps not be excluded as a possible explanation. These oft-recurring migrations from Central Mexico southwards resulted either in vigorous colonies — alien dominions, like that in Chichen Itza — or in a ruling upper class. Lehmann's statement that already in the 4th century the Pipil had settled in Salvador should perhaps be rounded off upwards with a century or two. These migrations ought, however, to be taken into account when we have to explain the occurrence of elements of the Teotihuacan culture in Guatemala and the trade relations with Peten Maya.

Toltecs and the Teotihuacan culture.

Charnay was of opinion that the various cultures of which he had studied remains during his travels in 1857 and 1880—1882 "had but one and the same origin — that they were Toltec".[54] Brinton had with equal assurance in 1868 denied the existence of the Toltecs. Charnay's work spurred him on to a renewed attack on the hard-killed Toltecs. His summing up was as follows: "Why should we try to make an enlightened ruler of Quetzalcoatl, a cultured nation of the Toltecs, when the proof is of the strongest that they are fictions of mythology".[55]

But the Toltecs have lived on in the literature and caused a great deal of confusion. The chroniclers' accounts of them vary, and different students apply the name of Toltecs to different peoples of different periods and in different parts of Mexico. Hypotheses and theories have been set up as facts, and on such foundation of sand the structure has been more and more added to. Seeing that the Toltecs and the inhabitants of Teotihuacan are frequently being given the same meaning, the Toltec question cannot altogether be left out of this brief résumé.

The accounts given by the chroniclers are extremely varying, so that they clearly cannot be unreservedly accepted even though the spokesmen have partly based their statements on picture-writings. Dynastic tables, connected historical accounts and exact datings extending back in time some 900 years (e. g. in Historia de los Reynos de Colhuacan y de México) are not apt to be very confidence-inspiring. According to different authorities, the Toltecs immigrated from different parts, and their origin is still more variegated. Their "empire" began at various dates ranging from 245 to 752 A. D., and the date of its subsidence is variously given between 969 and 1168. This only to mention a few examples. Any writer considering himself having more or less dated the rise and fall of the problematic Toltec empire, would then be able

[54] Charnay 1887: vii.   [55] Brinton 1887: 241.

197

among different chroniclers to pick out the exact dates he finds would serve his purpose. These exact dates given by the early authors are obviously to a great extent fanciful, for even if there existed original documents in the 16th century, these can hardly be supposed to be based on archaic ones. The shortness and unreliability of oral tradition, at any rate as regards any connected course of events, has been experienced by students of Swedish history. If the people of Teotihuacan possessed the art of writing, which by no means is certain, such writing must have been very little developed. Accounts vary, too, of the cause of the fall of the Toltec empire: volcanic eruption, excessive use of alcohol (pulque), over-refinement or coarsening of manners and customs, invasion by barbarians, epidemics, and — most frequently and most credibly — famine following periods of severe drought.

After the fall of their empire, migration took place. Traces of various kinds left by the emigrants, from buildings to codices, are supposed to have been observed in different parts of Mexico. Frequently such records are palpably incorrect. Mexican influence in Yucatan is as certain as the presence of elements of the Teotihuacan culture in different localities within the region of the Maya Old Empire. But as to time, the difference is very great, and the Mexican elements are besides of a different character and not to be explained by any single act of immigration.

By the name of Toltecs, the Aztecs seem to have denoted all high-cultured peoples existing before their time, and whose cultural inheritors they considered themselves to be. Tradition magnified actual facts, and the predecessors were wrapped in a fairyland lustre. As a wishful dream they depicted this brilliant, happy and peaceful age, "the good old days". Historical facts were woven into the narratives together with tribal tales and mythological conceptions. For the sake of clarity many writers have altogether avoided the term "Toltecs" and instead used the concrete conception, the Teotihuacan culture. The people of the next epoch, on the other hand, might be called Toltecs. For Sahagun differentiates between earlier and later Toltecs, and places the latter in Tula. Also in Historia Tolteca-Chichimeca and by Chimalpain and Torquemada, distinction is made between two different ethnic elements, or two different Toltec groups. Ixtlilxochitl expressly states that Teotihuacan was greater and more powerful than Tula.[56]

Lehmann recognized two Toltec empires.[57] The earlier of these came to an end about 600 A. D. His authority for this is mainly Sahagun's statement: "Porque por sus pinturas antiguas hay noticia que aquella famosa ciudad que se llamó Tula ha ya mil años o muy cerca de ellos que fué destruida".[58] As this was written in 1571, Lehmann figures it out as 571, rounding it off to 600. This first empire he considers, although without adducing any clear proof, having arisen roughly about the birth of Christ, or 250 years later.[59] Taking Sahagun literally, strikes one as rather optimistic, for "a thousand years" probably only means a long time ago. Teoti-

[56] Cf. Krickeberg 1937: 211—212.   [57] Lehmann 1921: 16 seq.   [58] Sahagun 1938, vol. 1: 8.
[59] Lehmann 1938 a: 188 seq.

huacan was the centre of Lehmann's first Toltec empire.[60] The second empire roughly coincides with that referred to below, which had Tula for its centre.

Just as the Archaic period, chiefly through Vaillant's researches, has been resolved into several consecutive cultures, so it is possible to divide up the Toltec era. Earliest of these cultures is that of Teotihuacan, named after its centre. The area of its distribution has not yet been determined with any claim to exactness. In it, the Chalchicomula district in Puebla has hitherto generally been included. This is not borne out by our researches. On the other hand we discovered a considerable amount of contemporary remains of habitations in the neighbourhood of Calpulalpan, in Tlaxcala. Of a numerous population and settlement of some considerable duration, evidence is seen in the enormous quantities of artifacts from the Teotihuacan culture that are found in Azcapotzalco. Cholula must have been an important centre during this period. Even its earliest structure, discovered in the interior of the large pyramid, is of Teotihuacan type, its orientation is identical with that obtaining in Teotihuacan, and the pottery finds are wholly similar.[61] The Teotihuacan culture was widely connected: the Gulf coast, Oaxaca and the Maya region under the Old Empire. It maintained intimate trade relations with, and probably established colonies in, Guatemala and El Salvador, and certain dying ripples of impulses may even have extended as far as Yucatan. With the Maya, intercourse seems to have taken place during Teotihuacan II and III, and with the Zapotecs during Teotihuacan III. The intense relations with the Maya would, according to the Goodman-Martínez Hernández-Thompson correlation have existed during the period A. D. 435—633. The cause of the downfall of the Teotihuacan culture remains unknown to us. It may be that there set in a slow decline, as nothing goes to indicate any sudden catastrophe caused either by natural forces or ravaging barbarian invaders. Perhaps emigration to the Maya region took place simultaneously with successive infiltration on the part of importunate, more primitive neighbours. This specialized, highly cultured society would in such case furnish an example of the modern conception of technical brittleness. Those of lower organization prove stronger, more adaptable and more resistant. Vaillant appears inclined to discern a slow decay: "The archaeological evidence at Azcapotzalco discloses a late period not found at Teotihuacan, where there was a rich if decadent culture, suggesting that long twilight of the Roman Empire found in the Byzantine civilization".[62] Even if the dating fixed by Lehmann of the Pipil in Salvador at ca. A. D. 300 be adjusted upwards by as much as three centuries, it would agree well enough with the Teotihuacan contact of A. D. 435—633. Even Sahagun's dating the downfall to 600 A. D. would, strange to say, also fit in. From this peak period of Central Mexican civilization, memory survived among the Aztecs mainly in the form of myths, legends and wishful dreams.

[60] Lehmann 1933: 150.   [61] Noguera 1937 a: 8 seq.; Marquina 1939 a: 14—17.
[62] Vaillant 1936: 326.

The later "Toltec culture" had Tula for its centre. This locality appears, from the geographical data and place-names contained in the historical sources, to have been the ruined city of the present Tula in the State of Hidalgo. Sahagun's Aztec spokesmen appear to have differentiated between Teotihuacan and Tula, and by the inhabitants of Tula have referred to Toltecs.[63] Up to the year 1940, when its archaeological exploration, properly speaking, was begun, Tula was chiefly known through Charnay's work and of some gigantic stone sculptures that had been moved to Museo Nacional in Mexico City. From their striking resemblance to sculptures in Chichen Itza he connected the two places with each other.[64] Several scientists, later on have studied the identities between the art of Chichen Itza and that of Tula and the Valley of Mexico.[65]

The archaeological explorations that have lately been begun and are led by Jorge Acosta have already given startling results. They have revealed that in this locality no traces whatever of the Teotihuacan culture are to be found among the artifacts.[66] Neither do the buildings show any points of resemblance, and are besides orientated exactly to the four points of the compass, which, as already mentioned, is not the case in Teotihuacan. Below artifacts from Aztec times, only such as derive from the Mazapan culture were encountered. This latter culture was first demonstrated by Vaillant and has been named after the place of its discovery, San Francisco Mazapan in Teotihuacan.[67] Vaillant located it between the Aztec and the Teotihuacan era. Above the Xolalpan ruin, referred to in the foregoing, we found graves from the Mazapan culture. Everything seemed to point to the subsequent settlers not even having known of the existence of the ruin.[68] In 1935 we examined a near-by grave constructed of hewn pieces of stone and roofed over with flat stone slabs. It contained a large number of mortuary offerings of Mazapan type, but nothing to connect it with either the preceding or the following culture could be discovered.[69] Pottery of Mazapan type has so far been recovered in various spots in the Valley of Mexico, Calixtlahuaca and Tula. Acosta considers that the archaeological finds prove the bearers of the Mazapan culture to have erected the buildings at Tula, and that consequently they must have been the historical Toltecs. As was the case in Teotihuacan, in Tula, too, the culture was from the beginning fully developed, so that its origin is to be found elsewhere, possibly in the Tarascan territory. During the Aztec era the city attained another period of prosperity, but its archaeological remains show that it was never abandoned — the Aztecs having moved in and finally assumed complete dominance.

That strangers coming from Mexico invaded Yucatan is confirmed by literary sources as well as by the existence of alien stylistic elements in art and architecture. Definite affinities between Tula and Chichen Itza can be seen. It is true that some

[63] Sahagun 1927: 387 seq., 436 scq., 1938, vol. 3: 109 seq., 136 seq.   [64] Charnay 1887: 343 seq.
[65] Spinden 1913; Seler 1915 b: 197—388; Tozzer 1930: 155—164; Morris, Charlot and Morris 1931.
[66] Acosta 1940: 172—194.   [67] Vaillant 1932: 489.   [68] Linné 1934: 75—86, 215—216.   [69] Linné 1938 a: 176.

few new elements have their counterparts in Teotihuacan. The city, for example, is orientated according to the same astronomical principles. It may of course not be impossible that impulses from the Teotihuacan culture found their way to this place. Even Palenque appears orientated in a similar way. But with Tula, Chichen Itza has many elements in common: ball-courts, serpent columns, Atlantean supports, Chac mool figures, descending gods, tigers in procession, eagles and other representations in relief, large columns with sculptured representations of warriors which have direct counterparts in Chichen Itza. The typical pottery is altogether absent. That of Chichen Itza appears largely related to that of Vera Cruz, while having but few points of contact with the pottery of the highland and none at all with the Teotihuacan culture. But only positive proofs are here to be attached with importance because different groups of the population had specialized in different arts and crafts. As it may be supposed that in ancient times the women, as generally in the America of our days, were the makers of pottery, it is not certain that conquering hordes preserved their ceramic culture. It is possible that the women did not accompany the invaders, who, when by intermarriages they had become re-domiciled, found themselves the possessors of an entirely new type of pottery. Sculptural art, on the other hand, is so closely similar as to make it appear as if the same artists had been at work at both places.

Even the later Pipil possessed elements pointing towards Tula as their origin, but here, too, the pottery has nothing in common with the Mazapan type. As already mentioned, they also brought with them elements from the Gulf coast. Among the Pipil who were the last to emigrate, Aztec elements are on the other hand clearly discernible.

According to Historia de los Reynos, the peak period of Tula lasted from 726 to 1070 A. D., but its decline began in 1064.[70] If to these dates be respectively added 52 years, better agreement is obtained with other authorities, such as Historia Tolteca-Chichimeca, viz. from 778 to 1116 A. D. The last-mentioned date would thus fix the emigration to Yucatan. Thompson has, however, pointed out that part of the elements supposed to have been carried to Yucatan by the immigrants were already in existence there.[71] Either was there a first wave of emigration at some earlier date, or the year 1064 (1116) is incorrect. The happiest solution would perhaps be that of finding, if possible, an intermediary between Tula and Chichen Itza, which could be made responsible, wholly or in part, for the Mexican infiltration of Yucatan. Another possibility is that of the Tula elements having been introduced into Chichen Itza during an earlier emigration led by Quetzalcoatl.

According to Historia de los Reynos, Quetzalcoatl was born in Acatl (Reed) in 843, became priest-king in 873, and died in 895.[72] As already mentioned, the

[70] Lehmann 1938: 60, 109—110.
[71] Sociedad Mexicana de Antropología, Boletín No. 2. Primera sesión de la Mesa Redonda sobre problemas antropológicos Mexicanos y Centroamericanos (del 11 al 14 de julio de 1941). P. 12.
[72] Lehmann 1938: 70, 75, 79, 93.

dates given by this authority should perhaps be advanced 52 years. This would date his birth to 895 and his death to 947. His span of life, 52 years, being regarded as a sacred cycle; the myths of partly astronomical import that have been woven about this culture hero, the leader of his people's emigration and subsequently deified, it all suggests a mixture of fantasy and reality. An important personage and religious conceptions have been merged together. He has been made a personification of myths and abstract speculations. In Sahagun's lengthy accounts of Quetzalcoatl and the Toltecs, the hero is represented as being at the same time both priest-king and god,[73] but a reference to him in Historia de los Reynos can be interpreted to mean that he was the first to be known by that name.[74] It is most probable that Quetzalcoatl, Quetzal-bird-serpent, was a title assumed by the priest-king. The title was either the name of a tribal god, or the god received his name through the priest-king. Be that as it may, there came into being a combination of god and man that the chroniclers' spokesmen were unable to separate. The death of Quetzalcoatl being connected with an eastward move may mean that he led the first emigration to Yucatan. According to the myth, he was reborn in the planet of Venus, which after having been invisible during eight days returns as the morning star. His alleged death on the ocean beach in the east does not need to have any foundation in fact. This is no doubt another instances of confusing Quetzalcoatl, the man, with the god symbolized by the planet Venus. The cycle of Venus began on the day 1 Acatl, Quetzalcoatl's birthday, and the planet was believed to return after 2×52 years. The 52-year period of the calendar, the myth describing the evening star's journey towards the east, its death and its resurrection in the form of the morning star, were thus interwoven with historical happenings.

Landa relates how Kukulcan, the feathered serpent, Quetzalcoatl's name among the Maya, arrived from the west and returned to his own country after having concluded his great work of civilizing organization.[75] He cannot, therefore have died on the way there. Seeing that the Mexican influence in Yucatan, according to Mayan sources, spans the period 1190—1450, and as Tula collapsed in 1116, the leader of the emigrants could not very well have had any home to return to. Thompson's pointing out, referred to in the foregoing, that Tula-Toltec elements appear in Yucatan prior to the fall of Tula, might be explained by someone called Quetzalcoatl — the first bearer of that name — having headed an emigration in the middle of the 10th century. If then he returned with alien notions, he may have sown religious dissension which subsequently resulted in giving up resistence to neighbours that were hammering at the gates, and in final emigration en masse. Reminiscences of Quetzalcoatl's emigration to Yucatan and his return to his homeland appear to have been handed down if we may judge by Moctezuma's address

[73] Sahagun 1927: 268—292, 387—398.   [74] Lehmann 1938: 104.
[75] Landa 1928, vol. 1: 62—69.

to Cortés and his speech to his sub-chiefs.[76] According to Cortés' relation, the tribal ancestors were said to have come with a great leader from a foreign country. To this he went back, returning from it once more, but finally again left for it, this time for good. He then told the people that he, or someone representing him, would come back to them and become their leader. Quetzalcoatl was expected to return in the year 1 Acatl, and as Cortés arrived in such a year, Moctezuma believed that then the time had come for Quetzalcoatl to resume supreme authority. By that belief bringing disaster upon himself and his people.

The later Toltecs were not altogether swept away. Part of those which remained were counted as a ruling class in the same way as the Pipil were in Guatemala. In Historia de los Reynos de Colhuacan y de México it is stated that in 1458 the chief of Toltitlán (near Cuautitlán) was of Toltec descent.[77] The chronicler Ixtlilxochitl also reckoned himself as being of Toltec extraction, for from them the ruling dynasty of Texcoco counted descent. It is possible that part of the population migrated to Colhuacan and continued to live at that place. The Olmeca and other peoples were by Sahagun looked upon as Toltecs that had remained behind.[78] Even the inhabitants of Teotihuacan appear to have partly counted themselves as descendants of the Toltecs.[79]

The intimate contact between the Teotihuacan culture and the Maya of the Old Empire has upset the prevailing conception that the Maya culture was the older and lending part. Seler and Lehmann went to extremes in the opposite direction: "Der gebende Teil sind die Mexikaner gewesen, der empfangende die Maya".[80]

Lehmann makes use of an earlier opinion of Seler's and gives it a dogmatic form.[81] These two authors slide the Toltec era back and the Mayan era forward, and consider that the former have enriched the Maya with a large variety of elements, such as hieroglyphs, stelae, a certain knowledge of architecture etc.[82] Whether the Teotihuacan culture actually included hieroglyphs is still an open question, and it would be more than remarkable if the pupils had to such a degree surpassed their teachers. Mrs. Nuttall's solution of the Toltec problem runs directly counter to that of Seler-Lehmann, holding that the Toltecs immigrated from the Maya country, while the ancestors of the Maya had come from Mexico,[83] and Maudslay, too, considers that Tula, Cholula and Teotihuacan were strongly influenced by the Maya.[84]

✻ ✻
✻

[76] Cortés 1866: 86—87, 98—99. [77] Lehmann 1938: 253. [78] Sahagun 1927: 428. [79] Guzmán 1938: 90—91.
[80] Lehmann 1922: 315. [81] Seler 1916: 85. [82] Lehmann 1933: 85, 99, 116, 146 etc.
[83] Nuttall 1926 a: 250—255. [84] Díaz del Castillo 1908, vol. 1, introduction: 50—53.

The foregoing exposition has many weak points. It seems clear, however, that the Toltecs of the chroniclers were the people that had Tula for their centre, and assumed the leading part in Yucatan. The points of resemblance between Tula and Chichen Itza are sufficiently strong for supposing that the emigrants from Tula directly continued their artistic creativeness in the service of religion in Chichen Itza. With the Teotihuacan culture, these Toltecs had nothing whatever to do. Of this epoch in the history of the country an echo survived in the Aztecs' conceptions of "the good old times".

Of neither of the above cultures has the history been cleared up. Neither how, when, or where development began, nor why, or when, it broke up. The insufficiency of the material — literary sources as well as archaeological investigations — still makes it impossible to discern even the main features. The connection between the two epochs, for connected they must have been, either directly or indirectly, has neither been made clear. Possibly the key to the problem of the rise of the Teotihuacan culture lies in Guatemala. From their relations with the Maya Old Empire, certain important data can be established. The well-developed stage of the Teotihuacan culture is directly connected with a period among the Maya which falls between 435 and 633 A. D. This is according to the correlation between the Mayan and the Christian chronology that is most generally accepted. Absolutely certain it is, however, not. Still, if a cultural connection can be shown to have existed between Teotihuacan and south-western U. S. A. via north-western Mexico, a new channel might be opened for the solution of the correlation question.[85] Through A. E. Douglass' dendrochronological method there is available an absolute dating of more than a thousand years of the cultural history in the Southwest.

Non-scientists are fain to connect the Teotihuacan pyramids with those of Egypt, and even some scientific students have in real earnest believed in such a connection. Less fantastic are those who maintain that fertilizing cultural currents have reached America from south-eastern Asia. But of late it seems generally agreed that the American cultures have developed without help from abroad.[86] Where and when the high cultures were built up, and how they were interconnected, are questions that have engaged the attention of many a scientist without any definite result having been attained.[87] That there is a great deal of agreement of opinions cannot be denied. Formerly it was held as an axiom that the cradle of the high cultures had stood in Middle America. Max Uhle, who has devoted a long life's work to the study of the South American high cultures, has summed up this general opinion in the following words: "Die Inspiration ging ... soweit wir bis jetzt sehen, fast in allen Fällen immer von Mittelamerika aus".[88] There may have been an interchange of influence; in some cases this was probable, in others, though extremely few, certain. Ideas and trade goods, for example, seem to have been interchanged,

[85] Cf. Ekholm 1939: 10.   [86] Nordenskiöld 1930, 1931.   [87] Krickeberg 1935; Lothrop 1940; Kidder II 1940.   [88] Uhle 1935: 47.

but from subjective opinions to conclusive proof the step is a long one.[89] The earliest traces of human culture that the archaeologist encounters in Mexico and Middle America are by no means of primitive types. If no earlier stages are to be found either here or in South America, the solution of this question will have to remain a matter of temperament. Either were the Indians in general inventors and discoverers of exceptional gifts, or had cultural acceleration been exceedingly speedy, or one or more cultural centres been annihilated by upheavals of nature, or else recourse must be had to the old-age last straw that never proved anyone's salvation: a bygone world in the Pacific Ocean—Atlantis.

[89] Cf. Kroeber 1940: 478—480.

Fig. 333. Pottery fragment with decoration in relief: half human face, half death's head. (Actual size) 35. 8. 542.

BIBLIOGRAPHY[1]

ACOSTA, JORGE R.
1940.   Exploraciones en Tula, Hgo., 1940 (Revista Mexicana de Estudios Antropológicos, tomo 4, pp. 172—194, 5 lám., 4 planos, Mexico 1940).

ANDREE, RICHARD.
1907.   Ethnologische Betrachtungen über Hokkerbestattung (Archiv für Anthropologie, neue Folge, Band 6, pp. 282—307, 2 pls., Braunschweig 1907).

APENES, OLA.
1936.   Possible derivation of the 260 day period of the Maya calendar (Ethnos, vol. 1, pp. 5—8, Stockholm 1936).

ARAGÓN, JAVIER O.
1931.   Expansión territorial del imperio mexicano (Anales del Museo Nacional de Arqueología, Historia y Etnografía, tomo 7, época 4a., pp. 5—64, Mexico 1931).

BALL, SYDNEY H.
1941.   The mining of gems and ornamental stones by American Indians (Bulletin 128 of the Bureau of American Ethnology, Smithsonian Institution, Anthropological Papers, no. 13, pp. 1—77, 5 pls., Washington 1941).

BANCROFT, HUBERT HOWE.
1883—1888. The history of the Pacific States of North America, vols. 4—9 (Mexico, vols. 1—6). San Francisco 1883—1888.

BARRETT, S. A.
1925.   The Cayapa Indians of Ecuador. 2 vols. (Indian Notes and Monographs, Museum of the American Indian, Heye Foundation, no. 40, New York 1925).

BATRES, LEOPOLDO.
1906.   Teotihuacan. Mexico 1906.

BENNETT, WENDELL C.
1939.   Archaeology of the north coast of Peru. An account of exploration and excavation in Viru and Lambayeque Valleys (Anthropological Papers of the American Museum of Natural History, vol. 37, part 1, New York 1939).

BENNETT, WENDELL C. and ZINGG, ROBERT M.
1935.   The Tarahumara. An Indian tribe of Northern Mexico. Chicago 1935.

BERG, GÖSTA.
1941.   Drinking-Tubes: some notes from Europe (Ethnos, vol. 6, pp. 98—108, Stockholm 1941).

BEYER, HERMANN.
1913.   Ueber die mythologischen Affen der Mexikaner und Maya (International Congress of Americanists. Proceedings of the 18th session, London, 1912, part 1, pp. 140—154, London 1913).

1922.   La controversia Mena-Gamio. (El Mexico Antiguo, tomo 1, núms. 10—12, pp. 283—289, Mexico 1922).

1927.   Review of Walter Krickeberg: Die Totonaken (El Mexico Antiguo, tomo 2, núms. 11—12, pp. 318—321, Mexico 1927).

1927 a. Algunos datos sobre los "yugos" de piedra prehispánicos (El Mexico Antiguo, tomo 2, núms. 11—12, pp. 269—278, Mexico 1927).

1930.   A deity common to Teotihuacan and Totonac cultures (Proceedings of the twenty-third International Congress of Americanists, New York, 1928, pp. 82—84, New York 1930).

[1] The bibliography only includes such authors as are quoted in the present work. For a wider range of bibliographical data concerning Teotihuacan the reader is especially referred to the publications of Gamio, Vaillant and Noguera, as well as to my previous publication (Linné 1934) and part of the literature mentioned on page 14.

BIRKET-SMITH, KAJ.
1929.   The Caribou Eskimos. 2 vols. (Report
        of the Fifth Thule Expedition 1921—
        24, vol. 5, Copenhagen 1929).
1929 a. Drinking tube and tobacco pipe in North
        America (Ethnologische Studien, vol. 1,
        pp. 29—39, Leipzig 1929).
BLACKISTON, A. H.
1910.   Archaeological investigations in Hondu-
        ras (Records of the Past, vol. 9, part 4,
        pp. 195—201, Washington 1910).
BLOM, FRANS.
1930.   Preliminary notes on two important
        Maya finds (Proceedings of the twenty-
        third International Congress of Ameri-
        canists, New York, 1928, pp. 165—171,
        New York 1930).
1932.   The Maya ball-game Pok-ta-pok, called
        Tlachtli by the Aztec (Middle Ameri-
        can Papers, Middle American research
        series, publication no. 4, pp. 485—530,
        The Tulane University of Louisiana,
        New Orleans 1932).
1934.   Summary of archaeological work in the
        Americas 1931—1932—1933. II. Middle
        America (Bulletin of the Pan American
        Union, December 1934, pp. 861—882,
        Washington 1934).
1934 a. A Maya skull from the Uloa Valley,
        Republic of Honduras. Historical back-
        ground (Studies in Middle America,
        Middle American research series, publica-
        tion no. 5, pp. 7—14, The Tulane Uni-
        versity of Louisiana, New Orleans 1934).
BLOM, FRANS and LA FARGE, OLIVER.
1926, 1927. Tribes and temples. A record of
        the expedition to Middle America con-
        ducted by the Tulane University of
        Louisiana in 1925. 2 vols. (The Tulane
        University of Louisiana, New Orleans
        1926, 1927).
BOEKELMAN, HENRY J.
1935.   Ethno- and archeo-conchological notes
        on four Middle American shells (Maya
        Research, vol. 2, pp. 257—277, New
        York 1935).
BREKER, CARL.
1888.   Beiträge der Ethnographie Mexico's (In-
        ternationales Archiv für Ethnographie,
        Band 1, pp. 212—214, Leiden 1888).
BRENNER, ANITA.
1931.   The influence of technique on the de-
        corative style in the domestic pottery of
        Culhuacan (Columbia University Contri-
        butions to Anthropology, vol. 13, 95 pp.,
        New York 1931).

BRINTON, DANIEL G.
1887.   Were the Toltecs an historic nationality
        (Proceedings of the American Philo-
        sophical Society, vol. 24, pp. 229—241,
        Philadelphia 1887).
BROWNE, JIM.
1938.   Antiquity of the bow (American Anti-
        quity, vol. 3, pp. 358—359, Menasha
        1938).
1940.   Projectile points (American Antiquity,
        vol. 5, pp. 209—213, 2 pls., Menasha
        1940).
BRÜNING, HANS H.
1898.   Moderne Töpferei der Indianer Perus
        (Globus, Band 74, pp. 259—260, Braun-
        schweig 1898).
BUTLER, MARY.
1936.   Ethnological and historical implications
        of certain phases of Maya pottery deco-
        ration (American Anthropologist, n. s.
        vol. 38, pp. 452—461, Menasha 1936).
CASO, ALFONSO.
1932.   Las exploraciones en Monte Alban. Tem-
        porada 1931—1932 (Instituto Panameri-
        cano de Geografía e Historia, publica-
        ción no. 7, Mexico 1932).
1935.   Las exploraciones en Monte Alban. Tem-
        porada 1934—1935 (Instituto Panameri-
        cano de Geografía e Historia, publica-
        ción no. 18, Mexico 1935).
1937.   Tenían los Teotihuacanos conocimiento
        del Tonalpohualli? (El Mexico Antiguo,
        tomo 4, núms. 3—4, pp. 131—143,
        Mexico 1937).
1938.   Exploraciones en Oaxaca. Quinta y
        sexta temporadas, 1936—1937 (Instituto
        Panamericano de Geografía e Historia,
        publicación no. 34, Mexico 1938).
CHARNAY, DÉSIRÉ.
1885.   Les anciennes villes du Nouveau Monde.
        Voyages d'exploration au Mexique et
        dans l'Amérique Centrale par Désiré
        Charnay 1857—1882. Paris 1885.
1887.   The ancient cities of the New World.
        Travels and explorations in Mexico and
        Central America from 1857—1882. Lon-
        don 1887.
CLEMENTS, FORREST E. and REED, ALFRED.
1939.   "Eccentric" flints of Oklahoma (Ameri-
        can Antiquity, vol. 5, pp. 27—30, 1 pl.,
        Menasha 1939).
COBO, BERNABÉ.
1895.   Historia del Nuevo Mundo. Tomo 4
        (La Sociedad de Bibliófilos Andaluces).
        Sevilla 1895.

CODEX BORGIA.
1904—1909. See Seler 1904—1909.

CODEX TROANO.
1930. Codex Troano. Fac-simile edition published by the Junta de Relaciones Culturales. Madrid 1930.

CODEX VATICANUS NR. 3773 (CODEX VATICANUS B).
1902. See Seler 1902 a.

CORTÉS, HERNANDO.
1866. Cartas y relaciones de Hernan Cortés al Emperador Carlos V (Edited by Pascual de Gayangos). Paris 1866.

CUMMINGS, BYRON.
1933. Cuicuilco and the Archaic Culture of Mexico (University of Arizona Bulletin, vol. 4, no. 8, Social Science Bulletin no. 4, pp. 1—56, Tucson 1933).

DANZEL, THEODOR-WILHELM.
1923. Mexiko II (Kulturen der Erde, Band 12, Hagen i W. und Darmstadt 1923).

DÍAZ DEL CASTILLO, BERNAL.
1908—1916. The true history of the conquest of New Spain. Edited and published in Mexico, by Genaro García. Translated by A. P. Maudslay. 5 vols. (Hakluyt Society, second series, vols. 23—25, 30, 40, London 1908—1916).

DÍAZ LOZANO, ENRIQUE.
1922—1923. Los restos fósiles cuaternarios y las culturas arqueológicas del Valle de México (Ethnos, 2a. época, tomo 1, no. 1, pp. 37—51, 3 pls., México 1922—1923).

DIESELDORFF, E. P.
1926—1933. Kunst und Religion der Mayavölker. 3 vols. Band 1—2 Berlin 1926, 1931; Band 3 Hamburg 1933.

DINGWALL, ERIC JOHN.
1931. Artificial cranial deformation. A contribution to the study of ethnic mutilations. London 1931.

DISSELHOFF, H. D.
1940. "Brujos" im Hochland von Ekuador (Zeitschrift für Ethnologie, Jahrg. 71, pp. 300—305, Berlin 1940).

DOERING, HEINRICH U.
1931. Altperuanische Gefässmalereien. II. Teil. Marburg/Lahn 1931.

DUPAIX, GUILLELMO.
1831. The monuments of New Spain. The first expedition in search of antiquities, undertaken in the year 1805 (Lord Kingsborough, Antiquities of Mexico: Comprising fac-similes of ancient Mexican paintings and hieroglyphics ... together with the Monuments of New Spain, vols. 4—6, London 1831).

1834—1836. Antiquités mexicaines. Relation des trois expéditions du capitaine Dupaix, ordonnées en 1805, 1806 et 1807, pour la recherche des antiquités du pays ... accompagnée des dessins de Castañeda ... 2 vols. Paris 1834—1836.

DURAN, DIEGO.
1867, 1880. Historia de las indias de Nueva España y islas de tierra firme. 2 vols. México 1867, 1880.

EKHOLM, GORDON F.
1939. Results of an archeological survey of Sonora and northern Sinaloa (Revista Mexicana de Estudios Antropológicos, tomo 3, pp. 7—10, Mexico 1939).

1940. Prehistoric "lacquer" from Sinaloa (Revista Mexicana de Estudios Antropológicos, tomo 4, pp. 10—15, Mexico 1940).

FEWKES, JESSE WALTER.
1907. Certain antiquities of eastern Mexico (25th Annual Report of the Bureau of American Ethnology, Smithsonian Institution, pp. 221—284, 36 pls., Washington 1907).

FOWKE, GERARD.
1896. Stone art (13th Annual Report of the Bureau of Ethnology, Smithsonian Institution, pp. 47—178, Washington 1896).

FRIEDERICI, GEORG.
1926. Hilfswörterbuch für den Amerikanisten (Studien über Amerika und Spanien, Extra-Serie, No. 2, Halle 1926).

FÖRSTEMANN, E.
1886. Erläuterungen zur Mayahandschrift der Königlichen öffentlichen Bibliothek zu Dresden. Dresden 1886.

GAMIO, MANUEL.
1922. La población del Valle de Teotihuacán. 3 vols. (Secretaría de Agricultura y Fomento, Dirección de Antropología). Mexico 1922.

1926—1927. Cultural evolution in Guatemala and its geographic and historic handicaps (Art and Archaeology, vol. 22, pp. 202—221, vol. 23, pp. 16—32, 70—78, 129—133, Washington 1926—1927).

GANN, THOMAS.
1918. The Maya Indians of southern Yucatan and northern British Honduras (Bulletin 64 of the Bureau of American Ethnology, Smithsonian Institution, Washington 1918).

1925. Maya jades (Congrès International des Américanistes, compte-rendu de la XXIᵉ session, Göteborg 1924, pp. 274—282, Göteborg 1925).

GANN, THOMAS and MARY.
1939. Archeological investigations in the Corozal District of British Honduras (Bulletin 123 of the Bureau of American Ethnology, Smithsonian Institution, pp. 1—66, 10 pls., Washington 1939).

GREENMAN, E. F.
1932. Origin and development of the burial mound (American Anthropologist, n. s. vol. 34, pp. 286—295, Menasha 1932).

GUZMÁN, EULALIA.
1938. Un Manuscrito de la Colección Boturini que trata de los antiguos Señores de Teotihuacán (Ethnos, vol. 3, pp. 89—103, Stockholm 1938).

HAMY, E. T.
1897. Galerie américaine du Musée d'Ethnographie du Trocadéro. 2 vols. Paris 1897.

HERRERA, ANTONIO DE.
1601. Historia general de los hechos de los castellanos en las islas i tierra firme del mar oceano. Madrid 1601.

HISTORIA DE LOS MEXICANOS POR SUS PINTURAS.
1883. See Phillips 1883.

HISTORIA DE LOS REYNOS DE COLHUACAN Y DE MÉXICO.
1938. See Lehmann 1938.

HOOVER, J. W.
1935. Generic descent of the Papago villages (American Anthropologist, n. s. vol. 37, pp. 257—264, Menasha 1935).

HRDLIČKA, ALEŠ.
1912. An ancient sepulchre at San Juan Teotihuacan, with anthropological notes on the Teotihuacan people (Reseña de la segunda sesión del 17 Congreso Internacional de Americanistas, México 1910, Apéndice, 5 pp., 1 pl., México 1912).

IZIKOWITZ, KARL GUSTAV.
1935. Musical and other sound instruments of the South American Indians. A comparative ethnographical study (Göteborgs Kungl. Vetenskaps- och Vitterhets-Samhälles Handlingar. Femte följden. Ser. A. Band. 5. N:o 1. Göteborg 1935).

JOYCE, THOMAS A.
1914. Mexican Archaeology. London 1914.

KELLY, ISABEL T.
1938. Excavations at Chametla, Sinaloa (Ibero-Americana: 14, Berkeley 1938).

KIDDER, A. V.
1932. The artifacts of Pecos (Papers of the Phillips Academy Southwestern Expedition, no. 6, New Haven 1932).
1935. Notes on the ruins of San Agustin Acasaguastlan, Guatemala (Contributions to American Archaeology, no. 15, Carnegie Institution of Washington, publication no. 456, pp. 105—120, 3 pls., Washington 1935).

1936. Important Maya discovery in the Guatemala Highlands (Maya Research, vol. 3, pp. 177—188, New Orleans 1936).

1936 a. Kaminaljuyu (Carnegie Institution of Washington, Year book, no. 35, pp. 130—131, Washington 1936).

1937. Guatemala Highlands (Carnegie Institution of Washington, Year book, no. 36, pp. 143—144, Washington 1937).

1938. Arrow-heads or dart points (American Antiquity, vol. 4, pp. 156—157, Menasha 1938).

1940. Archaeological problems of the Highland Maya (The Maya and their neighbors, pp. 117—125, New York 1940).

KIDDER, A. V. and THOMPSON, J. E.
1938. The correlation of Maya and Christian chronologies (Cooperation in Research. Carnegie Institution of Washington, publication no. 501, pp. 493—510, Washington 1938).

KIDDER II, ALFRED.
1940. South American penetrations in Middle America (The Maya and their neighbors, pp. 441—459, New York 1940).

KINGSBOROUGH, LORD.
1831—1848. Antiquities of Mexico: Comprising fac-similes of ancient Mexican paintings and hieroglyphics ... together with the Monuments of New Spain. 9 vols. London 1831—1848.

KRICKEBERG, WALTER.
1918—22, 1925. Die Totonaken. Ein Beitrag zur historischen Ethnographie Mittelamerikas (Baessler-Archiv. Band 7, pp. 1—55; Band 9, pp. 1—75, Berlin 1918—22, 1925).

1935. Beiträge zur Frage der alten kulturgeschichtlichen Beziehungen zwischen Nord- und Südamerika (Zeitschrift für Ethnologie, Band 66, pp. 287—373, Berlin 1935).

1936. Bericht über neuere Forschungen zur Geschichte der alten Kulturen Mittelamerikas. I. Die Grundlagen (Die Welt als Geschichte, II. Jahrgang, pp. 488—505, Stuttgart 1936).

1937. Bericht über neuere Forschungen zur Geschichte der alten Kulturen Mittelamerikas. II. Archäologische Ergebnisse [I. Teil] (Die Welt als Geschichte, III. Jahrgang, pp. 194—230, 4 pls., Stuttgart 1937).

KROEBER, A. L.
1937. Archaeological explorations in Peru. Part IV. Cañete Valley (Field Museum of Natural History. Anthropology, Memoirs. Vol. 2, no. 4, Chicago 1937).
1940. Conclusions: The present status of Americanistic problems (The Maya and their neighbors, pp. 460—489, New York 1940).

LANDA, DIEGO DE.
1928, 1929. Relation des choses de Yucatan (Relación de las cosas de Yucatan. Edition Jean Genet). 2 vols. Paris 1928, 1929.

LARSEN, HELGA.
1936. The 260 day period as related to the agricultural life of the ancient Indian (Ethnos, vol. 1, pp. 9—12, Stockholm 1936).

LEHMANN, WALTER.
1910. Ergebnisse einer Forschungsreise in Mittelamerika und México 1907—1909 (Zeitschrift für Ethnologie, Band 42, pp. 687—749, Berlin 1910).
1912. Berichte des K. Ethnographischen Museums in München, IV (1911) (Sonderabdruck aus dem Münchner Jahrbuch der bildenden Kunst, pp. 83—103, München 1912).
1920. Zentral-Amerika. Die Sprachen Zentral-Amerikas in ihren Beziehungen zueinander sowie zu Süd-Amerika und Mexiko. 2 vols. Berlin 1920.
1921. Altmexikanische Kunstgeschichte (Orbis Pictus, Band 8, Berlin 1921).
1922. Ein Tolteken-Klagegesang (Festschrift Eduard Seler, pp. 281—319, Stuttgart 1922).
1933. Aus den Pyramidenstädten in Alt-Mexiko. Berlin 1933.
1938. Die Geschichte der Königreiche von Colhuacan und Mexico (Quellenwerke zur alten Geschichte Amerikas, vol. 1, Stuttgart und Berlin 1938).
1938 a. La antigüedad histórica de las culturas Gran-Mexicanas y el problema de su contacto con las culturas Gran-Peruanas (El Mexico Antiguo, tomo 4, núms. 5 —6, pp. 179—198, Mexico 1938).

LEÓN, FRANCISCO DE P.
1939. Los esmaltes de Uruapan. México 1939.

LEÓN, NICOLÁS.
1905. Data about a new kind of hieroglyphical writing in Mexico (Proceedings of the International Congress of Americanists, 13th Session, New York, 1902, pp. 175—188, Easton, Pa. 1905).

LINDBLOM, G.
1941. Drinking-tubes, especially in Africa (Ethnos, vol. 6, pp. 48—74, Stockholm 1941).

LINNÉ, S.
1925. The technique of South American ceramics (Göteborgs Kungl. Vetenskaps- och Vitterhets-Samhälles handlingar. Fjärde följden. Band 29. N:o 5. Göteborg 1925.)
1929. Darien in the past. The archaeology of eastern Panama and north-western Colombia (Göteborgs Kungl. Vetenskaps- och Vitterhets-Samhälles Handlingar. Femte följden. Ser. A. Band 1. N:o 3. Göteborg 1929).
1934. Archaeological researches at Teotihuacan, Mexico (The Ethnographical Museum of Sweden, Stockholm. New series. Publication No. 1. Stockholm 1934).
1936. The expedition to Mexico sent out in 1934—35 by the Ethnographical Museum of Sweden (Ethnos, vol. 1, pp. 39—48, Stockholm 1936).
1937. Statens etnografiska museums expedition till Mexico 1934—35. De arkeologiska undersökningarna (Ethnos, vol. 2, pp. 267—300, 3 pls., Stockholm 1937).
1937 a. Hunting and fishing in the Valley of Mexico in the middle of the 16th century (Ethnos, vol. 2, pp. 56—64, Stockholm 1937).
1938. Zapotecan antiquities and the Paulson collection in the Ethnographical Museum of Sweden (The Ethnographical Museum of Sweden, Stockholm. New series. Publication No. 4. Stockholm 1938).
1938 a. A Mazapan grave at Teotihuacan, Mexico (Ethnos, vol. 3, pp. 167—178, Stockholm 1938).
1939. Blow-guns in ancient Mexico (Ethnos, vol. 4, pp. 56—61, Stockholm 1939).
1940. Dental decoration in aboriginal America (Ethnos, vol. 5, pp. 2—28, 1 pl., Stockholm 1940).
1941. Teotihuacan symbols (Ethnos, vol. 6, pp. 174—186, Stockholm 1941).

LONGYEAR III, JOHN M.
1940. The ethnological significance of Copan pottery (The Maya and their neighbors, pp. 268—271, New York 1940).

LOTHROP, SAMUEL KIRKLAND.
1926. Pottery of Costa Rica and Nicaragua. 2 vols. (Contributions from the Museum of the American Indian, Heye Foundation, vol. 8, New York 1926).

1927. Pottery types and their sequence in El Salvador (Indian Notes and Monographs, Museum of the American Indian, Heye Foundation, vol. 1, no. 4, pp. 165—220, New York 1927).

1933. Atitlan. An archaeological study of ancient remains on the borders of Lake Atitlan, Guatemala (Carnegie Institution of Washington, publication no. 444, Washington 1933).

1936. Zacualpa. A study of ancient Quiche artifacts (Carnegie Institution of Washington, publication no. 472, Washington 1936).

1936 a. Sculptured pottery of the southern Maya and Pipil (Maya Research, vol. 3, pp. 140—152, New Orleans 1936).

1937. Coclé. An archaeological study of Central Panama (Memoirs of the Peabody Museum of Archaeology and Ethnology, Harvard University, vol. 7, Cambridge 1937).

1939. The southeastern frontier of the Maya (American Anthropologist, n. s. vol. 41, pp. 42—54, Menasha 1939).

1940. South America as seen from Middle America (The Maya and their neighbors, pp. 417—429, New York 1940).

LUDENDORFF, HANS.
1936. Die astronomische Inschrift aus dem Tempel des Kreuzes in Palenque (Forschungen und Fortschritte, Jahrg. 12, Nr. 2, pp. 17—18, Berlin 1936).

LUMHOLTZ, CARL.
1904. Bland Mexikos indianer. 2 vols. Stockholm 1904.

MARQUINA, IGNACIO.
1928. Estudio arquitectónico comparativo de los monumentos arqueológicos de Mexico (Secretaría de Educación Pública). Mexico 1928.

1939. Atlas arqueológico de la República Mexicana (Instituto Panamericano de Geografía e Historia, publicación no. 41, Mexico 1939).

1939 a. Exploraciones en la piramide de Cholula, Pue. (Mimeographed, 1—19 pp., one plan). Mexico 1939.

MASON, J. ALDEN.
1935—1941. Reports on current archaeological work in Middle America (American Antiquity, vols. 1—6, Menasha 1935—1941).

1940. The native languages of Middle America (The Maya and their neighbors, pp. 52—87, New York 1940).

MAUDSLAY, A. P.
1913. Recent archaeological discoveries in Mexico (Journal of the Royal Anthropological Institute of Great Britain and Ireland, vol. 43, pp. 10—18, 1 pl., London 1913).

MENA, RAMÓN.
1914. Altares-incensarios a Chalchiuhtlicue y a Macuilxochitl (Memorias y Revista de la Sociedad Científica "Antonio Alzate", tomo 33, núms. 9—10, pp. 229—233, 3 pls., Mexico 1914).

MOLINA ENRIQUEZ, RENATO.
1925. Las lacas de México (Ethnos, tercera época, tom. 1, núm. 5, pp. 115—124, México 1925).

MONTELL, GÖSTA.
1936. Mexikanskt indianliv i forntid och nutid. Stockholm 1936.

1936 a. The expedition to Mexico sent out in 1934—35 by the Ethnographical Museum of Sweden. The ethnographical investigations (Ethnos, vol. 1, pp. 60—66, Stockholm 1936).

1937. Statens etnografiska museums expedition till Mexico 1934—35. De etnografiska undersökningarna (Ethnos, vol. 2, pp. 301—318, Stockholm 1937).

1938. Yaqui dances (Ethnos, vol. 3, pp. 145—166, Stockholm 1938).

MORRIS, EARL H., CHARLOT, JEAN and MORRIS, ANN AXTELL.
1931. The Temple of the Warriors. 2 vols. (Carnegie Institution of Washington, publication no. 406, Washington 1931).

MUELLERRIED, FRIEDRICH K. G.
1924 Algunas observaciones sobre los "cues" en la Huasteca (El Mexico Antiguo, tomo 2, números 1—2, pp. 20—29, 3 pls., Mexico 1924).

MUIR, JOHN M.
1926. Data on the structure of Pre-Columbian Huastec mounds in the Tampico region, Mexico (The Journal of the Royal Anthropological Institute of Great Britain and Ireland, vol. 56, pp. 231—238, 4 pls., London 1926).

NOGUERA, EDUARDO.
1932. Extensiones cronológico-culturales y geográficas de las cerámicas de Mexico. Mexico 1932.

1935. Antecedentes y relaciónes de la cultura Teotihuacana (El Mexico Antiguo, vol. 3, núms. 5—8, pp. 3—90, 33 pls., Mexico 1935).

1935 a. La cerámica de Tenayuca y las excavaciones estratigráficas (Tenayuca. Departamento de Monumentos, pp. 141—201, 62 pls., Mexico 1935).

1937. El Altar de los Cráneos Esculpidos de Cholula. Mexico 1937.

1937 a. Conclusiones principales obtenidas por el estudio de la cerámica arqueológica de Cholula (Mimeographed, 1—16 pp.). Mexico 1937.

1940. Excavaciones en Calipan, Estado de Puebla (El Mexico Antiguo, tomo 5, núms. 3—5, pp. 63—96, 27 pls., Mexico 1940).

1940 a. Excavations at Tehuacan. Translated and condensed by S. B. Vaillant (The Maya and their neighbors, pp. 306—319, New York 1940).

NORDENSKIÖLD, ERLAND.

1913. Urnengräber und Mounds im bolivianischen Flachlande (Baessler-Archiv, Band 3, pp. 205—255, 2 pls., Leipzig und Berlin 1913).

1916. Die Anpassung der Indianer an die Verhältnisse in den Überschwemmungsgebieten in Südamerika (Ymer, vol. 36, pp. 138—155, Stockholm 1916).

1921. The copper and bronze ages in South America (Comparative ethnographical studies, vol. 4). Göteborg 1921.

1926. Miroirs convexes et concaves en Amérique (Journal de la Société des Américanistes de Paris, n. s. tome 18, pp. 103—110, Paris 1926).

1928. Indianerna på Panamanäset. Stockholm 1928.

1930. Modifications in Indian culture through inventions and loans (Comparative ethnographical studies, vol. 8). Göteborg 1930.

1931. Origin of the Indian civilizations in South America (Comparative ethnographical studies, vol. 9). Göteborg 1931.

NUTTALL, ZELIA.

1886. The terracotta heads of Teotihuacan (The American Journal of Archaeology, vol. 2, pp. 157—178, 318—330, 2 pls., Baltimore 1886).

1903. The book of the life of the Ancient Mexicans ... an anonymous Hispano-Mexican manuscript preserved at the Biblioteca Nazionale Centrale, Florence, Italy. Part 1. Berkeley 1903.

1904. A penitential rite of the ancient Mexicans (Archaeological and Ethnological Papers of the Peabody Museum, Har-

vard University, vol. 1, no. 7, Cambridge 1904).

1926. Official reports on the towns of Tequizistlan, Tepechpan, Acolman, and San Juan Teotihuacan sent by Francisco de Castañeda to his Majesty, Philip II, and the Council of the Indies, in 1580 (Papers of the Peabody Museum of American Archaeology and Ethnology, Harvard University, vol. 11, no. 2, Cambridge 1926).

1926 a. The Aztecs and their predecessors in the Valley of Mexico (Proceedings of the American Philosophical Society, vol. 65, pp. 245—255, Philadelphia 1926).

ORDÓÑEZ, EZEQUIEL.

1905. Los Xalapascos del Estado de Puebla (Parergones del Instituto Geológico, vol. 1, núms. 9—10, Mexico 1905).

OVIEDO Y VALDÉS, GONZALO FERNANDEZ DE.

1851—1855. Historia general y natural de las Indias, islas y tierra-firme del mar Océano. 4 vols. Madrid 1851—1855.

PALACIOS, ENRIQUE JUAN.

1917. Puebla, su territorio y sus habitantes (Memorias y Revista de la Sociedad Científica "Antonio Alzate", tomo 36, 1916, p. 1—748, Mexico 1917).

1922. Hueyaltépetl (Anales del Museo Nacional de Arqueología, Historia y Etnografía, tomo 1, época 4a., pp. 179—192, 6 pls., México 1922).

1923. Otra ciudad desconocida, en Hueyaltépetl (Boletín del Museo Nacional de Arqueología, Historia y Etnografía, tomo 2, época 4a., pp. 21—35, 4 pls., México 1923).

1937. Arqueología de México. Culturas Arcaica y Tolteca. Mexico 1937.

PARSONS, ELSIE CLÉWS.

1936. Mitla, Town of the Souls, and other Zapoteco-speaking pueblos of Oaxaca, Mexico (The University of Chicago Publications in Anthropology. Ethnological Series). Chicago 1936.

PEÑAFIEL, ANTONIO.

1885. Nombres geográficos de México: catálogo alfabético de los nombres de lugar pertenecientes al idioma "Nahuatl". Estudio jeroglífico de la matricula de los tributos del Códice Mendocino. México 1885.

1890. Monumentos del arte mexicano antiguo. Ornamentación, mitología, tributos y monumentos. 3 vols. Berlin 1890.

1895, 1897. Nomenclatura geográfica de México. Etimologías de los nombres de lugar correspondientes a los principales idiomas que se hablan en la República. Atlas and 2 vols. text. México 1895, 1897.

1900. Teotihuacán. Historical and archaeological study. México 1900.

PÉREZ, JOSÉ R.
1935. Exploración del túnel de la Pirámide del Sol (El Mexico Antiguo, tomo 3, núms. 5—8, pp. 91—95, Mexico 1935).

PHILLIPS JR., HENRY.
1883. Notes upon the Codex Ramirez, with a translation of the same (Proceedings of the American Philosophical Society, vol. 21, pp. 616—651, Philadelphia 1883).

POLLOCK, H. E. D.
1936. Round structures of aboriginal Middle America (Carnegie Institution of Washington, publication no. 471, Washington 1936).

POMAR, JUAN BAUTISTA.
1891. Relación de Tezcoco, escrita en 1582 (Nueva colección de documentos para la historia de México. Publicada por Joaquín García Icazbalceta, tomo 3, pp. 1—69, México 1891).

POMO DE AYALA, FELIPE GUAMAN.
1936. Nueva crónica y buen gobierno (Université de Paris. Travaux et Mémoires de l'Institut d'Ethnologie, vol. 23, Paris 1936).

PONCE, FRAY ALONSO.
1873. Relación breve y verdadera de algunas cosas de las muchas que sucedieron al padre Fray Alonso Ponce en las provincias de la Nueva España. 2 vols. Madrid 1873.

POPE, SAXTON T.
1918. Yahi archery (University of California Publications in American Archaeology and Ethnology, vol. 13, pp. 103—152, 17 pls., Berkeley 1918).

POPENOE, DOROTHY H.
1934. Some excavations at Playa de los Muertos, Ulua River, Honduras (Maya Research, vol. 1, pp. 61—85, New York 1934).

PRESCOTT, WILLIAM.
1937. Der Untergang der indianischen Kultur. Die Eroberung Mexikos durch Ferdinand Cortez. Wien-Leipzig-Olten 1937(?).

PREUSS, KONRAD THEODOR.
1894. Die Begräbnisarten der Amerikaner und Nordostasiaten. Königsberg 1894.
1938. Das Tolteken-Problem (Mexiko) nach einer alten Bilderhandschrift und den

Anschauungen heutiger mexikanischer Indianer (Zeitschrift für Ethnologie, Band 69, pp. 446—451, Berlin 1938).

RADIN, PAUL.
1920. The sources and authenticity of the history of the ancient Mexicans (University of California Publications in American Archaeology and Ethnology, vol. 17, no. 1, pp. 1—150, 17 pls., Berkeley 1920).

REDFIELD, ROBERT.
1930. Tepoztlan, a Mexican village (The University of Chicago Publications in Anthropology, Ethnological Series). Chicago 1930.

RICHARDS, HORACE G. and BOEKELMAN, H. J.
1937. Shells from Maya excavations in British Honduras (American Antiquity, vol. 3, pp. 166—169, 1 pl., Menasha 1937).

RICKETSON JR., OLIVER G.
1925. Burials in the Maya area (American Anthropologist, n. s. vol. 27, pp. 381—401, Menasha 1925).
1931. Excavations at Baking Pot, British Honduras (Carnegie Institution of Washington, publication no. 403, Contributions to American Archaeology, vol. 1, no. 1, pp. 1—27, 25 pls., Washington 1931).
1935. Four pottery moulds from Guatemala (Maya Research, vol. 2, pp. 253—256, New York 1935).

ROMERO, JAVIER.
1935. Estudio de los entierros de la pirámide de Cholula (Anales del Museo Nacional de Arqueología, Historia y Etnografía, tomo 2, quinta época, pp. 5—36, Mexico 1935).

RYDÉN, STIG.
1936. Archaeological researches in the Department of La Candelaria, Prov. Salta, Argentina (Etnologiska studier, vol. 3, Göteborg 1936).

SAHAGUN, BERNARDINO DE.
1927. Einige Kapitel aus dem Geschichtswerk des Fray Bernardino de Sahagun aus dem Aztekischen übersetzt von Eduard Seler. Stuttgart 1927.
1938. Historia general de las cosas de Nueva España por el M. R. P. Fr. Bernardino de Sahagun. 5 vols. México 1938.

SAPPER, KARL.
1928. Mexico. Land, Volk und Wirtschaft. Wien 1928.
1936. Pipiles und Mayavölker (Ibero-Amerikanisches Archiv, Band 10, pp. 78—86, Berlin und Bonn 1936).

SAUSSURE, HENRI DE.
1858. Découverte des ruines d'une ancienne ville mexicaine située sur le plateau de l'Anahuac (Bulletin de la Société de Géographie de Paris 1858).

SAVILLE, MARSHALL H.
1899. Exploration of Zapotecan tombs in southern Mexico (American Anthropologist, n. s. vol. 1, pp. 350—362, 5 pls., New York 1899).
1909. The cruciform structures of Mitla and vicinity (Putnam Anniversary Volume, pp. 151—190, 13 pls., New York 1909).
1930. Toltec or Teotihuacan types of artifacts in Guatemala (Indian Notes, Museum of the American Indian, Heye Foundation, vol. 7, pp. 195—206, New York 1930).

SCHELLHAS, PAUL.
1904. Representation of deities of the Maya manuscripts (Papers of the Peabody Museum of American Archaeology and Ethnology, Harvard University, vol. 4, no. 1, Cambridge 1904).

SCHULTZE-JENA, LEONHARD.
1935. Indiana II. Mythen in der Muttersprache der Pipil von Izalco in El Salvador. Jena 1935.

SELER, EDUARD.
1895. Wandmalereien von Mitla. Eine mexikanische Bilderschrift in Fresko. Berlin 1895.
1900. Das Tonalamatl der Aubin'schen Sammlung. Eine altmexikanische Bilderhandschrift der Bibliothèque Nationale in Paris. Berlin 1900.
1902. Gesammelte Abhandlungen zur amerikanischen Sprach- und Alterthumskunde (Erster Band). Berlin 1902.
1902 a. Codex Vaticanus Nr. 3773 (Codex Vaticanus B). Eine altmexikanische Bilderschrift der Vatikanischen Bibliothek. Erläutert von Dr. Eduard Seler. 2 vols. Berlin 1902.
1904. Gesammelte Abhandlungen zur amerikanischen Sprach- und Alterthumskunde (Zweiter Band). Berlin 1904.
1904 a. Wall paintings of Mitla. A Mexican picture writing in fresco (Bulletin 28 of the Bureau of American Ethnology, Smithsonian Institution, pp. 243—324, Washington 1904).
1904—1909. Codex Borgia. Eine altmexikanische Bilderschrift der Bibliothek der Congregatio de Propaganda Fide. Erläutert von Dr. Eduard Seler. 3 vols. Berlin 1904, 1906, 1909.

1908. Gesammelte Abhandlungen zur amerikanischen Sprach- und Alterthumskunde (Dritter Band). Berlin 1908.
1915. Die Teotiuacan-Kultur des Hochlands von México (Gesammelte Abhandlungen zur amerikanischen Sprach- und Alterthumskunde, Fünfter Band, pp. 405—585, 81 pls., Berlin 1915).
1915 a. Beobachtungen und Studien in den Ruinen von Palenque (Aus den Abhandlungen der Königl. Preuss. Akademie der Wissenschaften, Jahrgang 1915, Phil.-Hist. Klasse, Nr. 5, pp. 1—128, 19 pls., Berlin 1915).
1915 b. Gesammelte Abhandlungen zur amerikanischen Sprach- und Alterthumskunde (Fünfter Band). Berlin 1915.
1916. Die Quetzalcouatl-Fassaden Yukatekischer Bauten (Aus den Abhandlungen der Königl. Preuss. Akademie der Wissenschaften, Jahrgang 1916, Phil.-Hist. Klasse, Nr. 2, pp. 1—85, 12 pls., Berlin 1916).
1923. Gesammelte Abhandlungen zur amerikanischen Sprach- und Alterthumskunde (Vierter Band). Berlin 1923.
1927. See Sahagun 1927.

SELER-SACHS, CAECILIE.
1922. Altertümer des Kanton Tuxtla im Staate Veracruz (Festschrift Eduard Seler, pp. 543—556, 7 pls., Stuttgart 1922).

SMITH, ROBERT E.
1937. A study of Structure A—I Complex at Uaxactun, Peten, Guatemala (Carnegie Institution of Washington, publication no. 456, pp. 189—231, 11 pls., Washington 1937).
1940. Ceramics of the Peten (The Maya and their neighbors, pp. 242—249, New York 1940).

SPENCE, LEWIS.
1923. The Gods of Mexico. London 1923.

SPINDEN, ELLEN S.
1933. The place of Tajin in Totonac archaeology (American Anthropologist, n. s. vol. 35, pp. 225—270, Menasha 1933).

SPINDEN, HERBERT J.
1913. A study of Maya art (Memoirs of the Peabody Museum of American Archaeology and Ethnology, Harvard University, vol. 6, Cambridge 1913).
1915. Notes on the archeology of Salvador (American Anthropologist, n. s. vol. 17, pp. 446—487, Lancaster 1915).
1928. Ancient civilizations of Mexico and Central America (Handbook Series No. 3,

third and revised edition, American Museum of Natural History, New York 1928).

STARR, FREDERICK.
1894. Notes on Mexican archaeology (The University of Chicago, Department of Anthropology, Bulletin 1, pp. 1—16, 4 pls., Chicago 1894).

STAUB, WALTHER.
1919. Some data about the pre-Hispanic and the now living Huastec Indians (El Mexico Antiguo, tomo 1, núm. 3, pp. 49—65, 5 pls., Mexico 1919).
1921. Neue Funde und Ausgrabungen in der Huaxteca (Ost-Mexiko) (Jahresbericht über die Ethnographische Sammlung in Bern, 1920, pp. 33—77, 9 pls., Bern 1921).
1921 a. Pre-Hispanic mortuary pottery sherd deposits and other antiquities of the Huasteca (El Mexico Antiguo, tomo 1, núms. 7—8, pp. 218—236, 11 pls., Mexico 1921).
1926. Ueber die Altersfolge der vorspanischen Kulturen in der Huaxteca (Nordost-Mexiko) (Jahresbericht über die Ethnographische Sammlung in Bern, 1925, pp. 12—24, 3 pls., Bern 1926).
1926 a. Le nord-est du Mexique et les indiens de la Huaxtèque (Journal de la Société des Américanistes de Paris, n. s. tome 18, pp. 279—296, 1 pl., Paris 1926).
1935. Archaeological observations in the Huaxteca (Eastern Mexico) (Maya Research, vol. 2, pp. 33—36, New York 1935).

STEINEN, KARL VON DEN.
1904. Ausgrabungen am Valenciasee (Globus, Band 86, pp. 101—108, Braunschweig 1904).

STIRLING, MATTHEW W.
1940. An Initial Series from Tres Zapotes, Vera Cruz, Mexico (National Geographic Society, Mexican Archeology Series, vol. 1, no. 1, pp. 1—15, Washington 1940).
1941. Expedition unearths buried masterpieces of carved jade (National Geographic Magazine, vol. 80, pp. 277—302, 16 pls., Washington 1941).

STONE, DORIS and TURNBULL, CONCHITA.
1941. A Sula-Ulúa pottery kiln (American Antiquity, vol. 7, pp. 39—47, 6 pls., Menasha 1941).

STREBEL, HERMANN.
1885, 1889. Alt-Mexiko. Archäologische Beiträge zur Kulturgeschichte seiner Bewohner. 2 vols. Hamburg und Leipzig 1885, 1889.

STRONG, WILLIAM DUNCAN.
1935. Archeological investigations in the Bay Islands, Spanish Honduras (Smithsonian Miscellaneous Collections, vol. 92, no. 14, Washington 1935).

TÁPIA, ANDRÉS DE.
1866. Relación hecha por el señor Andrés de Tápia, sobre la conquista de México (Colecciónes para la historia de México. Publicada por Joaquín García Icazbalceta. Tomo segundo, pp. 554—594, México 1866).

TENAYUCA.
1935. Tenayuca (Departamento de Monumentos, Mexico 1935).

TERMER, FRANZ.
1931. Zur Archäologie von Guatemala (Baessler-Archiv, Band 14, pp. 167—191, Berlin 1931).
1936. Die Bedeutung der Pipiles für die Kulturgestaltung in Guatemala (Baessler-Archiv, Band 19, pp. 108—113, Berlin 1936).
1936 a. Probleme der archäologischen Erforschung der Hochländer des nördlichen Mittelamerika (Forschungen und Fortschritte, Jahrg. 12, Nr. 10, pp. 126—127, Berlin 1936).
1941. Zur Geographie der Republik Guatemala. II. Teil (Mitteilungen der Geographischen Gesellschaft in Hamburg, Bd. 47, Hamburg 1941).

THOMPSON, J. ERIC S.
1930. Ethnology of the Mayas of southern and central British Honduras (Field Museum of Natural History, publication 274, anthropological series, vol. 17, no. 2, Chicago 1930).
1931. Archaeological investigations in the southern Cayo District, British Honduras (Field Museum of Natural History, publication 301, anthropological series, vol. 17, no. 3, Chicago 1931).
1939. Excavations at San Jose, British Honduras (Carnegie Institution of Washington, publication no. 506, Washington 1939).
1940. Archaeological problems of the Lowland Maya (The Maya and their neighbors, pp. 126—138, New York 1940).

TORQUEMADA, JUAN DE.
1723. Monarchia Indiana, con el orígen y guerras, de los Indios Occidentales etc. 3 vols. Madrid 1723.

TOSCANO, SALVADOR.
1940. La pintura mural precolombina de México (Boletín Bibliográfico de Antro-

pología Americana, vol. 4, pp. 37—51,
1 pl., Mexico 1940).

TOZZER, ALFRED M.

1921. Excavation of a site at Santiago Ahuitzotla, D. F. Mexico (Bulletin 74 of the Bureau of American Ethnology, Smithsonian Institution). Washington 1921.

1930. Maya and Toltec figures at Chichen Itza (Proceedings of the twenty-third International Congress of Americanists, New York, 1928, pp. 155—164, New York 1930.

TOZZER, ALFRED M. and ALLEN, GLOVER M.

1910. Animal figures in the Maya codices (Papers of the Peabody Museum of American Archaeology and Ethnology, Harvard University, vol. 4, no. 3, Cambridge 1910.

UHLE, MAX.

1935. Die alten Kulturen Perús im Hinblick auf die Archäologie und Geschichte des amerikanischen Kontinents. Berlin 1935.

VAILLANT, GEORGE C.

1930. Excavations at Zacatenco (Anthropological Papers of the American Museum of Natural History, vol. 32, part 1, pp. 1—197, 54 pls., New York 1930).

1931. Excavations at Ticoman (Anthropological Papers of the American Museum of Natural History, vol. 32, part 2, pp. 199—439, 40 pls., New York 1931).

1932. Stratigraphical research in Central Mexico (Proceedings of the National Academy of Sciences, vol. 18, no. 7, pp. 487 —490, Washington 1932).

1935. Chronology and stratigraphy in the Maya area (Maya Research, vol. 2, pp. 119—143, New York 1935).

1935 a. Excavations at El Arbolillo (Anthropological Papers of the American Museum of Natural History, vol. 35, part 2, pp. 137—279, New York 1935).

1936. The history of the Valley of Mexico (Natural History, vol. 38, pp. 324—340, New York 1936).

1938. A correlation of archaeological and historical sequences in the Valley of Mexico (American Anthropologist, n. s. vol. 40, pp. 535—573, Menasha 1938).

1939. The twilight of the Aztec civilization (Natural History, vol. 43, no. 1, pp. 38—46, New York 1939).

1939 a. An early occurrence of cotton in Mexico (American Anthropologist, n. s. vol. 41, p. 170, Menasha 1939).

1940. Patterns in Middle American archaeology (The Maya and their neighbors, pp. 295—305, New York 1940).

VAILLANT, SUZANNAH B. and GEORGE C.

1934. Excavations at Gualupita (Anthropological Papers of the American Museum of Natural History, vol. 35, part 1, New York 1934).

VALLE-ARIZPE, ARTEMIO.

1939. Historia de la Ciudad de México segun los relatos de sus cronistas. Mexico 1939.

WARDLE, H. NEWELL.

1905. Certain clay figures of Teotihuacan (Proceedings of the International Congress of Americanists, 13th Session, New York, 1902, pp. 213—216, 1 pl., Easton, Pa. 1905.

WASSÉN, HENRY.

1934. The frog in Indian mythology and imaginative world (Anthropos, Band 29, pp. 613—658, St. Gabriel-Mödling bei Wien 1934).

WAUCHOPE, ROBERT.

1934. House mounds of Uaxactun, Guatemala (Contributions to American Archaeology, no. 7, Carnegie Institution of Washington, publication no. 436, pp. 107—171, 9 pls., Washington 1934).

1938. Modern Maya houses. A study of their archaeological significance (Carnegie Institution of Washington, publication no. 502, Washington 1938).

WELTFISH, GENE.

1930. Prehistoric North American basketry techniques and modern distributions (American Anthropologist, n. s. vol. 32, pp. 454—495, Menasha 1930).

YDE, JENS.

1938. An archaeological reconnaissance of northwestern Honduras (Acta Archaeologica, vol. 9, Copenhagen 1938).

ZINGG, ROBERT M.

1940. Report on archaeology of southern Chihuahua (Contributions of the University of Denver: Center of Latin American Studies, I, 1940).

INDEX

188; lids to vessels, 74, 128—129, 169; mending by the »crack-lacing» method, 43, 176; moulds or mouldmade decoration, 66, 69, 75, 85, 90, 133, 143, 165—169, 173, 176, 181, 186; negative painting, 38—39, 161—162; pellets, 70, 74—75, 81—82, 90, 187; petrographic analysis, 38, 79, 176—177, 187, 195; plumbate ware, 178; roasting dishes, 39, 72, 186; shoe shaped vessels, 72, 185; spindle-whorls, 39—40, 69—70, 137, 158, 166, 185—186, 190; stamps, 47, 69, 74—75, 140, 166, 176, 181, 186; storing vessels, 69; Teotihuacan, 161—179, 181; three-handled vessels, 73; trade pottery, 37—38, 40—42, 47, 50, 98, 166, 175—179, 181, 190—191, 194—195; unfired 130—131; yellowish-red, 37—38, 55, 66, 75—76, 78—80, 90, 128, 133, 140—141, 143, 176—177, 181, 187, 190, 194—195. See also Clay figures; Comales; Molcajetes
Prescott, William: 16
Preuss, Konrad Theodor: 51, 105
Projectile points: 29, 32, 43, 47, 131, 134—136, 144, 180, 187
Prytz, Björn: 11
Pueblos in south-western U. S. A.: 151, 185
Pusilhá: 151
Pyramid of the Sun, tunnels into: 91, 165, 185
Pyrite: 126, 132, 146, 174, 180—181, 187

Quetzalcoatl: 82, 172, 177, 188, 196—197, 201 —203
Quimistlán, Puebla: 45

Radin, Paul: 147
Rain God: see Tlaloc
Ranchito de las Animas culture: 41, 53
Rasping bones: 148, 185
Rattles: 57, 74, 152
Redfield, Robert: 82
Reed, Alfred: 145
Reygadas Vértiz, José: 13
Richards, Horace G.: 151
Ricketson Jr., Oliver G.: 52, 66
Roatan Island, Honduras: 152
Roman y Zamora, Jerónimo: 36
Romero, Javier: 156
Ruiz, Bartolomé: 147, 151
Rydén, Stig: 79

Sahagun, Bernardino de: 42, 148—149, 169, 172, 198—200, 202—203
Salcajá-Momostenango, Guatemala: 80
Salvador: 82, 164, 195—197, 199
San José, British Honduras: 151, 156, 170, 181, 193
Santa Cruz Quiché, Guatemala: 170
Sapper, Karl: 116, 196

Saussure, Henri de: 49
Saville, Marshall H.: 52, 162, 193
Schellhas, Paul: 83, 172
Schultze-Jena, Leonhard: 196
Seler, Eduard: 16—17, 44, 49, 51, 74, 80—81, 83—84, 86, 146—147, 149, 151, 162—163, 169—170, 184, 191, 193—194, 196, 200, 203
Seler-Sachs, Caecilie: 168
Serna, Jacinto de la: 147
Shells and shell work: 29, 32, 69, 126, 132—133, 135—136, 139, 141, 143, 150—153, 190
Shephard, Anna O.: 177, 195
Sinaloa: 146, 162, 190
Skeletons and skulls: 29, 34—35, 54—55, 65, 71, 125—126, 133—138, 140, 143, 156, 184; object manufactured from part of human skull, 148
Slate: 132, 136—137, 141, 146
Smith, Robert E.: 155, 193, 195
Sociedad Mexicana de Antropología: 193, 201
Sonora: 185
South America: 39, 47, 50—51, 79—81, 145—146, 204—205
Spence, Lewis: 163, 169
Spinden, Ellen S.: 191
Spinden, Herbert J.: 88, 162, 193, 196, 200
Spindle-whorls: 39—40, 69—70, 137, 158, 166, 185—186, 190
Spinning: 157—160, 180
Stamps: 47, 69, 74—75, 140, 166, 176, 181, 186
Starr, Frederick: 86, 118
Staub, Walter: 44, 51, 191
Steinen, Karl von den: 51
Stirling, Matthew W.: 53—54, 155
Stone: axes, 44, 145, 187; balls, 44, 70, 145; bark-beaters, 155, 185; beads, 29, 35—36, 43—44, 58, 65, 70, 132—133, 136, 140, 146; knives, 145, 185, 187; metates, 33—34, 43—44, 49, 70, 122, 131, 145, 184—186; ornaments, 140, 144, 180; plasterer's floatstones, 145, 185 —186; ring from a ball-court, 23; rings, 104, 120, 145, 186; sculptures, 26—28, 44—45, 49, 122, 146, 180; smoothing-stones, 145; vessels, 29, 34, 43, 133, 140, 146, 162, 180; whetstones, 145. See also Jade; Mica; Mirrors; Obsidian; Projectile points; Pyrite; Slate; Tecali
Stone, Doris: 193
Strebel, Hermann: 41, 45, 53
Strong, William Duncan: 152
Strömberg, Elisabeth: 14, 156—160
Sucking-tubes: see Drinking-tubes
Swedish America-Mexico Line: 11
Swedish-Mexican Society: 11
Swedish Society for Anthropology and Geography: 11
Sylwan, Vivi: 157

Plate 1

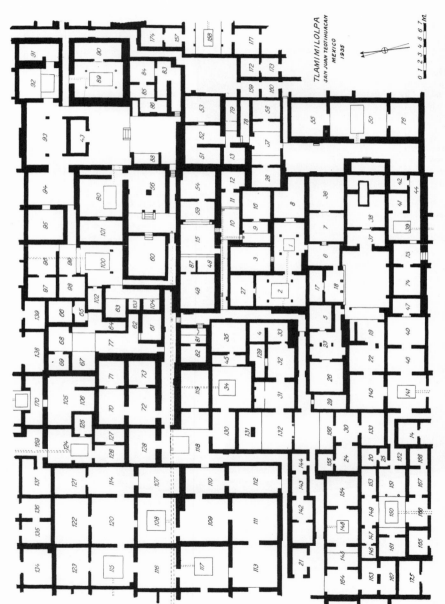

TLAMIMILOLPA
SAN JUAN TEOTIHUACAN
MEXICO
1935

0 1 2 3 4 5 6 7 M.

Plan of the excavated ruin at Tlamimilolpa, Teotihuacan.
Symbols: thin lines, tresholds; rectangles within rooms, forecourts; double dotted lines, drains. Cf. figs. 182—188.

Plate 2

Tripod vessel recovered in Cache 1 (cf. pp. 142—143). Scale, ca. ³/₄. 35.8.2126. On right: potsherd, trade ware, found below the third floor in Room 16; outer and inner surfaces (cf. figs. 328—329). Scale, ca. ¹/₂. 35.8.2501. Below: fragment of clay vessel from the Maya territory, found below the bottom floor of Room 21 (cf. fig. 331). Nat. size. 35.8.185.

Plate 3

Clay masks for incensarios. Scale, ca. ³/₄. Top: found below the third floor in Room 1. 35.8.2773.
Bottom: belonging to incensario from Burial 1. 35.8.2383.

Plate 4

Clay masks for incensarios found below the third floor in Room 1. Scale, ca. ³/₄. 35.8.2774 and 2775.

Plate 5

Clay masks for incensarios. Scale, ca. ³/₄. Top: found below the third floor in Room 1. 35.8.2776.
Bottom: found below the second floor in Room 6. 35.8.2777.

Plate 6

Textile fragments from Burial 1, Tlamimilolpa, Teotihuacan. 35.8.2220 a—h.

a) bast fibre, 27 × 31 mm.   b) cotton, 25 × 30 mm.   c) bast fibre, scale, ³/₂.   d) cotton, 15 × 40 mm.   e) earthenware dish with textile fragments, diam. 169 mm. 35.8.2194.   f) bast fibre, 20 × 34 mm.   g) cotton ca. 40 × 100 mm.   h) cotton, 19 × 34 mm.